Let them Dance

A Preparation for Dance and Life

Let them Dance
A Preparation for Dance and Life

Laurel Martyn

Illustrated by Margaret Mackie

DANCE BOOKS LTD
9 Cecil Court, London WC2N 4EZ

First published 1985 by Dance Books Ltd., 9 Cecil Court, London WC2N 4EZ.

ISBN 0 903102 89 7

Distributed in the USA by Princeton Book Co.,
P.O. Box 109, Princeton, N.J. 08540.

Design and production in association with
Book Production Consultants Ltd., 47 Norfolk Street, Cambridge.
Typeset by Kerrypress Ltd., Luton.
Printed by the Thetford Press Ltd.

Contents

Acknowledgements

I wish to thank all the people who, throughout my life, have helped me to realize my ambition to be a dancer, choreographer and teacher. My parents, husband and brothers have always given me encouragement and understanding and have made many sacrifices on my behalf. My teachers in scholastic subjects, music and languages have made my life interesting and rich. My teachers of dancing have been very distinguished and too many to enumerate. However, those with the greatest influence must be mentioned. In Australia, Kathleen Hamilton and Marjorie Hollingshed set me on the right path so I could continue my studies, without interruption, with my beloved Phyllis Bedells in London. Good fortune gained the interest of Dame Adeline Genée and Dame Ninette de Valois in my dancing and choreography and further allowed study with Madame Lubov Egorova in Paris. On my return to Australia, Madame Xenia Borovansky helped me to develop into a dancer capable of performing ballerina roles with the Borovansky Ballet. To all the people, dancers, choreographers, composers, designers and administrators who contributed so greatly to the Victorian Ballet Guild and Ballet Victoria, I owe much.

In establishing this dance course I had valuable assistance from teachers and students who acted as guinea pigs. In the preparation of the book I wish to thank especially Margaret Mackie for her illustrations and encouragement, Robin Grove M.A., A.T.C.L. Senior Lecturer, Department of English, University of Melbourne and Gwenyth Williams F.C.N.A. for their help in clarifying my thoughts and words and Frank M. Forster D.C., D.O. for his assistance with the notes on anatomy and the treatment of injuries.

Preface

Movement is Life. Things that grow in the soil or in the sea are stimulated by the elements. They are swayed by the wind or the tide and expand in the warmth of the sun. Animals rejoice in exerting themselves by running, jumping, spinning, bending and gliding, swimming and flying. They also enjoy controlling these activities. Very young children, in common with other young animals, experience joyous excitement in uncontrolled movement, but as they grow older learn the necessity of harnessing their energy for specific purposes, such as any type of sport, athletics or dancing. It is important that the joy of moving should be retained, even as it is brought under conscious control.

Some children know the direction in which their desires and talents lie. Others are guided into such activities as appeal to their parents or into activities which they think will benefit the child.

Dancing, especially ballet dancing, has become accepted as good for posture, ease of movement and assurance, therefore, many parents direct their children into this activity. It is sad to see children forced to take ballet-dancing lessons when they are not interested. However, I believe the majority of young children enjoy moving in an expressive way, be it beautiful or grotesque. The teacher must find what does interest these children, and use that as a starting point for extending their experience in movement until it embraces actual dance. Thus, I was asked to teach one young boy who had a posture problem. He showed no interest in the lesson until I asked if he played cricket. He confessed that he could not bowl straight. I then explained that as his body was not held straight his 'machine' could not work properly, since a machine must be assembled correctly so that each part is in alignment with the others. In this way, he came to understand how his body should be aligned as a unit and in relation to external objects and directions. He now bowls straight, and is working hard so that he will be able to high-jump! In fact, he is still learning dancing and is interested in it. Other children, of course, will find their interest stimulated in different ways. Perhaps too many young girls picture themselves as a 'ballerina' (forever static and ethereal!), posed in a pretty tu-tu. A good teacher will prove that *movement* leading to poses is equally important, and that one without the other does not make dance. Boys, on the other hand, usually like the excitement of movement; and when this excitement and enjoyment is fostered, the result is satisfying and stimulating to watch.

Unfortunately, the average approach to the teaching of dance puts so much emphasis on acquiring 'technique' that the aim of technique is lost, sometimes forever. On the other hand, there is also the danger of allowing mere 'expression' to be overemphasized, so that insufficient regard is given to the necessary technical means required to achieve an appropriate balance.

During thirty years as Artistic Director of Ballet Victoria and Director of its schools, I frequently found both professional and amateur dancers lacking in many of the basic skills required of them as performers and instruments for the choreographer's creativity. Principally, the basic skills lacking were: the ability to hear music other than as a tune; an appreciation of the value of rests; the use of phrasing and dynamics; comprehension of floor and aerial patterns and a feeling for the composition as a whole; communication with others in a sequence of movement; real understanding of what the body can achieve, and the ability to use it as an instrument of expression; or a real appreciation of the quality of movement. The lack of these accomplishments is very frustrating to a choreographer as well as to the dancer; and since these observations apply to a wide spectrum of the professional field, as well as to amateur groups, they point, I believe, to the reason why many people find both classical ballet and modern dance unfulfilling.

In this situation, what is needed is for teachers and students alike to begin from fundamentals. It is no use assuming, for example, that classical ballet can be taught to any body at any age. Classical dance places considerable strain on muscles, ligaments, tendons and joints. It also requires an ability to concentrate and comprehend complex movements, rhythms and space-patterns. Bodies and minds not sufficiently developed should not be subjected to this demanding training. So, from both the psychological and the artistic point of view I would say that a high degree of technical excellence is expected too early from developing youngsters. They seem to me like beautiful hot-house plants forced to flower – so lovely for one season, but unable to flower in the following one. The plant that grows at its own pace in a sympathetic environment will flower year after year.

I believe that no child should begin classical-ballet training before the age of nine or ten; and so I established preparatory schools for Ballet Victoria where younger children could learn some of the basic skills, and at the same time learn to control their movements within the capabilities of their age-groups. These schools accepted pupils from the age of five. That was our starting-age because, up to five, children are fully occupied with learning about living, are not easily separated from their mothers, have a limited command of language, and have not yet learnt to copy movements knowingly. At five, they can understand clear and simple explanations, and can imitate something demonstrated. Their movement repertoire has widened – for instance, they can usually hop, balance on one foot, and walk backwards, and so are ready to learn how to isolate and co-ordinate simple movements.

These preparatory schools operated for many years, and during this time a teaching system was worked out and put into practice. When children had completed the four years of this course, they usually found no difficulty in understanding proper ballet exercises when the time came for them to move into this discipline. On the other hand, if the rigours of a classical ballet training did not appeal or the physique was not suited to it, a good foundation had been laid for modern dance, jazz, folk dance, or, in fact, for any form of physical activity. This experience led me to clarify and codify the work of so many years, in the belief that the system could be useful to teachers and to students.

A system of training, however, should not be confused with a style of dancing. The individual style of teacher or dancer, or of national 'school' (such as that of the U.S.S.R.), is determined by *how* the system is used. Because we have different temperaments and modes of life, using a borrowed system will not mean that we dance alike. Style is created by the approach of the individual, group or nation to its art, and springs from within, not from without.

There are many organizations which have examination syllabuses, but these do not, as a rule, help the teacher with a system of teaching. An examination syllabus sets out the end result required for a certain standard of achievement, while a system sets out how to achieve that result. It also explains why, and states when, movements and exercises should be introduced over the whole programme.

This book endeavours to explain such a system in detail, so that the teacher may follow it or vary it as desired. Brief explanations of some of the more technical terms I use will be found in the Glossary at the back of the book.

Introduction

The aim of the course outlined in this book is to prepare the five to nine-year-old child for serious study in any field of movement, be it dance, sport, self-defence, or simply living. At the end of four years' study the pupil should have learnt to move freely with a good rhythmic sense, to understand the simple principles of movement, and to have a good feeling for line, style, and the emotional implications and expressive possibilities of both movement and music.

The book is divided into four parts in which I endeavour to show how choreography and the art of dance develop from the basics of movement combined and interwoven with time, weight, space and flow in all their aspects.

Part I: The art of teaching: a broad concept of dance and how to teach the individual and his body/instrument.

Part II: Awareness exercises: designed to make the dancer completely aware of the body/instrument and its relationships with time, weight and space.

Part III: Qualities of dance, governed by time, weight and space.

Part IV: Flow of movement: which draws all the former elements together into steps, mime and expressive movement, resulting in choreography and the art of dance.

There is an overlapping and co-ordination of the three later parts, aimed at developing a student with a well-balanced, supple and strong body, and an alert and keenly observant mind.

For each section there are examples of exercises, developed from the first through to the fourth year. These provide a means of evaluating the course as well as the progress of the child. However, the recommended exercises and ideas (showing how the desired result might be achieved), together with the plan of the lessons, are merely guides to help individual teachers create lessons of their own.

* * *

The Russian system of classical dance training makes use of the divided exercise: that is, exercises dissected with pauses which give time to register the feeling of every movement and position reached, as well as allowing time for self-correction by the student. Each component of an exercise or step must be understood and practised before being co-ordinated into the finished form, and no new exercise or movement is added to the vocabulary of the class without this careful preparation.

I have based this preparatory course on the Russian system; but whereas in the classical dance exercises are done at first slowly, gradually increasing the speed and eliminating pauses until the correct tempo and execution has been achieved, in this system I have reversed the process. In the first year, exercises are done quickly so that young untrained bodies can cope. In the following three years the speed is decreased until, at the end of the fourth year, there is sufficient strength of posture and understanding of movement to sustain the effort, energy and concentration required to begin the study of classical dance in the correct divided manner.

I have used both English and French names for steps and exercises as I believe the children should hear these in their lessons. In this way they become accustomed to the French terms of the classical dance at the same time as knowing their meaning.

Although more girls than boys learn dancing, it is important to encourage boys to take up what is, after all, a natural right. Until comparatively recently, men were equal partners with women or even dominant in the art of dance. Because of this, I have, throughout the book, purposely referred to the student sometimes as 'she' and at other times as 'he'.

I hope the ideas embodied in this book will serve as a text to help teachers and pupils enjoy the experience of real achievement in their chosen endeavour.

Discovery

Part I

The Art of Teaching

1. Principles of Teaching

The aim of the teacher is to convey knowledge in a way that enables students not only to understand but to make use of that knowledge. Teachers must therefore be sure of their subject and capable of explaining and demonstrating clearly and accurately.

For the teacher of dance a knowledge and mastery of the following is necessary:

1. The principles of teaching.
2. The basis on which the body/instrument functions.
3. The theory of the elements of dance.
4. Analysis of movement.
5. The theory of divided exercises.
6. The principle of lesson-construction.
7. The programme of study and exercise-progressions.
8. The contribution of time, weight, space and flow to dance.

Not until these things are understood will the teacher be able to convey to the students the correct technical and aesthetic qualities of exercises and steps being studied. A reasonably high standard of performance can then be expected.

The relationship between teacher and student is very important, and teachers must discover for themselves how to use personality and skills in gaining the confidence and respect of their students. At the same time, the teacher must have respect for students, be able to hold the interest of the class in the subject being studied and lead them on to further enthusiastic exploration of it.

It must be understood that dance is a disciplined art. This should be reflected in discipline in class by both teacher and student. The teacher must set the example of self-discipline in both the preparation and presentation of the lesson, as well as in the execution of it. It should be remembered that each student is an individual requiring individual physical and psychological attention. No student should be neglected in class, and each should be given individual corrections. However, every student should be encouraged to pay attention to the corrections given to others and apply them if applicable. Therefore, all corrections must be audible to the whole class, so that those not being directly addressed can use their critical sense to assess themselves in the matter under scrutiny.

Since the majority of dance students are girls, it is easy to fall into the habit of speaking only to 'girls'. Therefore it is important to address the male members of the class and encourage them to move in the manner of young men.

Enjoyment of movement and enthusiasm for mastering it, exploring its possibilities and using the knowledge gained, should be integral to the lesson. It should never be forgotten by teacher or student that the purpose of the lesson is to dance. The dance teacher is not teaching kindergarten or physical culture. He is teaching an *Art*.

So, enjoyment and discipline go hand-in-hand. Students must be made aware of a plan and an aim for each lesson, and the lesson's relation to the term and the year's work. They should have the desire to reach the standard required for their progress to a higher class. The teacher, therefore, must be clear about the purpose of each exercise, considered not for its own sake, but as it takes its place in the complete picture of dance and can be related to past, present and future study. This understanding should be conveyed to the students. For instance, although preparatory and joining steps, such as *coupé, glissade* and *pas de bourrée* must be learnt individually, once technical execution is correct they should be used with the more important step to which they belong. It should be explained that the quality of the preparatory or joining step, and the energy used to execute it, will vary in relation to its companion step. If such steps are from *Petit Allégro*, then the preparation and joining steps will also be small and light. If, on the other hand, the steps are from *Grand Allégro*, the impetus of preparation and joining steps will be bigger and more vigorous.

By such means, the relationship of exercises to the end result of the training – that is, dance – should be constantly pointed out to the students. Teacher and student should both recognize that an exercise is in response to a *need*. For example, feet must be strong and flexible because they provide an important part of the springing mechanism both for exploding from the floor and for absorbing the shock on landing: hence such exercises as *battement tendu*. Equally, the arm movements actively assist a dancer to co-ordinate, to travel, to turn, to spring and to balance, as well as adding aesthetic quality and line to movement. In fact, both teacher and student should constantly be asking why this or that exercise is being practised; 'what is it expected to achieve?' 'where will it be useful?' and 'when?'. If a student understands the reason for each exercise, and how it reinforces the others in the final achievement, progress will be more rapid and lasting.

In other words, mind and body belong together. The dance student must be able to think well and quickly, because it is the brain which dictates movement and enables it to be controlled. The instrument of the dancer is the body itself, and it must be trained to obey, But for this very reason, the mind must be interested and fully involved in the work; so it is the teacher's responsibility to foster this involvement and not allow mindless copying and endless repetition of exercises.

Likewise, the feeling for a movement is registered in the memory so that it can be repeated accurately. If the correct directions are not given by the mind, the correct feeling cannot be registered and will not be repeated exactly and easily. Memory is trained by repetition – thoughtful repetition, above all – and that is why it is recommended to repeat an exercise up to four times on one side (usually the right) before transferring it to the opposite side. The equal use of both hemispheres of the brain is most important to maintain balanced development of the individual. Should one side of the body be weaker than the other, then, for remedial purposes, more emphasis should be given to the weaker side. Our concentration, in fact, should always be on the weaker, not the stronger aspect of a student when performing a particular movement.

Corrections, however, should be positive, not negative. The pupil should be told that a movement should be done *so*, not that it is *not* done so. The correct movement will thus be explained, rather than the incorrect one. It is tempting to overemphasize or exaggerate when correcting students: this is dangerous, since it will surely create faults instead of achieving the desired result.

Frequently, students thinking they are making a movement in the required manner are in fact making a compensatory one. This is either because they do not fully understand what is being asked of them, or because they find the correct physical movement difficult to perform. Their error is often manifested, for example, in the movement of the shoulders and waist when the movement required is of the head and neck only. Similarly, the faulty lifting of the hip or over-use of the buttock muscles is often a compensatory substitute for the free use of the hip-joint, which should move quite independently of the rest of the body. Careful observation is necessary to ensure that movements are being achieved by the correct muscles and in the correct joints.

Students very rarely do an exercise wrongly on purpose. They think they are working correctly; so when a correction is made it will feel wrong. The students have to re-educate themselves to a new understanding of how the movement *should* feel, and must accept that what has felt right is in fact wrong. This is often hard to absorb and requires patient explanation by the teacher. A child can have stood crookedly for most of his life, and naturally feels out of balance when placed with the spine straight and the head erect. It takes much time and patience (on both sides) to rectify such postural faults. Frequently, parents have not noticed any imbalance, and most family doctors do not consider such postural defects very important. However, just as an incorrectly assembled machine will not function well, neither will an incorrectly assembled body.

Besides, there is no doubt that a well-placed body will allow the mind to work better then a badly-placed one. Slow learners respond to their school work in a more efficient manner as a result of dance training and better posture. It has been proven many times that children with disciplined bodies have disciplined minds and are bright at their school work.

Anatomy and Posture

The remedial value of well-taught dancing is widely recognized, and many small imbalances in structural and muscular development can be corrected or improved. Equally, physical defects can be created by bad teaching. Therefore, it is essential for teachers to understand the anatomical basis of movement. They must know how the muscles and joints are articulated and how they work; they must understand body-mechanics and some simple remedial exercises to help in the healthy development of the children under their care.

It is most important to know how to handle the child's body so as to correct faults in posture or show the appropriate use of a limb. In this remedial placing of the body the teacher's hands play a major role. For example: (1) *Spine*: to help the forward and upward release of the spine, place the middle finger of one hand on the crown of the head and the middle finger of the other hand on the base of the spine, that is, on the coccyx. This enables the student to feel the straight line between these two points. (2) *Shoulders*: to open the shoulder-blades, place the thumb and third finger on the inside edge of the 'wings' and open them out to the sides until the shoulder area is flat. If the blades protrude over-much for this correction, take one arm under the elbow and lift it up and out to the side until the shoulder area is flat; hold the shoulder in that position and lower the arm to *bras bas*; repeat with the other arm. It will then be found that when the hand has been turned upward in *bras bas*, the arm is in the correct position and the back is flat across the shoulder-blades. Check that the shoulders are down and 'falling apart'. (3) *Buttocks*: to release the buttock muscles downwards, place the hands over the muscles and massage them downwards without pushing the pelvis under. Remember that the pelvis must be straight. Move the whole weight forward until the pelvis is directly over the feet. The student will feel as if he is about to fall forward, but the spinal release will bring the stomach muscles into play and counter-balance the falling feeling.

Child-Child Correction
This is when one child corrects another after an exercise has been carefully explained and postural corrections demonstrated by the teacher. By explaining the movement to someone else, and by actually placing another body in the required position, children gain a thorough understanding of the exercise. As a result, the consequent application of this understanding to themselves is facilitated. The teacher must supervise this child–child correction, and help by showing how to make the right adjustments. Keen observation is essential by both teachers and pupils so that faults can be identified and new work picked up quickly and accurately.

Preparation for Movement
Correct usage of the body prevents injuries and accidents; carelessness causes them. Therefore the student must never be allowed to be careless or too hurried in preparing for and performing a movement. If time is allowed for concentration and control *before* commencing, the movement itself can be executed in a free and flowing manner. It follows that preparations should be given great attention, and not glossed over in order to get on with the

exercise: an exercise not fully prepared in thought will never be satisfactorily performed. This applies also to the finish of movements, which should be made positive and expressive, holding the final pose for a second or two so that the good gained by doing the exercise is not thrown away by dropping control of mind and body.

Voice and Music

The voice of the teacher, its timbre, quality and expression are important factors in the lesson. Time and rhythm are given by the voice, and it is by its inflexion, phrasing and accent that the type of musical accompaniment required is conveyed to the pianist and the students. For example, the introduction should lead into the music, so the inflexion of the voice will illustrate this; then the introductory chords played by the pianist will lead into the music proper on an upbeat in order to give the time, character and impetus to the music following. The finish should be on a downward cadence to give the character of a completed sentence. When the sequence embraces two qualities, these should be expressed by the use of the voice, and this example will then be copied by pianist and pupils so the correct contrast in feeling will be registered and executed. Movement should 'sing' through the body, and a musical voice can express this quality better than a wordy explanation. It is useful to ask the students also to count aloud in a singing tone during exercises, as in this way not only is the musical feeling captured, but the exact timing and co-ordination can be reinforced. Counting, moreover, requires a great deal of concentration and soon reduces any tendency to carelessness in the student's approach to his work. For very small children, counting time on their own is difficult as they tend to get either faster or slower, though it is important that they be able to keep strict time. Clapping exercises, therefore, measuring the distance of the hand-movements when opening between claps, will help to establish the understanding and feeling for strict time. Singing or speaking words or sentences can also help in establishing awareness of a regular beat.

In many ways, then, the musical accompaniment is of the utmost importance. It must co-operate with the movement in such a way as to underline its quality and reinforce its character. Tempo is also important and will be found to vary for different age-groups.

Marking Movement

The teacher need not be technically brilliant, but must be able to demonstrate accurately, showing the line and direction of *épaulement*, the co-ordination of head and arms with their active role of assisting the movements of the legs and body, as well as showing the aesthetic quality of each exercise or step. Anatomically, the use of limbs and body must be right, even though the rotation of the legs may not be one hundred per cent, or the legs lifted higher than forty-five degrees. The student will understand any teacher's inability to dance with full vigorous execution, but will certainly be confused if limbs are incorrectly placed, if line and quality are lacking, or if time is mangled.

The art of marking movements, therefore, should be studied by teacher and student alike. It is used by the teacher when demonstrating an *enchaînement* and by the student when learning it. Good marking uses all the right body-mechanics together with the qualities of time, weight, space and flow, except for the final full use of energy. Springs, for instance, must be marked in the exact timing required, with full use of *demi-plié* and with co-ordination of arms and head. All head, arm and body movements must be made with the actual purpose involved in the *enchaînement*. Thus the body feels lifted into the air without the final explosion of energy which actually propels it into the air. Similarly, the 'landing' must be cushioned as if the spring had indeed been executed. And the actual distance covered when a step is fully danced must also be covered when marking. In this way, not only the mind is exercised but also the body is prepared to execute the movement fully with the required time, quality and technical understanding. Yet energy is saved, for the teacher to teach and for the student to perform the *enchaînement* fresh and well prepared.

Teacher and Student Relationship

Teachers should not keep themselves in isolation but should talk and exchange ideas and experiences with other teachers of dance, teachers from different disciplines, and laymen of various backgrounds. Too often the dance world becomes divorced from reality and the people around it. This rarefied atmosphere makes for dried-up artificiality, cut off from the warm full-blooded reservoir of life which should be its rejuvenator and inspiration. Dancers are not beings apart (although they are mostly special people), but are PEOPLE WHO DANCE. Students, correspondingly, are PEOPLE WHO WISH TO DANCE. Too often they are regarded as passes, or failures, in examinations.

Examinations

Useful as a means of gauging the student's progress, they also test the confidence of the young dancer. But an examination should be regarded as a performance in which the examiner becomes the audience to be interested and pleased. I believe that, in examinations, the test should be not whether the student knows the examination syllabus, but whether she understands and can use the elements of dance, their co-ordination and expressiveness, in ways appropriate to the standard of achievement reached. For the purposes of this course, I would suggest that the teacher set the examination lesson in which all this is to be displayed. The student should be able to practise this lesson for a short time, and then present for the examination. If the examiner cannot judge the child's ability by watching a performance of a lesson, either the teacher has failed to present the work well (perhaps because some sections of training were neglected), or the child has not reached the standard required. I do not believe that a child should be judged on examination only; rather, in the yearly report to the parents, the whole year's work should be assessed. In this way a much truer evaluation of progress can be made and examinations can be seen in their proper perspective.

Creativity and Composition

A good teacher must be creative in order to retain enthusiasm and convey it to the students. There are many good textbooks on the teaching of modern creative dancing and dance in education and music. The teacher should be constantly reading and learning and every opportunity should be taken to develop ideas and concepts. A genuinely creative approach such as this makes it possible to avoid the boredom of endless repetition of the same dull set of exercises and steps, and a careful balance between creativity and repetition makes for a productive lesson.

Praise

Learning should be an interesting and exciting experience, as well as a challenge, so praise must be given when it is due – that is, when something is done exceptionally well. Doing it correctly is the norm, and the student should not expect praise for being correct. When faults are not found, obviously the work is satisfactory; but when they *are*, then something is wrong and must be put right. Here, patient help should be given. Self-indulgent tears must be discouraged. Even if an accident happens or a small injury is sustained it must be instantly forgotten, and concentration applied instead to the on-going work. If a mistake is made, the fault should not be dwelt upon but the correct execution immediately brought to mind and put into practice.

2. The Body/Instrument

A teacher of any art must understand the instrument or the materials with which the artist works. The dancer's instrument is his or her body. The dance teacher, therefore, is teaching both the budding artist and the 'instrument' at one and the same time. We have dealt with the artist as an individual; now let us consider the instrument itself.

The human body is a marvel of engineering: strong, yet delicate; complicated, yet extremely functional. A fundamental knowledge of its construction and working is essential so that no injuries are caused through faulty use of muscles and joints. Instead, we may hope that the body will be used correctly and not asked to move contrary to its construction and purpose. Injuries and misplacements will then happen only through real accidents, or though careless lack of attention on the part of the dancer.

The skeleton

The body is supported by the skeleton, which is comprised of bones held together at the joints by ligaments which are strong, flexible, fibrous tissue. The skeleton in its turn is supported by muscles attached to the bones by tendons – that is, strong cords, or bands of tissue. The muscles and bones protect and support the organs which are housed in the cavities of the skeleton: the brain in the skull, the heart and lungs in the chest, and the stomach and intestines in the abdomen.

The head and face is composed of twenty-two bones where are lodged, as well as the brain, the organs of special sense – the eyes, the ears, the nose and the tongue. The spine is made up of thirty-three vertebrae, held together by strong ligaments and separated by thick pads of cartilage which are called inter-vertebral discs. The ligaments allow the spine to be flexible, and the discs act as shock-absorbers. The spine itself is divided into several sections, according to placement and function:

there are seven *cervical* vertebrae which form the neck;

twelve *dorsal* vertebrae are attached to twelve curved rib-bones joined in front to the sternum to form the rib-cage;

five *lumbar* vertebrae hold the small of the back;

five *sacral* vertebrae are fused together to form the sacrum;

four *coccygeal* vertebrae make up the coccyx or tail. The pelvis is a large formation of bone which supports the lower spine and which is itself supported by the legs. The leg consists of:

the thigh bone or *femur*, which extends from the hip-joint to the knee-joint;

the shin or *tibia*, which extends from knee to ankle on the inside of the leg;

splint-bone or *fibula*, which is a long thin bone on the outside of the lower leg;

the knee-cap or *patella*, which is a flat bone covering and protecting the knee-joint;

seven *tarsal* bones and five *metatarsal* bones, which are found in the foot;

fourteen *phalanges* make up the toes.

The arm consists of:

shoulder-blade, or *scapula*;

the collar-bone, or *clavicle*;

the *humerus,* or bone of the upper-arm;

bones of the forearm: the *ulna*, on the side of the little finger, and the *radius*, on the side of the thumb;

the *carpal* bones, arranged in two rows of four, form the wrist;

five *metacarpal* bones make the frame for the palm of the hand and fourteen *phalanges* form the fingers and thumb.

The joints

There are four kinds of joints:

the ball-and-socket joint has a rounded head fitted into a socket, which allows movement in all directions – the hip and shoulder being typical;

the hinge joint allows movement in one direction only, like a hinge swinging backwards and forwards: for example, the elbows and fingers;

the gliding joint permits only very slight movement without rotation or hinge movement: for example, the joints between the tarsal bones;

the pivot joint allows one bone to rotate round the pivot of another: for example, the atlas, which is the uppermost cervical vertebra supporting the skull.

Movable joints are surrounded by an envelope of strong fibrous tissue which is called the capsule and is strengthened further by the ligaments on the outside. Inside, the joint is lined with the synovial membrane which secretes lubricating fluid to oil the cartilage-covered bone-ends, and allows them to move freely without irritation. When a joint bends, this is called 'flexion', and when it is straightened, 'extension'.

The muscles

Each muscle consists of thousands of fibres, roughly cylindrical in shape, which are attached to each end of muscle tendons. When stimulated by impulses from the brain, the fibres contract and the force of the contraction is transmitted through the tendons to the bones. Skeletal or Voluntary muscles move as a result of will or conscious purpose, and are extensible and elastic. The muscles of the organs work involuntarily.

If muscle-tissue is warm it responds to stimulation more rapidly than when cold, and so contracts quickly and there is a shorter latent period; when cold, however, its contraction is slower and weaker and the latent period is longer. If stimulation of a muscle continues after contraction has reached its maximum, the muscle gradually loses the contraction. This is known as muscle fatigue, and is due to an accumulation of lactic acid in the muscle, with fatigue at the junction of the stimulating nerve and the muscle fibre, resulting in the failure of the stimulus to reach the muscle fibres.

Stretching

Over-stretching, without allowing the muscle to return to its latent state, reduces elasticity, and so, although it may result in high extensions of the limbs, is ultimately detrimental to elevation. Active stretching exercises (that is, those done by the dancers themselves) are thus preferable to passive ones which are done to the dancer by another person. It is also more advantageous to do stretching exercises when the body has been warmed up by a good *barre*.

Very young children should not do any strenuous or demanding stretching, and so none has been recommended in this preparatory course.

Energy

To produce a contraction and return to the latent state, energy is required. This energy is derived from carbohydrate which is taken into the body in the diet, and from oxygen which is taken from the air and inhaled into the lungs. A proportion of carbohydrate is converted into glycogen and stored in the muscles. When the muscle is stimulated to contract, a complete series of chemical changes takes place which results in the production of the energy necessary for contraction and, as a by-product, heat. After muscle fibres have contracted, lactic acid is found to be present. The oxygen brought to the muscle by the blood is necessary for oxidation of some of the lactic acid into carbon dioxide and water, while the remainder is changed back into glycogen. The carbon dioxide is exhaled by the lungs. Excessive lactic acid in the muscles, because oxidation cannot keep pace with its production, results in pain which may take several days to pass.

Nervous tissue

Nervous tissue consists of nerve cells, which generate and receive impulses, and fibres which transmit the impulses. It is through the nervous system that the brain communicates with the body and with the outside world. Sensory nerves convey the senses of heat, cold, touch and pain, as well as receiving sight, sound, smell and taste. It is the sensory nerve ends which are stimulated in the skin by pain. They transmit the impulses *via* the sensory nerves and spinal cord to the brain for interpretation. The brain sends back messages by the motor nerves which stimulate and energize the muscles. As the nerve end enters the muscle it spreads into thousands of fibres. Although muscle fibres respond to stimulus, the strength of the response may vary, as the build-up of lactic acid or weak stimulus makes the responses weak. The nerves activate the fibres to achieve maximum stimulus. The autonomic nervous system regulates the involuntary functions of the body.

Vestibular apparatus

The vestibular apparatus, the body's balance mechanism, lies inside the skull, internal to the mastoid process, and it registers variations in pressure from both outside and inside the body. When we start or stop moving, when we lean on things or when we fix one part of the body close to another part, this apparatus should tell us what is happening. Likewise it gives us information about our spatial orientation and the way we are supporting our body against gravity on various surfaces, such as with the feet on the ground, or on the back when we lie down.

This is done by means of built-in spirit-levels, the so-called 'labyrinths'. These are cavities placed at right-angles in the planes of the skull which are filled with heavy gelatinous fluid. In contact with this fluid are a number of hairs projecting from the cavity walls. The weight of the fluid drags on the hairs in accordance with the head position, and, as the body rotates, the inertia of the fluid jogs it up and down against the hairs. These cavities also have a small cap called a cupula, which swings like a swing-door to and from a resting position. All of this sends information to the brain about body-position on the vertical and longitudinal axes, up, down, right, left, front, back, etc. It also gives information about acceleration and deceleration by the displacement of the gelatinous fluid. It does this more accurately if it is carried on a symmetrically balanced head.

A correct resting head balance, in which the vestibular apparatus can be carried on an even keel, provides a stable platform from which the special senses of the eyes, mouth, nose, ears and tongue can all work. All too often the vestibular apparatus sacrifices its primary position to the demands of the other senses – for example, the eyes to focus on or reject certain sights, the ears to pick up or block out certain sounds, and so on. The precariously developed head balance is easily disturbed by the bombardments of modern life and by the incessant desire to pick up or reject information through the special senses. It becomes a prime necessity that the correct, balanced resting position of the head be re-established.

The cardiovascular system

The cardiovascular system ensures the free flow of healthy blood from the heart through the arteries to its various destinations, and its return through the veins to the heart. As such, of course it is one of the life-supports of the body, which is nourished by the circulation of the blood while waste is carried by it to the organs of elimination.

Respiratory process

Another life-support is the respiratory system whereby air is drawn, with a muscular effort, into the lungs through the nose and respiratory tract, and exhaled by relaxation. This causes an exchange of gases between the air and the blood. The blood carries oxygen to the tissues, and absorbs moisture and carbon dioxide which it returns through the heart to the lungs for expiration. So good breathing is essential for the nourishment of the tissues and the replacement of energy at all times and especially during physical exertion in sport, dance or work.

Nutrition

The body cannot live without food, and should have sufficient to nourish, warm and energize without adding unwanted weight. It needs protein, carbohydrates, fats, mineral salts, vitamins and water. These foods are taken through the processes of the alimentary canal and the accessory organs where they are processed, absorbed and eliminated. A balanced diet of wholesome food should satisfy and not leave a craving for excessive sugar or bulk, thus it should not add unnecessary weight. An active person should not carry too much weight, as the various systems of the body become over-taxed and over-extended by having to cope with the excess burden. Neither should the body be under-nourished. Too often, following a foolish fashion, young dancers become really ill through under-nourishment. This can cause a psychological condition (*anorexia nervosa*) which requires the help of a specialist. Once these sufferers begin to eat again, they frequently put on all the unwanted fat – and more – and cannot then remove it. So, encourage your students to eat well and sensibly, and do not ridicule the 'fatties' into drastic dieting.

There are many publications on nutrition readily available, but the fundamental principle is to provide a well-balanced nourishing diet. This is best achieved by including fresh foods, rather than refined, processed, packeted, instant varieties and ready-cooked fast foods. Plenty of fresh fruit, salads and vegetables; wholemeal bread and flour (which, as well as being more nourishing, provide essential fibre); some protein with each meal (to lessen the desire for snacks and sweets) can be provided in such items as fish, poultry, cheese, eggs, soya beans, red kidney and lima beans, lentils, nuts, wheatgerm and yoghurt, as well as meat. Salt and white sugar should be used very sparingly, and vegetables steamed to preserve vitamins. As dance students use a great amount of energy, vitamin and mineral supplements are often recommended.

Injuries and First-aid

The teacher should be able to remedy minor problems in the instrument he is using without having to return it to its maker – a bit drastic when applied to the human body! But it is important to have some skills in this area.

As we have already seen, minor injuries such as bruises and strains to muscles, ligaments and tendons may be caused through insufficient warming-up, fatigue, or carelessness. The teacher should have first-aid equipment handy and know what to do to minimize the damage. If possible, ice should be available for immediate application to prevent swelling. A plastic bag full of ice wrapped round the injury and the limb elevated should prevent or limit bruising. If ice is not available, hot and cold compresses should be applied: three minutes hot and one minute cold, repeated five times, after which the limb should be elevated and the patient rested.

At night the application of a compress of castor oil on towelling and covered with plastic, bandage and a sock is advised. A pillow under the knee allows the lower leg to release tension. The weight of the bedclothes should be kept from the injured limb. In the morning, remove the compress and wash the limb with water and one teaspoonful of carbonate of soda. To assist movement, the next day the foot should be stood in a bucket of warm water and the ankle moved; a bath may be more appropriate for other injured parts. During the day the limb should be used normally and no attempt made to 'save' it.

Castor oil plasters can be used for any muscular spasm or pain, together with a hot-water bottle on the injured part for about one and a half hours.

For stiffness or swelling in the joints take a warm bath in which two pounds of epsom salts has been dissolved, soaking for as long as possible. An epsom salts compress is good for bruises.

Since tension aggravates most conditions, it is important to help the patient release the tension caused by the pain. For a back injury: lie the patient on the floor, face down, with a pillow under the hips and another under the chest, and apply a castor oil compress covered with a hot-water bottle, until there is a reduction in the pain. Then turn the patient onto the back with the knees drawn up and together and the feet apart. Flatten the small of the back onto the floor, place the hands on the stomach and relax.

If the injury is too severe to respond quickly to these remedies, advise the parents to seek the services of a doctor or chiropractor. During the period necessary for recuperation, the student can do many floor exercises which do not place any strain on the injured limb, and so keep in practice. In addition, watching lessons during this time should be advantageous, as observation can be heightened and a critical sense developed.

3. The Elements of Dance

Dance is made up of many elements, not all of which are necessarily used in every composition, neither does every part of the body have to move: for instance, the eyes can dance while the body is still, the hands can turn and twist, the trunk can sway or the toes can wriggle. However, total dance uses every part of the body and most, if not all, of the elements. These are:

1. *Control:* this includes control of the muscles, of time and speed, of quality, and of the use of space.

2. *Transference of weight:* complete transference, to the support is essential for balance in stillness and in motion.

3. *Balance:* this includes posture in stillness and motion, as well as balance of pattern and shape in personal and general space.

4. *Line:* body and movement line are both functional and aesthetically pleasing.

5. *Jumping:* elevation adds dimension to dancing emotionally as well as physically.

6. *Turning:* learning to turn adds another element which can be used on the floor and in the air, and includes part, full, or multiple turns, twists and spirals.

7. *The use of head and arms:* apart from being under control, the head and arms play an important part both mechanically and aesthetically.

8. *Travelling:* the ability to move the body along the floor and in the air in general space produces freedom in movement and pattern and adds an exciting quality to dance.

9. *Bending:* this includes bends of every part of the body, from the feet to the neck, and allows full use of personal space.

10. *Falling:* the falling element adds drama as well as full use of the levels of space.

11. *Time:* included are music, breath rhythm, phrasing and dynamics.

12. *Quality:* the use of weight and time–weight qualities supplies the expressive and artistic side of dance.

13. *Direction:* the direction in which the body faces and moves through space adds dimension to the figure and the movement pattern.

14. *Co-ordination:* through co-ordination of each part of the body with the various elements of the dance, mechanical and aesthetic flow of movement will result.

15. *Group and partner work:* communication with each other and the use of complex patterns become possible when dance involves more than the solo performer.

It will be seen in the next section ('Movement analysis') that every exercise and step is comprised of various elements, and the understanding of these and how they blend makes the execution complete and artistically satisfying.

4. *Movement Analysis*

Movement analysis means that the function of each part of the body in a given exercise or step is first understood in isolation, and then in time-relation with all the other parts. This is necessary because the limbs and torso are complex combinations of moving parts; thus

the *head and arms* include the fingers, the hands, the wrists, forearms, elbows and upper arms, the neck and eyes;

the *body* consists of the shoulders, chest, ribcage, diaphragm, waist, hips, buttocks and stomach;

the *legs* include the thighs, knees, shins, calves, ankles, feet, insteps, soles and toes.

When the dancer is aware of the whole body, together with co-ordination, time, quality and pattern, and uses all these in one single movement, and later in phrases, then in dances and ballets dancing will be meaningful both to the performer and to the audience.

In the section of sample exercises I have divided the movements to relate to the beat of the musical bar. The part played by the legs and feet is explained, then that of the head and arms. When the individual function of each part of the limbs or trunk has been analysed in isolation during the process of learning a basic movement, such as that of the breathing movement, these details are not repeated each time the basic movement is used. However, they must be constantly revised and remembered in detail by the teacher and the pupil.

Corrections

When analysing movement it is helpful to have a check-list of corrections applicable to the various elements in the step being studied. Such corrections can be divided into

(*a*) *Standard corrections:* balance of posture must, at all times, have first priority, making sure that the spine is released forward and upward, and the neck is free with the shoulders open and down. Having established this, check the following (numbers refer to the list of elements set out on pp. 00–00: line (4); control (1); use of head and arms (7); time (11); quality (12); direction (13); co-ordination (14). These corrections apply to all movements

(*b*) *Specific corrections:* these relate to the elements involved in the *specific* exercise or step being studied, and will vary accordingly. For example, in *pas de chat* gallop the following elements (numbered from the list on pp. 12–13) are incorporated:

3. Balance in posture throughout the step, before, during and after the spring.

2. *Transference* from the springing foot to the landing one, then once more to the springing foot.

4. Line of the body in the upward curve from take-off, at the height of the jump, and in the downward curve.

1. Control of the springing mechanism of the feet, knees, calves, shins and thighs.

7. Use of the arms (not the shoulders!) to actively assist the jump, and the use of the head and eyes to give direction and purpose to the step.

5. *Jumping* high in the air is characteristic of this step.

8. *Travelling* is on a straight line forwards, sideways or backwards.

9. *Bending* of the ankles, knees and hips for the *demi-plié* (before and after the spring) is required.

11. Time is 2/4, and the height of the spring is on the upbeat count of '&'.

12. Quality is light, with a soft cat-like landing.

13. Direction of movement can be to any given point, moving forwards, sideways or backwards.

*14. *Co-ordination* of all aspects allows the movement to flow into one harmonious whole which shows the character and shape of the step.

*Denotes standard corrections

By such study of the elements the teacher's critical sense is heightened, faults are recognized at their point of origin, and so are more easily corrected.

5. The Divided Exercise

There is so much to think about before even the simplest movement can be made. It is essential, therefore, to give the child time to think *before* making the movement, so that it can be fully prepared and executed properly. In classical dance, the introduction to an exercise, which in its finished form is completed in the counts of '& – 1', will, in its first progression, be in eight bars of slow 4/4. Take, for example, *battement tendu*:

	Face the *barre*, and on four chords place the hands on the *barre*.
Bar 1.	Think of the correct posture. Transfer the weight onto the left leg.
Bar 2.	Slide the right foot along the floor in line with second position until the heel begins to lift because, through releasing the spine upwards, the placement of weight does not alter from the supporting leg.
Bar 3.	Continue sliding the ball of the foot until it, too, is lifted and only the big toe remains on the floor in second position.
Bar 4.	Hold the position, think of releasing the spine and register the position of the body and legs. Make necessary corrections.
Bar 5.	Lower the foot onto the ball as the spine is released and the leg drawn back along the same line of second position towards first.
Bar 6.	Lower the foot until the whole sole draws into first position.
Bar 7.	Transfer the weight back on to two feet.
Bar 8.	Hold the position thinking of the correct lifted posture.

Second progression of the same exercise:

This progression should move more smoothly. As before the *tempo* is 4/4.

	On four chords, prepare with the hands on the *barre* and transfer the weight to the supporting leg.
Bar 1.	Extend the leg to second position as in the first progression (above);
Bar 2.	Hold the position, thinking and lifting the body;
Bar 3.	Close the leg in the same manner to first position, while releasing the spine.
Bar 4.	1,2,3, Transfer to two feet and pause, preparing to repeat the *battement tendu*;
	4, Transfer the weight on to the supporting leg, ready to repeat the movement.

Third progression:

The third progression is done sideways to the *barre*, and eliminates the pauses.

The weight remains on the supporting leg during the sequence of four *battements tendus*, and the transferences are made during the preparations and with the final closing of the arm to *bras bas*.

Fourth progression:

The fourth progression completes the *battement tendu* in one bar of 4/4.

Fifth and final form:

The fifth is completed in one bar of 2/4, and the final form is reached when two *battements tendus* are executed in one bar of 2/4.

To consolidate the experience of the exercise, repeat the movement four times on one leg before transferring to the other leg or to a new direction.

In this manner the final form of all exercises is reached so that the understanding of mechanical execution is achieved together with the correct quality and character of movement. When movements of the arms and head are added, there must be time to think of their co-ordination with the leg movements at frequent points in the exercise; hence the use of pauses during its execution.

These examples are for classical dance proper, and should be spread over about three years' training. For the preparatory course, the first progression may be too slow for a particular age-group such as Fourth Year. Should this be the case, speed up the exercise, as shown on p. 74 under *battement tendu* for Fourth Year. At all times, however, the teacher should work out how to divide exercises most advantageously, and also encourage the students to do so. This enables pupils to make self-corrections and attack their work with intelligence and enthusiasm. The use of the divided-exercise principle makes teaching and learning much easier and progress, therefore, more rapid.

6. The Principles of Lesson Construction

The year's study programme

There should be a clearly defined programme of work to be achieved in one year of study, and it should be seen to lead from the previous year to the following one. How much of the programme can be covered depends on the aptitude of the students and the preparation of lessons by the teacher. The programme must be carefully compiled to ensure nothing is added without adequate preparation, and each aspect of dance should be covered so that progress in all the elements goes forward at an even pace and the careful and logical development of the year's programme is fulfilled. If this is done, teaching and learning become easy, rewarding and a great joy.

Teaching progressions

It is helpful to divide the year into sections of, say, five or six lessons. This is equivalent to one week of full-time training and may have to be extended since, in the majority of schools, the student takes fewer lessons each week. When work is not very consistent and lessons are far apart the child cannot retain as much as with daily work, so the Progression may have to be spread over a longer period until the required standard has been reached. However, to divide the work into sections provides a control over the year's programme and an aim more easily comprehended than that of a whole year – so long as the overall plan is always kept in mind.

Each Progression adds the next move forward in certain areas, while previous work in others is continued; thus old work goes together with new exercises, and steps are added at the appropriate time in a pattern of logical development. Only one new element should be added at a time in order not to overcrowd the concentration or the exercise.

Lesson content

Time should be allotted to each section of the lesson, so that no part of the whole of dance is neglected. Each element and aspect should progress with the others on an even front, so that a complete dancer is being produced. No element can be left until *later*, as the bad habit of (say) not using the head movement with the arms, will be impossible to correct and that dancer will always have a stiff, unyielding appearance. Again, if turning in a simple form is not introduced early in the training, it will become a stumbling-block later, instead of being accepted as a natural part of dancing. With these principles in mind, I turn now to the practical business of lesson construction.

7. The Programme of Study and Exercise Progressions

The basic plan for a lesson in the childrens' dance course is loosely constructed on the same format as that of a classical lesson. This is a tried and proven structure, and will prepare the student for further study in classical dance if that opportunity presents itself.

1. *Warm-up:* Both the body and the mind must be attuned to the environment of the dance studio. It is a special place in which one is a dancer; and so an introduction to the lesson should be devised to help create this feeling. It should involve the elements (described on pp. 12–13) of control and balance and posture (1 and 3); line (4); use of head and arms (7); travelling (8); time (11); quality (12); direction (13); co-ordination (14). At the end of this warm-up period the student should be physically and mentally prepared to learn and to enjoy the lesson.

2. *Exercises for isolation and co-ordination:* Equivalent to classical *barre* work, these should cover all parts of the body in isolation and co-ordination, and be done sitting or lying on the floor, standing at the *barre*, or in the centre of the room. They must include the elements from (1) to (13), with the exceptions of jumping (5), travelling (8), falling (10), and group work (15).

3. *Slow controlled movements:* These are the equivalent of *Adagio* in classical dance. Construct the exercises on walking and posing, solo, in groups or pairs and in various floor patterns. This section contains all the elements except jumping (5) and, possibly, falling (10).

4. *Turning:* Equivalent to *pirouettes*, this section includes all the elements with the exceptions of jumping (5) and travelling (8), which will be added in later study.

5. *Small springs:* This is equivalent to *Petit Allégro* in classical dance, and all the elements are used here except travelling (8) and turning (6), which will be added in later study.

6. *Big springs and dance steps:* At a later stage this section will become *Grand Allégro*, but until that day arrives the student should experience the feeling of covering much space and using big bounding springs. Such movement is the culmination of dance experience in the imposed learning situation, and thus all elements are involved.

7. *Folk dance:* This adds a dance which can be shown to the parents or audience ('Look, I'm dancing . . .!') or a mime scene to encourage communication in movement.

8. *Improvisation:* In this section all the elements are used in accordance with the creative ability and imagination of the student.

Sample Plan of a Lesson

Using the appropriate work for each level, this can be adapted for classes from First Year to Fourth Year.

1. *Warm-up:* Use locomotive steps travelling in a simple pattern – say, in a circle around the studio, anti-clockwise, then clockwise. Incorporate time, quality and space-awareness.

2. *Exercises:* Include isolation and co-ordination exercises for the legs, body, arms and head. Posture and the technique of the locomotive steps used in the warm-up are improved, and the awareness of time and quality is heightened.

3. *Slow controlled movements:* Use walking steps and poses in a floor pattern, perhaps the same as in the warm-up. Following these with corrective exercises to cover all the elements and the aspects of music, quality, directions, and co-ordination needing improvement.

4. *Turning:* Add a turning movement to the steps of (3). For example, do the step three times and add the turn on the fourth phrase. Follow this with corrective exercises for turning.

5. *Small springs:* For this section, use the same rhythm as in (4), or the same pattern, or both. Follow with exercises to correct faults.

6. *Dance steps:* (see p. 143): Say, gallops, using the same pattern or a slight variation of it; and again follow with corrective exercises for the steps – for example, the divided exercise appropriate to the class.

7. *Folk dance:* Do one step of a folk dance and add a new one if time and progress permit; or, do one sentence of a mime scene. This will gradually develop with the addition of one step or one sentence at a time. Stress the understanding of music, quality and the use of space and directions.

8. *Improvisation:* In this section, study the music and discuss all its aspects. Give exercises for any that need work. Check that all the aspects have been considered, and then perform the dance as decided on by the students, as a solo, or in a small or large group.

Concentration Span

There may appear to be a great deal of work to get through in a lesson of one hour's duration, but since the span of a child's concentration is not very long, the work can be divided into short and simple sections, rather than long and complicated ones. If the exercises, except those for Isolation, are spread throughout the lesson, arising as need dictates and related directly to the step being studied, there will be no need to present them in one long section during which the children can easily become bored. Repetition of steps and exercises which have been developed logically gives the children a sense of security in the lesson, while at the same time allowing them to make definite progress.

With very young children it is useful to break up the lesson with 'talking time' several times during the hour. In this way silence can be maintained for the active part of the lesson. Placing a finger on their lips also helps them to achieve silence. In Second, Third and Fourth Years there should be no problem in maintaining discipline for one hour. However, the Third-Year lesson should, if possible, be extended to one and a quarter hours, and the Fourth-Years' to one and a half hours.

Balance of Content

The lesson should include both imposed and free learning. the proportions of which will be dictated greatly by the types of children in the class. Very uninhibited children need more imposed learning to help them gain self-discipline, while inhibited children need more free exploration and expression to enable them to become more out-going.

8. Time, weight, space and flow: their contribution to dance

There are many good books on Rudolf Laban's work on the principles of time, weight, space and flow of movement, and it is to the advantage of a teacher to study these since Laban's insights apply to all movement and all dance. No matter what technique is used, be it jazz, ballroom, character, contemporary or classical, if these principles are kept in mind, dance will retain its essential qualities.

A feeling for rhythm and music, quality, the use of space and orientation in it, with the flow of movement through all exercises and steps, can be introduced in easily understood progressive exercises. A grasp of these principles will widen the horizon and enlarge the vocabulary of students, and will be particularly valuable in improvisation and their own creative dances. In this way, the endless shapeless meandering which so often passes for improvisation can be avoided. In any case, awareness of every part of the body, and of the flow of movement through it, uniting the whole moving picture, is essential and must be encouraged early in training if dancing is to be a joy. When dancers do not experience the full pleasure of dancing, the audience cannot be expected to supply this need, and both parties therefore will be unsatisfied.

All aspects of dance are interdependent, and the examples given under one heading necessarily contain material which also belongs elsewhere. The student must learn to connect one subject to another, and amalgamate the knowledge gained into one harmonious whole. The division of study into headings, and of exercises into divided progressions, is only for the basic understanding and mastering of the elements involved. It should not become a way of life! On the contrary, both teacher and student should understand that it is the ultimate fusion of all these elements which produces and enriches dance; and it is in improvision that this goal can be attained, even in the early stages of training. Later, the same understanding should facilitate the development of the artist in the professional dance student, who too often becomes so engrossed in the mastery of technique that the qualities of dancing are lost and have to be painfully regained when she or he is required to perform in a dance company on stage.

The following exercises are merely guides as to how to interest the student and educate him in these various aspects of movement and dance. It is the individual responsibility of each teacher to grasp the principles and out of them create his own exercises with imagination and insight. The field for creative teaching in these areas is limitless, and the study of some of the many excellent books on the subject is recommended.

Music and the awareness of time

With the aid of time, rhythmic floor and aerial patterns are made visible. The rhythm needs time to become a statement, and the pattern takes time to create. Neither can be comprehended instantaneously, but must unfold to the ear and eye. Speed governs the length of time required to do this, as quick movements take a shorter time to draw a pattern or complete a rhythm than slow ones.

Time is measured by metre; thus, metre is the measurement of a unit of time duration. Dance, when accompanied by music, is metric: it uses the beats of the music to gauge the duration of the movement in semi-breves, minims, crochets and quavers. The basic beat is the crochet, which approximates to the heart-beat. The understanding of metric time measurements and their time signatures should be part of the child's early training, for the use of metre gives control over movement, as it is a means of judging the amount of energy required to achieve the effect desired.

To be 'in time' means that movements coincide with the beat. However it is quite common for a dancer to hear the sound and *then* react to it, thus creating a delayed action movement which gives the impression of melancholy and lassitude (qualities which can be expressively employed in the right circumstances). To be truly 'in time', the movement must arrive at its appointed destination on the exact beat of the music, so that the two are simultaneous. This indicates the importance of anticipation and preparation, and the use of the lead-note or, in dancing, the '&' or upbeat on which the movement is prepared or even commenced. In the early stages of training the preparation is extended to two beats; later it becomes one, and later still a half-beat or '&', as technical accomplishment progresses and speed is increased.

Rhythm

Rhythm is a force, active and creative, which makes a sense of 'being' or 'doing'. A rhythmic pattern is produced when the speed varies during a movement, as in a fox-trot; slow, slow, quick, quick, slow. Repetition of a pattern creates composition. The same or varied lengths of sound may be used with varied accents and stresses, with contrasts of silence or counter-activity. The rhythm may alter within the one time signature, the steps may vary and change in rhythm; and, as the manipulation of rhythm and movement repeats, changes, develops and becomes more complex, choreography is born. Rhythm appeals to the young, and through it they can be taught a sense of time. As everything in nature is governed by a natural rhythm, it follows that a sense of physical well-being will result from an awareness of rhythm in everyday life. Perfecting movements in time results in control and co-ordination and a balanced harmony of mind and body. It is normal for the whole body to respond to rhythm: one *hears* a sound and *feels* a rhythm. We walk, we breathe, and the heart beats with natural rhythm; and if this is reinforced by physical exercises, the understanding and use of rhythm will permeate the whole of living and make physical and mental activity easier. The teacher should move and speak rhythmically, to express this quality in normal movements as well as in dance.

Non-metric rhythm

Rhythm such as this comes from a natural force, and is not dictated by anything external, such as drum-beats or music. When music has been fully absorbed, non-metric and breath-rhythm can be introduced, as it is equally important for the student to feel this natural pulse. First, he should be fully aware of what he wishes to accomplish, and should move with purpose instead of, as too often happens, moving in a vague and senseless fashion, or with hyper-active lack of control. Breath-rhythm creates and controls the energy required to make the desired movement. The use of time–weight in non-metric exercises allows the student to give total attention to the quality, and so find the intrinsic rhythm of the movement itself, rather than its being imposed from the outside.

The use of metre in dance relationships (as a duration framework on which to work) is helpful in movement and mime conversations. A takes four bars to ask a question, then B answers in another four bars. Later, this can be allowed to move more freely into non-metric movement conversation, which will have a more natural and spontaneous effect.

Phrasing

Phrasing in movement is very important, as it allows the breath-rhythm to control the use of energy required. It facilitates the free flow of movement and the ease with which such movements can be executed, because it places the breath in the logical place for relaxation and renewed gathering of energy. The use of the rhythmic elements or the shape of the melody makes musical phrases. The juxtaposition of qualities also creates phrases in movement, as the change in quality requires the use of breath-rhythm, which, in turn, necessitates a finish of one quality and the beginning of the next. Movement without music is phrased by breath-rhythm or by the aerial or floor pattern used.

An *enchaînement* is a sentence of movements or steps, and, like a sentence of words, it must have a preparation, a middle and an end, as well as meaning. Also, like a sentence, it must be phrased, or it lacks sense and is difficult to execute. The rhythm and phrasing of an exercise or *enchaînement* act as framework for the movements and, as an aid to memory, provide easy points of reference.

Poses

While movement makes a phrase, a pose acts as punctuation and has the value and importance of various punctuation marks. Unless good phrasing and punctuation are used in dance, it, like speech, will be monotonous and dull. It is important to remember always that DANCE IS MOVEMENT BETWEEN POSES.

Thus a pause in dancing is arrested or suspended movement, which, like a rest in music, adds a sense of depth to the dimensions of length and breadth. A rest is silence for the duration of the sound it replaces. With understanding and restraint, interesting choreographic use can be made of rests by moving through them in order to obtain a specific effect.

Accent

The use of accents and dynamics adds greatly to the meaning of rhythmic patterns. Accents vary in weight, and the gradual or instantaneous release of energy from the initial attack creates dynamics in movement. Accents may fall on the first or any following beat of the bar, and exercises should be devised to correspond with the accent in the music. The ability to change accents to make a syncopated beat should be developed as the student progresses.

Melody

Melody places sounds in a pattern of pitch which, in movement, may be conveyed by a pattern of levels in space. This provides a simple exercise for very young pupils who can be asked to follow the melody's pattern through space.

Harmony

Harmony combines a succession of sounds vertically, and may retain the melody above or below the harmonies. As the student absorbs music and begins to understand some of its nuances, she should be encouraged to listen to harmony and react to it. Very interesting group exercises can be evolved from such beginnings.

Form

The appreciation of form should be encouraged from the earliest years. The value of climax, and its relation to the overall pattern, should be expressed in the form of each *enchaînement*, dance or improvisation. It is important, therefore, to recognize repeated musical phrases, to be able to repeat an appropriate movement, or to make one in direct contrast. In the first years, simple movement phrases should be used, where repetitions will create the basic form (AA). A progression to Binary form (AB), and then Ternary form (ABA) should follow later, while in the Third Year a study of Rondo form

(ABACA) and Canon form should be possible. By the Fourth Year, the student should be ready for work on a Theme and Variations. All these forms may be included in Improvisations: for instance, Binary form could be expressed by day and night, while Ternary could be wind, rain, wind. The possibilities for ideas in the teaching of form are limitless.

Musical terms

As well as recognizing time signatures, children should know and be able to use expressively simple musical terms relating to speed and quality. In short, a musical education should be part and parcel of technical dance training, because all the subtleties of music apply to movement also, and the movements themselves require these subtleties to fulfil their purpose. Unfortunately, really musical dancers are very rare. Most can keep in time, some can dance rhythmically and in phrases, some understand counter-point and can interpret the nuances in the music's content and quality. Many cannot react to *accelerando* or *ritardando*, to *crescendo* or *diminuendo*. Many do not understand dynamics. But the truly musical dancer understands and uses them all.

'Quality' and the awareness of weight

The awareness and understanding of weight and its distribution throughout the limbs and body are essential for the educated control of the physical side of dancing, and will be discussed later. But I should say at once that attention to the use of weight results in a better quality of movement. The section on transference of weight (p. 84) is mainly concerned with symmetrical distributions. In later exercises, in both classical and modern dance, we must work for the control of asymmetrical movements and poses; but for the purpose of the preparatory course, the use of asymmetry should be encouraged in the students' individual explorations in Improvisation only. The teacher should suggest that this area be investigated, and give advice and assistance as the student strives to use and understand asymmetry in movement, and in poses on the floor and in the air. The general work of the class, however, will be concerned with more regular forms.

Heavy and light movements

The contrast between heavy and light movements, and the infinity of gradation between these two poles, should be studied, as it is the mastery of weight quality which gives expression to movement. Heaviness itself is a passive attitude to weight, in which there is neither strong nor light tension. In heaviness there is no will to move or direct the body to control itself: allied to slow time, therefore, it may produce languid, sad, or tragic reactions in the mover and observer; when allied to quick time, the result is comic because of its total absurdity. Lightness, on the other hand, can be used throughout the whole range of speeds: slow lightness has a dreamlike quality, while quick lightness tends to be active, bright and crisp. The student should explore all the variations of time–weight relationships, and so enlarge her range of expressive movement.

A firm movement, being strong and forceful, is executed as though against

23

resistance, and the energy thus projected into space results in a strong movement, or, if withheld, in a strong position or pose. A light movement, by contrast, is fine, delicate, sensitive and buoyant, and thus uses very little tension. The body floats and feels carried in the air when moving or still. Strong movements use the centre of gravity, while light ones use the centre of buoyancy to counter the pull of gravity.

Judgement

Any physical activity requires judgement and decision; the more highly skilled the activity, the greater must be the mental awareness when quick judgements and decisions are to be made.

For example, to reach a certain place in a given time requires one to assess the speed necessary to enable the distance to be covered in the time available. The effort generated before the start propels the body through space, and must be continued – if necessary, increased – during the journey to a goal. This exemplifies the strong-sustained type of movement, and involves the feeling of the weight of the body being propelled through space. In dance, it is used in running and in movements which require continuing effort during their execution. More particularly, it is used for the purpose of expressing such emotions as anger, determination and dominance, since it is powerful and persevering. If the impetus on the other hand is light, like blowing thistledown or trailing a chiffon scarf, the movement will follow through lightly in a continuous line or pattern which gives a dreamlike, peaceful and quiet feeling.

Effort action

To throw or bowl a ball, the purpose of the action must be known beforehand, and the effort needed to achieve it gathered, then released, in the impetus attack. The reaction to this is the flight of the ball. So we can see that the effort action is in the preparation, while the apparent action is really a reaction to the initial impetus generated in the preparation. The same principle applies to hitting a ball with a bat, a racquet or stick of any kind, as in cricket, tennis, golf or snooker. In dancing, if the effort (prompted by the awareness of weight) is put into the preparation, the movement itself will be released, like the ball, to follow its destined path, and so will be allowed to achieve its desired effect and quality. According to the degree of force put into the preparation and the initial action, so the reaction will be strong and forceful, or light and delicate. If the release of effort is sudden, the feeling of the reaction will be energetic, athletic and vigorous, or sharp, crisp and bright. If the release is sustained, it will be slow and firm, or floating and light.

Mental approach

The mental approach and physical feeling towards weight results in dance quality. The attitude of mind to time–weight relationships directs the amount of expression put into, and reflected from, a certain movement, and enriches it with aesthetic quality. The gradations between strong–continuous, light–

continuous, strong–sudden, and light–sudden movements are innumerable. By selecting the correct blend of action and reaction, and employing his understanding and interpretation of time–weight qualities, the sensitive artist can express in his own individual style exactly what he wishes to convey.

Time–weight relationships

In the first years of study, the student should learn to understand the use of weight and its relationship to time in simple exercises, steps and improvisations. In mime, the many shades of feeling, expression, emotion and meaning depend on these two important elements. (Further suggestions for the teacher will be found in the exercises 'Weight related to effort and time', on p. 131).

The awareness of space

The awareness of space around the body, and the individual attitude to it, dictate how that space is used. One person's attitude may be directed in a set, self-oriented path, with no feeling for what is beyond himself, and so that person lives in a void. Another may explore and enjoy the space around him, and find it full of interesting people and things. These attitudes in turn affect each person's relationships with others and with the world outside. Very young children like to be close to others, and are often afraid of wide open spaces. As they grow up, this fear and the need for the security of others disappear in varying degrees. It is generally understood that space means freedom, both mentally and physically, and so the exploration and acceptance of space is a most important part of early movement training. For our purposes, we may make a distinction between personal and general space.

Personal space

This is the sphere around the stationary body, in which the limbs and torso can extend in all directions and at all levels. Movement may be made away from or towards the centre of the body, with the limbs extended away from or close to it. Various shapes can be assumed as the body moves through personal space: for example, the shape can be long and narrow, small and compact, wide, round, in the shape of the letters S and Y . . . and so on.

General space

General space is used when travelling either a short distance or a long one, at any level and in any direction. The patterns can be direct paths, or more complicated shapes and figures, such as X, O, T, Z, 8, 3, . . . and so on.

It is the awareness and understanding of space which help to give assurance in everyday life, in mixing with other people, in playing sports, in self-defence, or in driving a car. One is aware of space by observation through the eyes, and through the sense of feeling in the skin. This awareness leads to anticipation of emerging patterns. By looking, measuring, and judging space one can avoid an object or a person, pass, retreat, circle: one can arrest movement and meet without colliding, touch gently, or attack.

Judgement

When the assessment of distance is incorporated with a sense of speed (time) and energy (quality and weight), the ability to make a correct judgement is developed. This is essential for an accident-free life, and it is those in whom these qualities are highly developed who excel at sports, dancing, or driving. Having made the judgement, great concentration is required to achieve the goal. The eyes must not be taken off the ball so its speed and line of flight can be calculated to enable the catch to be cleanly taken. Judgement of the amount of energy to put into a throw or hit takes into account the distance to be covered. Likewise in dancing, the eyes must see clearly and positively to make judgements of the energy needed to cover a given distance; they then follow the path of the movement, and by these means complete the picture drawn in the air for the onlooker to see.

The exploration of space under the stimulus of ideas and emotions helps us express feelings and respond to the feelings of others. In this way, better self-understanding is gained, as well as empathy with others.

Exercises

Exercises in the use of space are an integral part of every class and it is most important that the beginner, from the very first, feels the necessity for being oriented in the space of the classroom and in relation to other students. When doing floor exercises, the body must be correctly placed and aligned accurately in the required direction. Balance and symmetry of the body are dependent on the dancer becoming as aware as possible of both his personal and general space.

In order to help the student to grasp quickly the direction in which he is asked to move or face, it is desirable to teach first the points of the stage or studio, and always to refer to their numbers.

The Points of the Stage

Upstage Opposite Prompt   Upstage Prompt

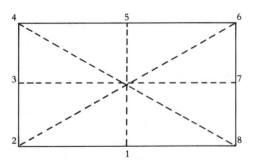

Downstage O.P.   Prompt

Audience/Teacher

Directional terms

Diagonale	....	diagonal
En manège	....	travelling and turning in a circular pattern around the stage
De côté	....	to the side
En avant	....	to the front
En arrière	....	to the back
Devant	....	in front
Derrière	....	at the back

Within the square of the stage are the basic patterns of movement: the circle, with varying lengths of radius according to the size of circle required; the cross, from 1 to 5 and from 3 to 7 or reverse; the *en diagonale* from 2 to 6 and from 8 to 4 and reverse.

Numerous variants of these basic shapes are possible. Straight patterns can be in the form of I, X, E, T, etc.; angular ones can be 7, V, W, etc.; rounded patterns may be curved, circular or spiral, as C, O, 6, 3, etc. When using these more complex figures, students should understand them in relation to the basic patterns, and an awareness of stage centre and of the directional numbers as points of reference is essential in judging and following a pattern.

The awareness of flow

The dancer's sense of freedom in movement and of spontaneous expression through improvisation is a valuable asset which should not be clouded through over-emphasis on technique for its own sake. Most children like to dance, or at least express their feelings through movement which is dance. Technique, I believe, should be the means by which one dances better; so, concurrently with exercises and steps, improvisation should be included in every class for young children and for the once-a-week student. Through improvisation, students can enjoy movement and experience the benefit gained from exercise, while developing a deeper understanding of dance. Technique thus assumes its proper role; while, since every child has *some* potential, improvisation may be the best way to find and develop what the individual student can do.

Formal steps

Every part of the body should be used in improvisation, so that a complete feeling of harmony of the head and limbs with the body is experienced. This feeling of completeness must then be retained in formal exercises and steps: in this way, each part of the class reinforces the other.

Partners and group-work

In improvisation the student is introduced to working with a partner or in a group, as well as dancing solo. Working with groups or partners, empathy is fostered as people express their feelings and moods through the manner in which they move and react.

27

Improvisation and training

It is in improvisation that the result of training can be seen and judged. If the child can use the mechanical facility gained in the Awareness Exercises section – if she or he can jump, balance, turn, bend, use the line of the body, co-ordinate movements of the head, arms, body and legs, and use the arms actively to assist movement – then real progress has been made. If he can use the floor and aerial patterns in both personal and general space, relate to and communicate with others, move rhythmically, express the quality of music, show a sense of presentation in performance, the requirements of a dancer have been prepared.

Improvisation, therefore, should be a performance, and not a self-indulgent exercise. An experience shared is of more value than one hoarded to oneself. The child learns that dance can be a means of conveying his ideas, emotions and stories to someone else. Thus the main purpose of improvisation is to dance and create the desired effect by means of a technique gained in exercises and with the use of accompaniment and surroundings.

Fundamentals of improvisation

In accordance with the principles of understanding each aspect of a movement while keeping the overall picture in mind at all times, concentrate on one aspect of improvisation at a time, so that as wide a range as possible can be used in the final performance. Place the emphasis on:

1. *Music:* time, tune/levels, quality, form, phrasing, and rests.
2. *Words:* Activities: dart, shoot, linger, creep, fly, collapse, whirl, float, etc.

Conditions: cold, hot, hungry, happy, angry, afraid, etc.

Imitations: people of various types; animals; flowers; trees, etc.

Happenings: showday; a picnic; a lost toy, etc.

Imaginings: A walk in space; smoke, bouncing a ball; storm at sea, etc.

The student must *think* about the subject, and see it in his imagination before it can be turned into movement. So, sit or stand still while listening to the music and think, then try to recreate the image of the mind.

When working on improvisation:

1. Present the theme, and discuss it.
2. If it is based on music, listen and discuss the music.
3. Explore suitable movements and practise them.
4. Combine selected phrases so as to make some form.
5. Check that floor patterns, levels, space, speed and quality are being clearly conveyed at all times.
6. Final performance, combining all that's been done.

Themes can be set by the teacher or chosen by the children. It is a good idea to set two, and let the children suggest the third, and later reverse the ratio.

Devising a programme

In the First Year, solo work is probably all the children can cope with; but in the Second Year they can dance in pairs. In the Third Year, introduce dances in threes and fours, and in the Fourth Year, work in larger groups as well as in the smaller ones. Dancing with others can be done by performing the same movement at the same time, or slightly after (as in a canon), or by doing the opposite in shape and level, time and quality. The rhythm can be copied, counterpointed, or augmented. The form of a conversation can be used. Meeting, approaching, parting, passing, avoiding or merging patterns can be incorporated in the improvisation. When working in threes, make use of splitting, linking, passing between and going through. In fours, the work can be in a group, two pairs, a square, or a diamond. In fives, a circle can be made, or an asymmetrical pattern of two and three. Full use should be made of all these possibilities.

It is also interesting to work on a specific part of the body, such as using head and arms only. Movement can be led by the shoulder, the elbow, the wrist or the hand (palm, fingertips, sides, back, etc.). If using the body or trunk only, the movement can be led by the chest, the pelvic girdle, or the waist. Remember that the centre of gravity is in the pelvis, and strong actions come from there which can lead forward, sideways, backwards or *en diagonale*. The centre of buoyancy is in the chest, and the waist is the link between the two centres.

Improvisation and performance
The use of properties can expand ideas and develop theatrical quality in a dance, but it should not be relied on as the sole means of inspiration. Scarves can represent many things, such as part of a costume, or scenery, or a floating cloud. Use balloons, hoops, ropes, feathers, boxes . . . and lots of imagination!

If improvisation is the culmination of a lesson, it leads to the equivalent of *Grand Allégro* of the classical dance, and fulfils the purpose of the training. To dance for the enjoyment of both performer and observer develops the budding artist's powers of presentation. However, it must be understood that 'presentation' has nothing to do with forced smiles or unnatural expressions, or with a visible awareness of the presence of an audience. The audience must be felt to be present, not constantly looked at. Presentation is the ability to convey emotion, content, quality, truthfully and simply by clear movement-pattern and phrasing, so that each member of the audience identifies with the performer and the situation being conveyed.

The choreographer
Improvisation and folk dance provide the necessary experience on which the choreographer can develop his art aided by the techniques of movement and stagecraft, and a thorough knowledge and appreciation of music.

Part II

Awareness Exercises

The Body/Instrument

Exercises are designed to help the dancer to dance better. They are meant to heighten body-awareness, and so add to the pleasure experienced by moving in an expressive manner. The movements which make up these exercises are also embodied in the steps. So the various qualities found in steps should be practised in exercises, as well as the different speeds which give each step its special character.

If the system of dividing exercises is applied, both teaching and learning are made easier and the results are more lasting. The following examples are to show the way to break up exercises into their basic divisions. However, it must be remembered that the divided exercise *must not become a way of life*: it is only a way to the required accomplishment. Therefore, avoid dwelling over-long on the division, and move on as soon as each part is mastered until the final form is reached.

It is better to do an exercise a few times well – say, from two to four times, followed by a rest, and then repetition – rather than many times carelessly and badly. To instil the feeling into the mind and body, the movement is done four times on the right, then repeated on the left.

Exercises *en croix*:

Exercises which are executed *en croix* – that is, to the front, side, back, and side – are taught in the following manner: *à la seconde*, *derrière*, and lastly *devant*. This is because, in certain aspects, the movement *à la seconde* is the hardest, and once correct posture can be maintained and maximum rotation has become habitual in the second position, it follows that *derrière* and *devant* will be easier. *Derrière* is taught next because again, it is more difficult to achieve the correct directional line *derrière* than *devant*. The most difficult aspect of *devant* is in keeping the two hip-bones in alignment; but if they have been correctly placed in the first two directions, the placement *devant* is easily understood. So it will be seen that by studying the most difficult direction first, the others are naturally and easily added.

When teaching an exercise to the side which ultimately closes *devant* and *derrière* alternately, do it four times closing *devant*, turn and repeat on the other side. In a later lesson, do the same closing *derrière*. When fully understood, alternate the closing. If moving to the fourth *derrière*, do the movement four times, turn and repeat on the other side. Later, do the same to fourth *devant*.

31

When the time comes to execute the movement *en croix*, do it twice only in each direction.

Moving in a circle

When doing a step in a circle, start anti-clockwise, and then repeat clockwise. This means that the first direction is to the right, and the second to the left. As the right is usually easier for most people, the step itself can be concentrated on while the direction causes no problem; and when the direction to the left is likely to cause worry, the step has already been learnt.

Observation

The student must observe a movement accurately, then she should be called on to recall and execute it correctly. All exercises and steps should be reversed as soon as possible, so that the area and scope of movement is widened. Students should be able to reverse any movement by themselves quickly and accurately, once the habit has been instilled. Sensitivity and quality should be encouraged in every exercise, be it at the *barre* or in the centre.

***

In the following exercises, the divisions are numbered according to the year of study. However, some classes make quicker progress than others, and these divisions must be flexible to meet the needs of each class.

Basic Exercises

Before any constructive work can be done, a foundation must be laid on which to build. In this section, certain positions and movements have been singled out to form this foundation. These consist of:

1. The *correct posture* and *placement of weight*, without which nothing can be achieved.

2. The *rotation of the legs* in the hip-sockets, which is required for certain positions and movements.

3. The *basic positions* of the feet and arms which establish points of reference for movements.

4. *Preparations and finishes* which provide the beginnings and ends of exercises and steps.

5. The correct manner of kneeling, sitting and lying before exercises are included here.

6. The *révérence* which creates a respectful attitude to the teacher and the art being studied.

Exercises for Posture

It is the first priority and responsibility of the teacher to correct posture before subjecting the student to difficult exercises and steps. The body should be held in an aesthetically beautiful and functional posture to allow the muscles and joints to move freely and beautifully with no injurious effects to the physique. Good posture or placement enables movements to be co-ordinated rhythmically and a balanced harmonious picture maintained in both movements and poses at all times.

In these four years of training the aim is to achieve correct posture and the ability to sustain it for a reasonable length of time. In accordance with the Alexander Principle of the use and functioning of the body (the study of which I strongly recommend), the spine should be released upwards so the head is free, the shoulders relaxed and open and allowed to fall down and apart (they should never be pinched back), the back straight, the stomach supported and the centre of balance directly over the middle of the feet.

First Year

1. a. To release the spine forwards and upwards, let the child imagine a balloon is tied to the top of his head. The balloon will float the body forwards and upwards with an accompanying feeling of growing taller.
See that there is no straining to achieve this correct posture.
Tempo 4/4.   On four chords, prepare by standing in first position parallel with the arms at the side of the body.
   Bars 1–4.   Stand tall imagining the head is being lifted up by a balloon tied to a piece of string from the top of the head;
   Bars 5–8.   Relax and prepare to repeat once.
At first stand for only two bars until the understanding and strength have been gained. Then increase the length of time. In this exercise the child also learns to understand that stillness is positive and not negative.
1.b.   Lie on the back on the floor. Make sure the body is lying straight and correctly aligned in a given direction. Note that in all exercises lying on the back, the face must be directly to the ceiling.
Tempo 4/4.   On four chords, prepare with the hands resting on the stomach.
   Bar 1.   Press the centre of the spine down to the floor. Breathe in;
   Bar 2.   Release the spine and open the hands to the side on the floor. Breathe out.
Practise no more than four times, rest, then repeat.

Second Year

2.a.   Repeat exercise 1.b. with the arms down by the sides of the body.
2.b.   Now repeat 1.b. with the arms extended to the side at shoulder level. The elbows should be relaxed and the palms on the floor.
2.c.   Lie on the back and bend both knees so the back can become quite flat. Place the hands on the stomach.
Tempo 4/4.
   Bar 1.   Extend the right leg fully, keeping the placement of the back;
   Bar 2.   Bend the knee again.
Do no more than four times with the right then repeat with the left. Later, extend the legs alternately and later still, extend both legs together.
2.d.   At the end of the second year, standing with the feet in parallel first, face the *barre* and hold it with both hands. Think about posture and correct it. This is done only if the necessary strength has been acquired. Should this not

be the case, wait until the Third Year to introduce the exercise in the upright position.

Third Year

3.a.   Exercise 2.a. is now done lying on the back with the arms above the head in parallel position, elbows relaxed and the palms turned inward.

3.b.   Exercise 2.d. is now standing in a slightly rotated first position of the feet.

Fourth Year

The exercise for posture is now included with positions of the feet at the *barre*.

Notes: When lying down, the legs and feet should be stretched in parallel position and the heels should not be lifted from the floor. Keep the shoulders released downwards and the chest open.

Make sure that the appropriate rotation exercises have been studied and understood before incorporating the turn-out in posture exercises. For relaxation of the spine, as well as a memory check on correct placement, lie on the back with the head supported on a book about one to one and a half inches thick (according to the age and size of the individual). Bend both knees and place them together with the feet in an open parallel second position. Place the hands folded on the stomach. Stay in this position with the whole spine touching the floor, for some minutes. This is very beneficial for any age or occupation.

Rotation Exercises

These exercises are designed to prepare the student for rotated positions of the feet and legs by making him aware of the deep muscles at the back and inside of the thighs which actively turn the leg in the hip-socket. Rotation is essential for later study of the classical dance when turn-out of the legs in the hip-sockets is both functional and aesthetic. Correct rotation can only be achieved if the posture of the body is held so as to allow the muscles and joints to move freely. Rotation exercises are introduced in the Second Year when the first rotated positions of the feet are used.

Second Year

2.a.   Sit on the floor with the legs stretched in front in correct alignment.

Tempo 4/4.   On four chords, correct the uplift of the spine, place the finger tips on the floor in second position, slightly forward of the shoulders, with the elbows released. Stretch the feet.

Bar 1.   Flex the feet, starting with the toes then the ankles. That is, 'go through the foot';

Bar 2.   Allow the toes, ankles, knees and thighs to fall outward rotating in the hip-sockets;

Bar 3.   Return to the parallel flexed position;

Bar 4.   Going through the feet, fully stretch them.

Note: This exercise can be added to that for *pliés* after each exercise is understood separately.

2.b.   Stand in parallel second position facing the *barre* with both hands lightly placed on it. Move the right heel forward rotating the leg on the ball of the foot only as far as comfortable, while maintaining correct alignment of the body. Now move the left heel forward to meet that of the right in a comfortable first position. Do not allow any wriggling into position and keep giving the direction to lengthen and release the spine forward and upward. Return to parallel and repeat.

Third Year

3.a.   Exercise 2.a. is now done lying on the back. Make sure the spine is released and lies flat on the floor. There is no movement in any part of the body other than that in the muscles at the back and inside of the thighs, the calves and the feet. The arms can be by the sides or in second position with the wrists and palms flat on the floor. The face should be looking to the ceiling.
3.b.   Exercise 2.b. moves both heels forward at the same time. Aim to improve rotation without distortion.

Tempo 4/4.   On four chords, place the hands on the *barre* opposite the shoulders and correct the posture while standing in parallel second position.

Bar 1.   Move both heels forward to first position;
Bars 2–3.   Hold the position and correct the posture;
Bar 4.   Return to parallel second.

Repeat three times.

Fourth Year

4.a.   Do exercises 2.b. and 3.b. standing in the centre.
4.b.

Tempo 4/4.   Prepare sitting on the floor with the finger tips touching the floor in second position. Stretch the legs to the front.

Bar 1.   1,2,   Stretch the feet in parallel first;
           3,4,   Rotate the legs in first position;
Bar 2.   1,2,   By moving the heels outward underneath the toes, rotate the legs in to a small open parallel position;
           3,4,   Rotate the legs outwards;
Bar 3.   1,2,   Move the heels under the toes into second position parallel;
           3,4,   Rotate the legs;
Bar 4.   Hold the position;
Bar 5.   1,2,   Turn the legs to parallel by rotating them so the toes are over the heels;
           3,4,   Rotate by bringing the heels to a small second position;
Bar 6.   Repeat Bar 5. returning to first position;
Bar 7.   Repeat;
Bar 8.   Return to parallel first.

Repeat three times.

Learning positions

4.c.   Combine foot work, knee bends and rotation.

Tempo 4/4.   On four chords prepare in the butterfly position (soles of the feet together and knees open to the sides). Place the finger tips in second.

Bar 1.   1,   Draw the knees together;

2,   Stretch the legs and feet in parallel first;

3,   Flex the feet;

4,   Rotate the legs;

Bar 2.   1,   Return the legs to parallel first with the feet still flexed;

2,   Stretch the insteps and toes;

3,   Draw the knees up to parallel *retiré*;

4,   Return to the butterfly position.

Repeat the exercise three times, relax and repeat.

Note: This is the finished form of the exercise. When introducing it, take it slowly with pauses. Use combined exercises when the basics are understood.

Positions of the feet

By the end of the Fourth Year, the five positions of the feet, which are the basis for executing all movements in the classical dance, have been prepared and understood. At the same time the correct posture has been consolidated. In the following exercises, the degrees of rotation refer to the angle made by each leg from the position of parallel first. Teach the positions in the following order and progressions.

First Year

First Position

1.a.   Place the feet in parallel first position with the heels, ankles and calves touching at the same level. The weight must be evenly placed on both feet with all five toes on the floor. Teach simultaneously with the exercise for posture and in the same manner.

1.b.   Later, probably in the later part of the year, allow a slight turn-out of the legs, no more than fifteen degrees while making sure the heels are touching. It is recommended to hold the position and posture from four to eight bars of 4/4 *tempo*. Relax and repeat.

Second Position

1.c.   Place the feet parallel side by side approximately one and a half times the length of the foot distant from one another. The heels must be level and the weight equally distributed on both feet. All five toes must be on the floor and the toes, ankles and knees must face the same direction making one straight line of the leg. Maintain correct posture. Rotate this position also at the appropriate time of training.

Fourth Position

1.d.   Place the feet in parallel position, one in front of the other the distance of one step. The weight must be equally placed on both feet with all five toes on the floor. Again the toes, ankles and knees face the same direction in one straight line. The hips must be level and not allowed to turn from the front. Maintain correct posture. Rotate slightly at the end of the year.

Second Year

First Position

2.a.　After the introductory exercises for rotation in the hip-sockets, allow the rotation to increase to twenty-five degrees. Make sure the weight is placed on the whole foot and the rotation is of the whole leg.

Second Position

2.b.　Allow each leg to rotate in the hip-socket from twenty-five degrees to forty-five degrees keeping the heels level and the toes, ankles and knees in one line. The weight being placed equally on both legs and the maintenance of correct posture are essentials.

Fourth Position

2.c.　Increase the rotation to forty-five degrees. With the weight on the balls of the feet, be sure to rotate by moving the heels forward, to the line of the toes (not the toes back to the line of the heels), as this movement is the basis for all changes of direction on the full foot.

Third Year

3.a.　Consolidate the rotation at forty-five degrees of first, second and fourth positions.

Third Position

3.b.　Introduce this position only when the rotation at forty-five degrees has been mastered. The feet stand one in front of the other, the heel of one foot tightly pressed to the centre of the other. The weight must be placed equally on both feet with all five toes on the floor. Do not allow the weight to fall back on the heels. Make sure the ankles are crossed. The body must be well lifted and correct posture held.

Fourth Year

4.a.　Increase the rotation in first, second, third and fourth positions to the individual child's maximum while observing all the previous rules.

Fifth Position

4.b.　Teach this position at the end of the fourth year and then only to the individual child's maximum turn-out. In the ideal classical fifth position the feet stand, turned out, one in front of the other with the toe of one foot closely pressed against the heel of the other. However, this can only be achieved in much later training. The centre of balance is between both feet with all five toes on the floor. Do not allow any rolling either backwards to the little toes or forward to the big toe. After fifth position is mastered third position is very seldom used.

Recommended exercise for all positions for all years

Tempo 4/4.　On four chords prepare.

　Bars 1–2.　Hold the position. During this time the teacher should remind the student of the directions he must give himself in order to achieve the correct position and posture;

　　Bar 3.　Relax;

　　Bar 4.　Take the position once more.

Teach facing the *barre* with two hands placed lightly on it directly opposite the shoulders with the elbows released down. Correct posture is maintained by lengthening forward and upward. Full rotation demands that the toes are turned to the side in one line with the heels, ankles, knees and shoulders. (Do not force the rotation if there is any distortion of the limbs and body.) This rotation is in the hip-socket and is achieved by the use of the deep muscles at the back and inside of the thigh. The use of these muscles causes the buttocks to firm and pull together. The turn-out should be isolated from the straightening movement of the pelvis which is held quite still during the leg rotation.

Changing from one position to another

Teach first at the *barre* and later in the centre. The placement of the hands on the *barre* is very important. The fingers and thumbs should be together and lightly rest on the top of the *barre*. The hands must be exactly opposite the shoulders and the elbows allowed to fall down in one line with the hands and shoulders. There must be no weight or strain on the hands. When changing the weight from first to second position, the hands must slide along the *barre* in order to stay opposite the shoulders and keep the body in the correct alignment. The head must be held upright and look straight ahead.

First Year
1.a.   Use a simple step to change from one position to another.

Second Year
2.a.   When brushes have been studied, change the positions with the brushing movement at Second Year level. Use both parallel and slightly rotated positions.

Third Year
3.a.   Teach facing the *barre*, with two hands lightly placed opposite the shoulders. Change positions with brushes held on the floor as for this year and use both parallel and rotated positions.

Fourth Year
4.a.   Teach facing the *barre* with the use of correct *battement tendu* to change rotated positions. Combine the exercise for posture with the change of position in the manner described below.

Tempo 4/4.   On four chords prepare the arms with the breathing movement. Place the hands on the *barre*.

Bar 1.   Stand in first position and think of the posture;
Bar 2.   Change to second position;
Bar 3.   Hold the position and make the necessary corrections;
Bar 4.   Change to first, third or fifth position;
Bar 5.   Hold the position;
Bar 6.   Change to fourth position;
Bar 7.   Hold the position;

Bar 8.   Return to first position.

Note: Use this same exercise for each year adapting the timing and using the appropriate positions being studied.

Positions of the Arms

The arms play a very important part in dance of any kind. They are the basic means of expression and give the finishing line to various poses. Their use is indispensible for correct co-ordination and gives active assistance in all movements, especially in turning and jumping. Correct placement and movement of the arms are the hallmark of the educated dancer. The arms should be free, light, floating, open, generous and expressive.

There are three basic positions of the arms; first, second and third. When mastered, together with better understanding of posture, these positions may be used at varying levels, that is, *demi* and *grand* positions. *Demi* positions are used with small poses and steps and *grand* ones with high poses and big jumping and travelling steps. They can also be combined to make additional poses and *port de bras*. However, teach the basic classical positions in the following order; *bras bas*, first, third and then second. When these positions have been mastered, introduce the *demi*-positions. In the Third and Fourth Years, combinations of these positions may be used, for example, the right arm in second and the left in first; the right arm in third and the left in first or second and so on. Often these composite positions are included in five positions of the arms when they are called third and fourth and the basic third position is referred to as fifth. However, the naming is unimportant as long as the principle is understood. When learning the composite positions, it is useful to place one arm at a time until the feeling for the position has been established, and only then move both arms simultaneously.

Teach the correct use of the head and eyes with each arm position so that their use becomes habitual.

Before introducing curved positions of the arms in Second Year, exercises for curving them should have been studied, see Isolation Exercises for *allongé*, p. 43 and Control Exercises for the elbows and *allongé*, p. 80.

The position of the hand and fingers should be studied before commencing the arm positions.

Position of the Hand

Extend the arm with a released elbow and the palm turned down. The hand forms one line with the arm so the wrist is not 'broken'. The fingers should be held lightly together, the fingertips aiming to the same point in the distance. The second and third fingers touch one another, the first and little ones are allowed to extend slightly upwards away from the palm while the thumb lies freely, without strain, under the first finger. The second and third fingers curve in towards the thumb in rounded positions and extend in straight ones. They also lead the opening of the arms from a curved position and extend to trail when lowering the arm. The use of the fingers, together with the softening of the elbow when lowering, gives fluidity to arm movements and avoids over-use of the wrists with its consequent flapping effect.

First Year

Parallel Positions

1.a. *Arms low.* Allow the arms to hang freely by the sides with the palms of the hands towards the body. The arms should be free from the body and allowed to curve slightly.

1.b. *First position.* Raise the arms from arms low directly in front of the body to a height a little above the waist. The elbows are extended but not locked. The fingers are also extended but not strained, the palms are turned down to face the floor. The position is parallel, each arm opposite its own shoulder. The head inclines slightly to allow the eyes to look at one hand.

1.c. *Demi-first position.* Lift the arms to half way between arms low and parallel first position. The arms are extended as in first with the palms towards the floor. The head inclines slightly to allow the eyes to look at one hand.

1.d. *Third position.* Continue the line of first position upwards until the hands are just visible without looking up. The palms are facing away from the body, the fingers extended but not strained. The hands are in one line with the wrists, elbows and shoulders. The elbows should not be locked as they should still have a softened feeling. The shoulders must remain down and not be lifted with the arms, but should feel open and apart. The chest must be open, the diaphragm not protruding and the back held upright and quite still. The head is free and the eyes look slightly up to the hands. It is essential to maintain correct posture by releasing the spine upward, even at the expense of the height of the arms as this will increase with understanding and work.

1.e. *Second position.* The arms are extended to the sides slightly in front of the body at the same height as first position. The elbows are extended but not locked. The fingers also extend softly with the palms turned down to the floor. The head and eyes should look straight ahead and the hands be just visible without turning to look at them.

1.f. *Demi-second position.* This is half the width and half the height of second position and is executed in the same manner.

Second Year

2.a. *Bras bas.* The correct form of *bras bas* is introduced in Second Year and used from then on. It is a preparatory position from which most movements of the arms commence. The arms are held low in front of the body but not touching it, being extended a little way from the body. The distance between the hands is only small, say, two or three inches. The fingers are grouped together with the palms facing upwards. The arms form an oval shape with the elbows pointing away from the body to the sides.

2.b. *First position.* The arms are lifted from *bras bas* in front of the body to the height of the diaphragm and are lightly curved at the elbows and wrists to form an oval as in *bras bas*. The palms turn towards the body. The elbows and fingers are in one curved line. The shoulders fall apart and down and the chest is open. The hands are from two to three inches apart. The back and spine must be held straight and the body released upwards from the pelvis. Make sure there is no movement in the body or raising of the shoulders as the arms are lifted. Do not allow the hands and wrists to droop but keep them in line with the forearm, the elbows and the upper arm.

2.c. *Demi-first position.* This is the same curved position as first but only half its height.

2.d. *Third position.* The arms form the same oval shape as in first and *bras bas* positions. They are lifted in front of the body until the hands are just visible when looking straight ahead. The oval of the arms frames the face. The palms turn towards the dancer's face. The rules of Posture must be observed.

2.e. *Second position.* The arms form an arc of a big circle in front of the body at the height of first position. The palms face the centre of the circle. The fingers should be able to be seen when looking straight ahead, this means the wrists are in line with the chest and the arms are not too far back. The student must be conscious of the relationship between the wrists, elbows and chest. The elbows face the back, the shoulders are down, the chest open and the rib-cage closed.

2.f. *Demi-second position.* The same curved position as second but only half its width and height.

Third and Fourth Years
The positions are exactly the same as for Second Year. Here is an example exercise for all years.

Tempo 4/4 or slow 3/4. Stand in a comfortable first position in the centre.

Bar 1. Copy the position as demonstrated;

Bar 2. Correct it as the teacher describes it;

Bar 3. Hold the position, thinking about it;

Bar 4. Relax.

Note: The exercises for curving the arms in Control exercises (p. 000) should be used here to assist the understanding of these positions and prepare the correct relative placement of the wrist, forearm and upper arm.

Changing from one position to another
How the arms change from one position to another is the basis of the graceful and beautiful movements of *port de bras* as well as having a very practical and functional role in dancing.

First Year
1.a. *From Arms Low to First Position Parallel*

Tempo 2/4. Stand in first position of the feet with corrected posture. On two chords, prepare with the arms in low position.

Bar 1. Lift the arms to first position leading with the second and third fingers and the wrists. The elbows are softened;

Bar 2. Hold the position, correcting it and the posture, look to one hand;

Bar 3. Slightly softening the elbows and stretching the second and third fingers, allow the fingers to trail and lower the arms to arms low, follow one hand with the head and eyes;

Bar 4.   Hold the arms in low position and raise the head and eyes erect.
Repeat once then relax and repeat looking at the opposite hand.

1.b.   *From First to Third Position Parallel*

Tempo 2/4.   Prepare on two chords.

Bar 1–2.   Lift the arms to first position parallel;

Bar 3.   Continue to lift with the fingers and wrists leading and with softened elbows, to third parallel, look to the right hand;

Bar 4.   Hold the picture;

Bar 5.   Lower to first parallel softening the elbows and allowing the fingers to trail;

Bar 6.   Hold the position in first looking to the right hand;

Bar 7.   Lower to arms low;

Bar 8.   Hold the arms and lift the head and eyes erect.

Repeat then relax. Repeat looking to the left hand.

1.c.   *From Arms Low to Parallel Second Position*

Tempo 2/4.   Prepare on two chords. Lift and lower the arms to second position in the same manner and timing as in the previous exercises. As the movement is mastered, the arms may lift a little higher than the shoulders thus making a 'flying' *port de bras*.

Notes: The body must be held still during all arm movements so that the arms alone make the movement in isolation from the rest of the body. When the positions and changing of them have been mastered, the pauses may be eliminated and the movement made continuous.

It is not recommended to use the opening movement from first to second or from third to second until the correct classical positions are studied in the Second Year.

Second, Third and Fourth Years

From Second Year on, the curved positions of the classical dance are used as well as the parallel ones. Before learning to change curved positions the movement of *allongé* should be understood.

a.   *Allongé.* This is the lengthening and stretching of the lower arm, with a slight circular movement downward, from a curved to a straight position in which the palms are turned to face the floor. The upper arm is held still in a rotated position with the inside of the elbow facing front. Only the lower arm moves and there is no breaking of the wrist so that, when correctly understood, this movement does not lead to the flapping of the wrist, which mannerism often passes for *allongé*. The *allongé* movement is always accompanied by a deep breath so that lift, rhythm and dynamic impetus are added to the movement of the whole body.

Allongé is explained fully and put into use in the Isolation section under 'For classical arm positions and *port de bras*'. (p. 81)

b.   *From Bras Bas to First and Third Positions*

When lifting and lowering the arms from *bras bas* through first to third, there is no change in the oval pattern of *bras bas*. On the way up, the thumb and first finger lead the way. The forearm is rotated to make the curve in the elbow. On the way down, the side of the little finger and hand leads the way.

c.   *From First to Second Position*

To open from first to second position the movement begins with the second and third fingers and the forearm opening to a wider curve and then the whole arm, held in that position, continues to open until it reaches second position. The inside of the elbow does not change shape but is held in the same relative position to the hand and wrist, that is, they all face the centre of a larger circle.

d.   *From Second to Bras Bas*

To lower the arms from second to *bras bas*, *allongé* the arms, allow the elbow to soften a little and begin the downward movement while the second and third fingers extend. Lower the elbows and forearm in a continuous movement until the elbows reach the correct position for *bras bas*. They are then arrested while the forearm and hand continue down to complete the oval of *bras bas*. The head and eyes turn to look over one hand and follow the movement down then are lifted to look over the shoulder away from the *barre* or in *épaulement* direction in the centre. If working *en face* in the centre, finish looking forward.

Third and Fourth Years

e.   *From Third to Second Position*

To open from third to second extend the second and third fingers, open the forearm until it is just past the side of the head and then cut the air with the sides of the little finger and hand, without alteration to the pattern, until they reach second position. To maintain the movement pattern from halfway between third and second, the upper arm is slowed down and rotated so the elbow faces the back. The upper arm is arrested when it reaches second and the forearm and hand continue to complete the picture.

Preparations and Finishes

No exercise or step should be executed without a correct preparation or introduction. Movement cannot begin from nothing. It can result from the explosion of forces gathered together and compressed which, when released, result in explosive expansion. Equally, it can begin through the use of the principle of the pendulum. The natural athlete or dancer will have this understanding built-in and, instinctively, will use the correct impetus for each movement. However, instinct must be reinforced by knowledge and the study of impetus is imperative for both the gifted and the not so gifted.

The explosive impetus is gathered in the *demi-plié*, the release of which results in *relevés* and springs. The pendulum principle is used when the *relevé* or spring is preceded by a small preparatory step such as a *glissade*. This preparatory step, in its turn, is preceded by a deep breath and a slight opening of the arms to *demi-seconde*. This slight opening, together with the breath, is referred to as the preparatory breathing movement and is described in Preparations.

It is most important to understand that this preparatory breathing movement is an on-going one into the *port de bras* proper and not an isolated unassociated action. As you do not push a pendulum from its still position but, instead, pull it back and let go to start it swinging so, the arms open a little before swinging through *bras bas* into the upward pattern of the *port de bras*. Arm movements are, of necessity, based on circular patterns and so must follow the laws of circular movement by which they gain a free, rhythmical beauty. The degree of effort in either preparation, explosion or pendulum is directly related to the force and speed required in the step which follows.

Equally important is the finish of each exercise or step so that the body and the pattern it has made may come to rest.

It is recommended to use two or four chords for preparations and two additional ones after the end of the musical phrase for finishing movements.

All years

1.a.   *Preparation and finish for the feet*

Tempo 2/4. or 4/4. Stand in first position parallel or rotated.

Bar 1.   Transfer the weight to one leg;

Bar 2.   Point the working foot to the front, side or back, parallel or rotated according to the standard and requirement of the step;

Bar 3.   Hold the position;

Bar 4.   When used as an exercise, close the leg to first position. When used as a preparation, commence the step from the *dégagé*.

Preparations for the arms

1.b.   *Breathing movement.* This small movement prepares for all *port de bras*. From *bras bas*, the fingers and forearm only are opened a little to the side. The head and eyes follow one arm. The body is well lifted and a deep breath is taken in preparation for the movement that is to follow. The arms then return to *bras bas* ready to continue into the next movement. This will be referred to in future as the breathing movement and precedes all arm movements. Use two bars of 2/4 *tempo* or one of 4/4.

1.c.   *To Pick Up the Skirt*

Tempo 2/4.   Prepare with the breathing movement on two chords.

Bar 1.   Look at the right hand and pick up the skirt between the thumb and middle finger;

Bar 2.   Lift the skirt to *demi-seconde*, keep the elbow curved and the wrist in the same line. Follow the hand with the head and eyes;

Bar 3.   Hold the position;

Bar 4.   Look *en face*.

Practise also looking to the left hand. Later use both arms simultaneously.

1.d.   *To Place the Hands at the Waist*

Tempo 2/4.   Stand in first position with the arms in low position or *bras bas*. Prepare with the breathing movement on two chords.

Bar 1.   Lift the right arm to *demi-seconde* with the palm turned to the floor. Look to the right hand;

Bar 2.   With an inward circular movement, place the hand on the waist; follow the hand with the head and eyes;

Bar 3.   Turn the head *en face*;

Bar 4.   Hold the position.
Practise also with the left arm and later with both arms together.

Finishing Movements for the Arms
1.e.   *From Holding the Skirt*
Tempo 2/4 or 4/4.
Bar 1.   Release the skirt looking to the hand;
Bar 2.   Lower the arm to *bras bas* following it with the head and eyes;
Bar 3.   Look erect;
Bar 4.   Hold the position.
Practise with the arms separately and later together.
1.f.   *From the Hands at the Waist*
Bar 1.   Extend the arms to *demi-seconde* with the palms up; follow one hand with the head and eyes;
Bar 2.   *Allongé* and lower to *bras bas*; follow with the head and eyes;
Bar 3.   Look erect;
Bar 4.   Hold the position.
Practise with each arm and later with both together.

As soon as possible, make a complete exercise from the preparation movements of the arms and feet and their finishing movements. To begin with, prepare the arms then the feet and finish with the feet and the arms last. Later move the arms and feet simultaneously. All exercises and steps must be commenced with a preparation and completed with the appropriate finish.
Note: It will be noticed that certain movements from the section on Isolation should be studied before some of the basics can be executed correctly. In the construction of a lesson, a small amount of work on each aspect of the course should be covered and the development in each section should proceed at an equal pace so an overall balanced education in movement is achieved. Therefore, all the basics will not be taught to First Year students before including other work. By the end of the First Year all the basics for that standard should have been achieved and fully understood.

1.g.   *Taking and Giving the Hands*. Grabbing the hand of one's partner is unsightly and disturbing to the line of movement and quality of performance. It also creates the wrong feeling towards the partner, unless antagonism is intended! So, from the First Year, the taking and giving of hands correctly is a basic necessity for harmony between the dancers and for the pleasure of the audience.

To Commence:
Tempo 4/4.   Stand in a circle.
Bar 1.   Each child makes a *port de bras* with the right arm, from *bras bas* through first position to *seconde*, following the hand with the eyes and head. Finish with the palm turned upward and look to the dancer on the right;
Bar 2.   Each then turns the head to the left to look at the dancer on the left;

Bar 3. Make a *port de bras* with the left arm from *bras bas* through first to *seconde*, *allongé* the forearm lifting the hand a little and gently place the downward turned palm on the upward held one of the dancer on the left;

Bar 4. Turn the heads to the centre or in the direction of the movement to follow.

To Finish:

Bar 1. Look to the left and lift the hand from the partner's then allow it to fall to the side following the movement with the eyes and head;

Bar 2. Turn to look to the right, *allongé* and lower the right arm in the same manner. Look *en face* to finish.

Kneeling

First Year

1.a. *Tempo* 2/4. On two chords, prepare in first position parallel of feet, arms low.

Bar 1. Step forward on the right leg; arms in parallel demi-first position; look forward;

Bar 2. Kneel on the left knee allowing the body to bend forward; place the palms on the floor opposite the shoulders;

Bar 3. a, to kneel on one knee, straighten the back;
b, to kneel on two knees, place the right knee alongside the left and curl up on two knees; place the forehead on the floor;

Bar 4. Unroll the back and place the palms on the knees.

Note: Be careful not to allow any sickle on either foot in the kneeling position on one knee or sitting on two.

Second Year

2. a. Do the same as for First Year in two bars instead of four and not bending forward as far as in Bar 3. of 1. a.

Third Year

3. a. *Tempo* 2/4. Prepare in first position with the arms in low position.

Bar 1. Step forward on the right leg; lift the arms to first parallel;

Bar 2. Kneel on the left knee keeping the back straight; hold the arm position;

Bar 3. To kneel on two knees, draw the right knee to the left; hold the arms;

Bar 4. Sit back and place the hands on the knees.

Fourth Year

4. a. Use the Third Year kneeling exercise but with the arms in second position parallel.

4. b.   *Tempo* 4/4. Prepare in first position, arms low.

Bar 1.   Step back onto the right knee, keep the foot pointed and the lower leg in a straight line. Slightly rotate the left leg; lift the arms to parallel second;

Bar 2.   To kneel on two knees, join the left leg to the right; keep the back erect.

Note: The arms can be varied at the discretion of the teacher. Practise on both the right and left legs.

All Years

Sitting

1. a.   *Tempo* 4/4. Prepare in first position of the feet, arms low.

Bars 1–3.   Kneel on two knees;

Bar 4.   Sit on the right thigh; place the right hand on the floor at the side;

Bars 5–6.   Swing the legs round to a straight position in front of the body; lift the arms to first parallel;

Bar 7.   Bend the knees to a crossed position (or whatever position is required). Place the arms as required;

Bar 8.   Hold the position. Think about posture.

Lying Down

1. b.   Continue the exercise for sitting from Bar 6:

Bar 7.   Place the sides of the hands on the floor behind second position;

Bar 8.   Slide the sides of the little fingers back in a V–shape as the body rolls down through the spine.

Standing Up from Lying on the Back

1. c.   *Tempo* 2/4.

Bars 1–2.   Bring the head up and lead with the forehead to a sitting position; lift the arms to first parallel.

Bars 3–4.   Swing the legs round to the side; kneel on two knees; arms in first;

Bar 5.   Kneel on one knee by stepping forward on one leg; open the arms to second;

Bar 6.   Consolidate the balance;

Bar 7.   Stand up and join the kneeling foot forward to the other;

Bar 8.   Lower the arms.

Promenade

I would recommend that the lesson commence with an 'entrance' or *promenade*. This gives practice in walking and the feeling for a special place when one dances either in the studio or on stage. Use a pattern round the room, in a circle or into lines and finish with a *révérence* to the teacher. This helps greatly in establishing discipline, attention and a 'special' feeling for dancing. During the *promenade*, stage presentation can be encouraged with the turn of the head towards the audience, a pleasant expression on the face and alertness in the body.

Révérence

All lessons should begin and end with a *révérence* to the teacher/audience.

First Year

Girls

1. a. *Tempo 2/4.* Stand in parallel first position, arms low.
   Bars 1–2. Pick up the skirt, look to the front;
   Bar 3. *Demi-plié* in parallel first and incline the head slightly forward;
   Bar 4. Stretch the knees and look erect.

Boys

Bars 1–2. Place the hands on the hips;
Bar 3. Slightly incline the head;
Bar 4. Look erect.

Second Year

Girls

2. a. *Tempo 2/4.* Stand in a slightly rotated first position.
   Bar 1. Pick up the skirt or open to *demi-seconde*;
   Bar 2. Step forward transferring the weight to one leg, hold the arms and look forward;
   Bar 3. Bend both knees and incline the head;
   Bar 4. Join the back leg to the supporting one and stand erect.

Boys

Bar 1. Place the hands on the hips;
Bar 2. Step forward to parallel first;
Bar 3. Incline the head and the waist very slightly;
Bar 4. Stand erect.

Third and Fourth Years

Girls

In the same *tempo* and manner step to the side; place the working foot at the back in the *cou-de-pied* position *par terre* and curtsey correctly (see exercise for *cou-de-pied* p. 75).

Note: Remember that the instep and toes must fully stretch before stepping on to the leg and correct posture must be maintained throughout. The *révérence* should thank the teacher for giving the lesson or the audience for its applause.

Boys

Step to the right side and join the feet in parallel first;
Open the right arm to *demi-seconde*;
Incline the head and upper body;
Recover and lower the arm to the side;
Repeat to the left.

Isolation Exercises

These exercises are to identify and move each part of the body independently from the others. Left and right limbs must be educated to equal strength and flexibility. In this way, when the time comes to co-ordinate them, each movement is understood and controlled.

Feet, Ankles and Toes

The feet should be instruments of expression, aware of the floor through the sensitivity of the toes, ball of the foot and the heel. The student should explore the many shades of feeling of which the feet are capable. The exercises strengthen the muscles, loosen the joints and make the feet strong and flexible for future springs, rises and all travelling steps as well as providing a stable base on which to stand. When standing, make sure that all five toes are on the floor and that there is no rolling of the ankles either forward or backward. When sitting with the legs stretched out in front, the ankle bones should be as close together as possible. This means the toes will be slightly apart. A partner holding the feet in place is a great help in feeling and maintaining this correct placement of the feet.

First Year

1. a.   To suitable musical accompaniment, shake the feet, circle the ankles, wriggle the toes and use simple forms of flexing and stretching the ankles and toes.

1. b.   *Tempo 2/4.*   Sit on the floor with the legs stretched out in front in correct alignment, the back straight and upright, the head free, the shoulders down and apart, the palms on the floor in second position and the spine released upwards. On two chords prepare the position of the arms.

Bar 1.   Flex the feet, leading with the toes then the ankles;
Bar 2.   Hold the position;
Bar 3.   Stretch the ankles, insteps and point the toes to the floor;
Bar 4.   Hold the position.

Repeat three times.

Notes: Do all the exercises four times correctly with full energy, relax and then repeat the exercise to gain strength and stamina. To do the exercises more often tires the muscles but does not strengthen them.

It is helpful to create games of exercises such as saying: 'Come here toes' with the flexing and 'Go away toes' with the stretching.

1. c.   When the movements are understood, the feet can alternate with the use of 'Come here Peter, come here Paul . . . Go away Peter, go away Paul'.

Note: It is helpful for children to say or sing the words with the movement of the feet. Alternately they can use the words 'Right' and 'Left'.

Second Year

2. a.   Use 4/4 *tempo* for exercises 1. a. and 1. b. and take one bar for each movement thus allowing more time for concentration and better execution. When the back is held strongly enough, the hands can be used in co-ordination

with or in opposition to the movements of the feet. Reinforce the movement of 'going through the foot'.

2. b.   The exercise can now be done lying on the back with the body correctly aligned in the required direction. Hold the arms to the side in second position.

Use 4/4 *tempo* and aim to eliminate the pauses.

Third and Fourth Year

3. a.   The simple exercise as used in Second Year can now be done in the astride sitting position. In this position the legs are open to the maximum and the back upright. The knees must point to the ceiling. Make sure the toes, ankles and knees are always in one straight line with one another (see Astride Sitting, p. 57). The *tempo* may be speeded up as long as each movement is clear and decisive.

3. b.   Either sitting or lying on the back; in parallel or rotated position of the legs.

Tempo 4/4.   Prepare on two chords.
    Bar 1.   1, 2,   Lift the right leg slightly off the floor;
             3, 4,   Flex the foot;
    Bar 2.   1, 2,   Stretch the ankles, insteps and toes;
             3, 4,   Lower the leg.

Repeat three times with the right then do four times with the left leg.

3. c.   This exercise is to improve brushes.

Tempo 4/4.   Prepare by sitting on the floor. Flex the feet.
    Bar 1.   Lift and stretch the right foot;
    Bar 2.   Flex and lower the leg.

Execute four times with each leg and later alternate them. Take the full four counts to lift and lower so as to gain control. Pauses may be used if considered necessary.

3. d.   After exercises for rotation have been mastered, 3. c. can be done with the legs rotated to the child's maximum. Lying on the back, it can also be done to the second position.

3. e.   The next progression is to do the same exercise lying on the stomach lifting the leg directly behind the shoulder. Do not try to lift the leg too high, a couple of inches is sufficient. Both hips must remain on the floor and no strain be shown in the body. The arms can be in sphinx position or, with the finger tips touching, turn the head to the side and lie it on the hands.

Demi-pointe or Platform

This is to identify the *demi-pointe* and to prepare for rises high on the ball of the foot.

It also helps to 'go through the foot' when alighting from rises or springs. In the classical dance there are four degrees of rising on the *pointes*: quarter, half, three-quarters and full *pointe*. In this course the use of the highest rise the child's feet will allow is recommended without, of course, rising on the full *pointe*.

First Year

Platforms

1. a. *Tempo* 2/4. Prepare standing in the first position parallel. On four chords place the hands on the waist.

Bar 1. Bend the right knee to allow the right foot to rise on to the *demi-pointe* platform;

Bar 2. Hold the position;

Bar 3. Lower the heel;

Bar 4. Hold.

Practise four times with each leg, rest and repeat. At first the child will make the movement on one count but when possible take the full bar to complete the movements.

Rises

Towards the end of the First Year, introduce rises on both *demi-pointes* with straight knees. It is most important to keep the legs straight and well pulled up. The ankles must also be pulled up and the weight not allowed to fall back on to the little toes. The weight of the body should be well forward so there is no transference visible when rising or lowering. Give the direction to release the spine forward and upward before, during and after the rise.

1. b. *Tempo* 2/4. Stand in parallel first and prepare the arm position.

Bar 1. Rise slowly taking the full bar and controlling the balance;

Bar 2. Balance while releasing the spine;

Bar 3. Slowly lower the heels still concentrating on the release of the spine upwards;

Bar 4. Hold.

Work four times, rest and repeat. Later, add simple arm movements such as 'flying'. Of course the children have been using these movements in 'fairy runs' but it should be explained that the exercise is to enable them to do the step better.

Second Year

In Rotated Positions

2. a. Introduce the rises in a rotated position of the legs in first and second. Use 2/4 or 4/4 *tempo* with pauses.

2. b. Now add a *demi-plié* before the rise in both parallel and rotated positions.

Tempo 4/4. Prepare the arms.

Bar 1. 1, 2, Bend the knees;
         3, 4, Stretch the knees;

Bar 2. 1, 2, Rise;
         3, 4, Balance;

Bar 3. 1, 2, Lower the heels with straight knees;
         3, 4, Bend the knees in *demi-plié*;

Bar 4. 1, 2, Stretch the knees;
         3, 4, Hold.

Note: The knees must always be straight before the heels leave the floor and until they return to it before the *demi-plié*.

Third Year

With Arms

3. a.   Continue with the previous exercises and add the use of arms. Lift the arms to the required position with the rise and lower them as the heels lower. The movements of the feet and arms must take the same length of time and be well co-ordinated. Use with slow arm swings as follows:

Tempo 3/4.   Prepare with breathing movement;

Bar 1.   *Demi-plié*; swing the arms to *bras bas*;

Bar 2.   Rise on *demi-pointes*, swing the arms to first position;

Bar 3.   Lower the heels and *demi-plié*, lower the arms to *bras bas*;

Bar 4.   Stretch the knees and swing the arms up to *demi-seconde*.

Repeat three times, rest and then repeat the exercise. The arms may also swing up to third position. Reverse the movement of the arms so that they are in first to commence and *demi-seconde* on the rise.

Fourth Year

On One Foot

Introduce rises on one foot at the *barre*. The working foot can be placed in parallel or rotated *retiré* position.

4. a.   *Tempo 4/4.*   On two chords, prepare the hands on the *barre*.

Bar 1.   1,2,   Rise on both *demi-pointes*;

3,4,   Lift the right leg in *retiré*;

Bar 2.   1,2,   Lower the leg to the *demi-pointe*;

3,4,   Lower both heels together going through the feet.

4. b.   *Tempo 4/4.*   Prepare by placing the hands on the *barre*.

Bar 1.   1,2,   Lift the right knee in *retiré* with the toes fully pointed and placed on the inside of the supporting knee;

3,4,   Hold;

Bar 2.   1,2,   Rise on the *demi-pointe* on the left leg;

3,4,   Hold;

Bar 3.   1,2,   Lower the supporting heel being careful to go through the foot;

3,4,   Hold;

Bar 4.   1,2,   Lower the working leg to first position;

3,4,   Hold.

Repeat three times, rest then repeat on the right leg.

4. c.   Later, lift the working leg at the same time as rising on the other.

4. d.   Add a *demi-plié* before and after the rise.

Note: The co-ordination of rises with arm swings is an excellent preparation for springs in which the arms actively assist the propulsion into the air from the *demi-plié*. Be careful to maintain correct posture throughout. Release the spine upward so the head and neck are free, the shoulders apart and down, the chest open and no strain is visible. There should be no movement in any part of the body other than in those actively engaged.

Knees and Hips

These exercises are to free the joints and strengthen the muscles for future rises, springs, poses and steps. They prepare for the study of exercises in classical dance and will be called by those names.

Retiré

In preparation for *adagio*, *pirouettes* and Steps.

First Year

1. a.   *Tempo 2/4.*   Sit on the floor, stretch the legs out in front in parallel and see the body is correctly aligned. On two chords, prepare with the back straight and the palms of the hands on the floor in second position. The shoulders must be released downward.

> Bar 1.   Draw up both knees keeping the soles of the feet on the floor;
> Bar 2.   Hold the position;
> Bar 3.   Stretch the knees and feet straight in front;
> Bar 4.   Hold.

Repeat three times, rest and repeat four more times.

Second Year

2. a.   In the same *tempo* and manner as 1. a. draw one leg up to *retiré* four times, then the other leg. Stretch the feet in the *retiré*. Fingertips should now be placed on the floor. Later delete the pauses and use the legs alternately.
2. b.   Repeat 2. a. still in parallel position standing at the *barre* and then in the centre. Hold the arms in a chosen position in the centre.

Third Year

3. a.   *Tempo 4/4.*   In the sitting position, continue to work on pointing the feet and add a flexing movement when both legs are stretched.
3. b.   Do 3. a. lying on the back.
3. c.   Continue to work on 2. b. the standing progression, quickening the *tempo*.

Fourth Year

4. a.   *Tempo 4/4.*   Prepare lying down with the legs in parallel first position, the arms in second position with the palms on the floor and the elbows released.

> Bar 1.   Draw one knee up to parallel *retiré*, with the feet pointed;
> Bar 2.   Rotate both legs in the hip sockets allowing the *retiré* to open freely to the side;
> Bar 3.   Return both legs to parallel position;
> Bar 4.   Stretch the working leg.

Do four times on each leg.

4. b.   In the same manner as 4. a. hold the rotation of both legs during bar 3. and lower the working leg in the rotated position. Turn both legs parallel on the last beat of the bar.

4. c.   Standing facing the *barre*, do the exercise in rotated positions. Add a rise on *demi-pointe* on the *retiré*.

4. d.   Add a *demi-plié* on the supporting leg before the rise after the working leg is in *retiré*. This should be at the *barre* and only when the foundation is strong enough to execute the movement correctly.

Notes: In *retiré* position the toe of the working foot should be on the inside of the supporting knee. Make sure the ankle, heel, instep and toes of the working foot are in one straight line so as to avoid a sickle foot in any of the exercises.

When adding a *demi-plié* before the rise, make sure the knees are straight before allowing the heel to leave the floor and that the heels are down before repeating the *plié*. The heels must alight gently but firmly on the floor without any bumping.

On the introductory chords, make sure the weight is transferred directly over the supporting leg *before* the working leg is lifted. Releasing and lengthening the spine is of the greatest importance. There must be no strain in the body, arms or neck. The movement is done smoothly and under control in even *tempo*.

Pliés

In this preparatory course only the *demi-plié* is used. The bending and stretching of the knees, to a greater or lesser degree, is used in all dance steps. There is an infinite variety in their use and expressive quality. The student should understand that the *demi-plié* used to propel the body upward in a rise or spring is different from that which cushions the return to the floor. The amount of effort needed for each step should be compressed into the preparatory full or *demi-plié* and is dictated by the quality and activity of that step. Therefore it is necessary to judge the amount of effort to be put into the preparatory *plié*. Equally, the effort to make the landing *demi-plié* act as a break and shock absorber must be understood for each individual step. There is no more important movement in dancing.

First Year

1. a.   *Tempo 2/4.*   Stand in first position parallel. On four chords, prepare by placing the hands on the waist, holding the skirt or placing the arms in any desired position.

   Bar 1. Using the full bar of music bend both knees equally over the toes; keep the back straight and free from strain; keep all five toes on the floor and do not allow any rolling over, either forward or backward on the ankles; keep the body and arms still by releasing the spine upwards;

   Bar 2. Take the full bar to stretch the knees;

   Bar 3–4. Hold still.

Repeat three times, relax and repeat.

1. b.   Sit, correctly placed, with the palms in second position on the floor.

Tempo 2/4. On four chords, prepared by drawing up the knees and allowing them to fall open to the sides to touch the floor if possible.

   Bar 1. Draw the knees together;

Astride sitting

Bar 2.　Stretch out in front in parallel;

Bar 3.　Flex the feet;

Bar 4.　Stretch the insteps and toes;

Bar 5.　Draw the knees up in parallel;

Bar 6.　Allow the knees to fall open;

Bar 7–8.　Hold the position correcting the posture by releasing the spine upward.

Repeat from once to three times according to strength and the ability to concentrate. In this exercise the bends of the hips, knees and feet are combined.

Second Year

2. a.　Repeat 1. a. in the same manner and *tempo*, standing at the *barre* in slightly rotated first and second positions of the feet. Later do it in the centre using the breathing movement of the arms.

2. b.　No. 1. b. is done in the same manner but in 4/4 *tempo* lying on the back.

Third Year

3. a.　Add the third position and improve the *plié* in rotated positions to forty-five degrees at the *barre*.

3. b.　Add arm swings to the exercise in the centre making sure the arms are in *bras bas* in the *plié*. This is an excellent preparation for springs and rises.

Fourth Year

4. a.　Add rises in the divided manner at the *barre*.

4. b.　Add rises in the divided manner with arm swings, in the centre.

Notes: Make sure the knees, ankles and toes are in one straight line. Allow the hip-joints, knees and ankles to bend freely. Release the spine upward. Without allowing any strain, bend as deeply as possible keeping the body upright and the heels on the floor. Do the bend and stretch in even *tempo* and fill out the music so developing elasticity in the muscles. Do not allow any sitting in the *plié*, remembering that a *plié* is a movement, not a position and it must not stop until the legs are once more straight.

Astride Sitting

This is a useful position in which to do certain exercises as it gently stretches the inside of the legs. Do not force the stretch as this can be injurious. Introduce only in the Second Year.

2. a.　*Tempo* 4/4.　Sit on the floor. On four chords, prepare with the legs in parallel first, the hands on the knees, elbows released and the back well lifted.

Bar 1.　1,2,　Draw up the knees parallel; the hands rest on the knees; head erect;

　　　　3,4,　Allowing the feet to turn to a rotated first position with the soles on the floor, the knees fall apart to the butterfly position; slide the hands to the ankles;

Bar 2.　Slowly slide the feet and legs to a very open second position, as wide as possible;

		place the hands on the knees and relax the elbows;
Bar 3.	1,	Flex the feet and see that the toes and knees face directly to the ceiling and that the knees are pulled up;
	2,3,4,	Hold the position;
Bar 4.	1,	Fully stretch the ankles, insteps and toes;
	2,3,	Draw the feet into the butterfly position; hold the hands on the knees with the elbows relaxed;
	4,	close the knees into parallel position as for the commencement of the exercise.

Repeat three times.

Note: Make sure the weight is not back on the buttocks but that the pelvis is straight and the spine released in correct placement of the body.

The Back, Stomach and Waist

The back muscles must be strong to hold the placement of the spine and prevent any whiplash in energetic movements. They must also be elastic so the back can bend in graceful movements and poses.

The stomach muscles must be strong to support the internal organs.

The waist is the link between the upper and lower body and it is by the use of this link that dimension is added to the harmony of two sensitive parts of the dancing instrument.

All Years

Slide onto the back from a sitting position, 'nubble by nubble', as described in Lying Down in the section on basics. Bring the arms down to the sides and up to first parallel. Roll up to a sitting position leading with the crown of the head feeling pulled up by the arms.

Spinal Resiliences (Bounces)

This exercise is to strengthen and stretch the spine in order to make it more elastic. It also helps to loosen the hip joints. It gives support to the back in later poses, steps and springs and assists in the flowing movements of the body in the dance.

First Year

1. a. *Tempo 2/4*. Sit on the floor with the legs stretched out in front in first position parallel. On four chords, draw the feet up until the soles are touching and the knees fall apart in the butterfly position. Release the spine upwards and place the hands to rest on the ankles.

Bars 1-4.	Leading with the crown of the head, slowly bend forward until the head is resting on the floor. Allow the elbows to open along the knees;
Bars 5-8.	Unfold the body by rolling up through the spine, the head being the last thing to reach the erect position; the hands are on the ankles and the elbows relaxed.

Repeat three times, rest and repeat.

Note: This exercise can be made more interesting for small children by calling it 'Grumpy Backs and Happy Backs', using the appropriate facial expression and saying the words at the same time.

1. b. In the second half of the First Year, the exercise can be developed as follows:

Tempo 4/4. On four chords, prepare as for 1. a.

Bars 1–2. Curl over;

Bars 3–4. Bounce the head forward eight times, one on each beat of the music;

Bars 5–6. Uncurl to the upright position;

Bar 7. Lift the arms to parallel first, following the right hand with the head and eyes;

Bar 8. Lower the arms to rest on the ankles, keeping the back straight and the head erect.

Do four times, rest and repeat looking at the left hand.

Second Year

2. a. *Tempo 2/4.* Prepare as for the First Year exercises.

Bar 1. 1, Bend forward, leading with the crown, until the head rests on the feet;

2, Gently bounce the back replacing the head on the feet;

Bars 2–4. Bounce six times;

Bars 5–8. Slowly unfold to the upright position, the head being the last to arrive.

Use the arms as for the First Year. Do no more than four times, rest and repeat if necessary.

2. b. *Tempo 2/4.* Prepare the hands on the knees with the elbows relaxed along thighs, the legs being stretched out in parallel first.

Bars 1–8. Repeat the exercise 1. a. in the same time and manner with the legs in parallel first;

Slide the hands down the shins to the ankles and hold them there during the bounces; allow the elbows to fall on the outside of the legs towards the floor; return to the original position at the end of the exercise.

Repeat three times.

2. c. Before introducing this next progression, astride sitting position should have been learnt (see p. 57).

Tempo 4/4. Prepare for the astride sitting position.

Bars 1–2. Take the astride position as in Isolation.

Bars 3–4. Flex the feet; Eight bounces bending directly forward; the palms are placed on the floor in front of the shoulders with the elbows relaxed;

Bars 5–6. Unfold the spine; point the feet; return the hands to the knees;

Bar 7. Return to the butterfly position; then close the knees to parallel;

Bar 8. Stretch the legs to parallel first.

Do no more than four times.

Third Year

3. a.   *Tempo* 4/4.   Amalgamate the three previous exercises by the addition of four chords for the transition from one position to another.

Note: To open the legs from parallel first to astride sitting, release the spine upwards and open both legs simultaneously. Maintain the placement of the hips so that the legs do not roll either forwards or backwards.

Fourth Year

4. a.   Before introducing this progression, turns at the waist should have been studied (see p. 66);

Tempo 4/4.   Prepare in the astride position, turn the upper body to face directly over one leg, fully stretch the feet, place the hands, palms down, on the floor on either side of the leg with the elbows relaxed.

Do the exercise in the same manner and timing as previously or it can be amalgamated with other bounces in various timings and combinations. For example, one bounce over the right leg, one in the centre, one over the left and one in the centre. Leave out the extra chords for changing position as it will now take place on the upward movement of the bounce.

Note: Be careful of the placement of the hands in each position. The exercise can also be done with flexed feet.

Cat Stretch
This is to make the spine supple and resilient.

First Year

Table Back

1. a.   *Tempo* 4/4.   On four chords, prepare by kneeling on two knees in correct alignment with the hips and shoulders. Softly place the palms flat on the floor in front of the shoulders, not too close to the knees. Make a table back with the knees directly under the hips and the feet pointed. Keep the spine and neck in one straight line.

> Bar 1.   Hold the table position and think about it;
> Bar 2.   Continue to hold and think;
> Bar 3.   Sit back on the feet;
> Bar 4.   Prepare the table position for a repetition of the exercise.

Repeat three times.

Note: Various games can be invented to help maintain stillness in the holding bars of music; for example, pretend to be a table which is being laid for dinner, hold still for the knives and forks . . . now a plate of hot soup which must not be spilt.

Second Year

2. a.   *Tempo* 4/4.   On four chords prepare in the table position.

> Bar 1.   1,2,   Arch the middle of the back;
>   3,4,   Hold the position;
> Bar 2.   1,2,   Return to table position;
>   3,4,   Hold.

Repeat three times.

Note: In this exercise the arch can also be dropped down and returned to table position. Make sure that the neck remains in one line with the spine and is not dropped either forward or backward.

Third Year

3. a. *Tempo 4/4.*   Prepare in the same manner.
      Bar 1. 1,2,3,   Arch upward and hold;
             4,   Return to the table position;
      Bar 2. 1,2,3,   Drop the arch and hold;
             4,   Return to the table position.
Repeat no more than three times, rest and repeat.

Fourth Year

4. a. *Tempo 6/8.*   The exercise 3. a. is done in the same manner but the pauses are deleted and the movement completed in one bar of 6/8 thus preparing for a proper sequential flow through the spine. Later, use different *tempi* and vary the accents and dynamics.

Sphinx and Swallow Positions
To prepare for bends of the back. Introduce this exercise towards the end of the Second Year as it requires real concentration.

Second Year

2. a. *Tempo 2/4.*   On four chords prepare the following position: lie on the stomach in correct alignment, place the arms in the sphinx position, that is, with the elbows beside the ribs and the lower arm directly forward with the palms on the floor. The head is straight with the forehead on the floor. If the spine is lengthened this position will not be uncomfortable.
      Bar 1.   Lift the upper body a little without altering the placement of the head and neck, keep the elbows on the floor;
      Bar 2.   Hold the position;
      Bar 3.   Slowly lower the body in the same posture, to the floor;
      Bar 4.   Hold the position.
Repeat three times, rest and repeat.

Third Year

3. a. *Tempo 2/4.*   Prepare as for the previous exercise.
      Bar 1.   As in 2. a. lift the body;
      Bar 2.   Keeping the neck lengthened, turn the head over the right shoulder and lift the body a little higher allowing the elbows to lift only fractionally from the floor;
      Bar 3.   Return to the half lifted position with the head turned to the floor;
      Bar 4.   Lower the body gently to the commencement position.
Look twice to the right and twice to the left.
Note: Remember to give the direction to lengthen the spine throughout the exercise.

Fourth Year

Swallow Position
4. a.   *Tempo 4/4*.   Prepare by lying on the stomach with the arms in parallel third and the head straight.

   Bar 1. Slowly lift the upper body keeping the same relationship between the arms, the head and the upper spine;

   Bar 2. Slowly lower the body.

Repeat three times only.

Note: Be careful not to allow any strain by trying to lift too high. Remember that straining weakens the muscles.

4. b.   In the same timing and manner, lift the legs in parallel first while keeping the torso and arms in place.

4. c.   If at the end of the fourth year the student has sufficient strength, both the body and legs may be lifted at the same time.

4. d.   Lift the right arm and leg then the left. Also lift them in opposition.

Head and Eyes

Head movements and positions are an integral part of the dance. Turning, inclining, fixing and holding positions gives an educated and disciplined look to a dancer. From the first, focusing the eyes in the direction of the movement must be concentrated upon and strongly underlined. The correct 'glance', together with the movement, adds expression from within to that of the movement itself. The beauty of a pose is made up of the expression of the face, highlighted by the use of the eyes, and the harmony of the arms, body and legs. From a technical point of view, the ability to 'spot' while turning the head swiftly and accurately, is essential.

Turning the Head and Eyes

First Year

1. a.   *Tempo 2/4*.   Prepare in a standing, sitting or kneeling position, the arms held at the discretion of the teacher.

   Bar 1. Turn the head and eyes to the right keeping the rest of the body still;

   Bar 2. Focus the eyes on a particular spot and hold the position;

   Bar 3. Return the head and eyes to the front;

   Bar 4. Focus on a particular spot.

Repeat to the right three times, rest, and do four times to the left. When mastered in this manner, alternate the sides making sure that the eyes focus each time the head turns.

1. b.   In the same manner and timing, look down, with a lengthened neck, to a spot well in front of the feet and return to the upright position.

Second Year

2. a.   Add the movement of the head and eyes slightly upward without dropping the neck back. The eyes will look up at an angle of approximately

forty-five degrees from horizontal. This is about the same angle as the downward glance.

2. b.   Make the turns of the head and eyes more exact by looking to corner 2 then to point 3, etc. A game can be made out of this by asking the children to look quickly from one point of the room to another (see points of the stage, p. 26).

2. c.   *Tempo 4/4.*   Make a 180 degree turn of the head in four bars. Prepare looking to point 7.

> Bar 1. 1,2,3,   Slowly turn the head to point 3;
>
>   4,   Hold the position;
>
> *or*
>
> Bar 1.   1,   Quickly turn the head;
>
>   2,3,4,   Hold.

Third Year

3. a.   In the same manner and timing, from the erect position, look up forty-five degrees return to erect, look down forty-five degrees and return to the erect position. Take great care to curve the neck and not allow it to drop.

3. b.   Do the 180 degree turn, alternating from side to side without the pause in the erect position, in two bars of 4/4.

Fourth Year

4. a.   *Tempo 4/4.* Make circular patterns of the head and eyes by joining the horizontal and vertical positions in quarter, half and full circles clockwise and anti-clockwise. Prepare by turning the head to the side.

> Bar 1.   Move from the side to the downward position;
>
> Bar 2.   Continue the circle to the opposite side;
>
> Bar 3.   Continue to the upward position;
>
> Bar 4.   Complete the circle to the beginning position.

Note: Make sure the eyes always focus quickly and accurately.

See that the body remains quiet and peaceful and the spine is released upward so the neck is always lengthened. It is important never to crush any vertebrae.

Inclined Positions of the Head and Eyes

These positions should be learnt in conjunction with the rounded positions of the arms in Second Year and are later incorporated in the actual *port de bras.* The inclination of the head is governed by the direction of the eyes and should be a natural and habitual part of arm movements. The head must be independent from the shoulders and not incline into an exaggerated, uncomfortable, stiff-necked position.

Second Year

2. a.   *Tempo 4/4.* Stand in first position with the arms in *bras bas.* On four chords, prepare the right arm in first position;

> Bar 1.   Look into the right palm; inclining the head to the left.
>
> Bar 2.   Return to the upright position.

Repeat three times and on two additional chords *allongé* and lower the arm to *bras bas*. Repeat the exercise with the left arm looking to the left palm and inclining the head to the right.

Later do the same with the arms in *demi-first* and third positions. When the positions are understood the exercise can be done with the head and eyes only.

2. b.   In this progression, lift the head and eyes with the arm to first position as before then follow the hand as it opens to second position. Return the arm to first with the head still inclined, look erect and lower the arm. Use 4/4 *tempo* with pauses in each position taking eight bars of music. Later eliminate the pauses.

2. c.   Now follow the arm from *bras bas* to third position and on its return through first to *bras bas*. Pause, while learning, in first position and third and later only in third.

Note: It will depend on the progress of the class when the progressions are introduced, for instance it may not be until the Third Year that the pauses can be eliminated.

Third Year
3. a.   Continue to work the head and eyes in the same manner with and without the arm movements.

Fourth Year
To loosen and free the neck, make circular movements clockwise and anti-clockwise with inclined head only, that is, keeping the face and eyes to the front. First, make a quarter circle, later half and later still a full circle.

4. a.   *Tempo 4/4.*   Stand erect, the arms in *bras bas* or in second position with the palms turned upward.

> Bar 1.   Look up at forty-five degrees;
> Bar 2.   Release the neck to incline to the right side to its maximum without any movement in the shoulders;
> Bar 3.   Look down at forty-five degrees keeping the neck stretched forward;
> Bar 4.   Look erect.

Repeat three times then repeat to the left. Later continue the movement to make a full circle.

Eyes
Exercises reinforce the use of the eyes in orientation and balance. They also strengthen them. Hold the head erect during the exercises and allow only the eyes to move.

First Year
It is a help for the very young to place a finger on their chins as a point of reference towards point 1.

1. a.   *Tempo 2/4.*   Prepare standing in first position or sitting in a comfortable upright position facing point 1.

> Bar 1.   Turn the eyes to the right side;

Bar 2. Focus on a particular spot;

Bar 3. Look erect;

Bar 4. Focus.

After four times, rest then repeat this time looking to the left.

1. b. Look up four times then down four times. When these movements are mastered, alternate the directions. At first give pauses for control and later vary the speed of the movement from slow to fast according to the ability of the child to focus quickly and accurately.

Second Year

2. a. Join the outside positions of side, down, side and up, clockwise and anti-clockwise, into a diamond shape.

Third Year

3. a. Now add the diagonal cross movement. Pause, at first, in the erect position and later without the pause.

Fourth Year

4. a. Join the eight points of the circle, slowly with pauses at first and later getting quicker without the pauses.

4. b. Many composite patterns can now be drawn with the eyes.

Note: Make sure that the eyes focus at the end of each movement and that the rest of the body remains still. Maintain correct posture.

To rest the eyes, close them for a few seconds and place the heel of the hand lightly on the eyelids.

Waist and Shoulders

For the Shoulders: These exercises are to free the shoulders so the arms can move without restriction. They help the student become aware of the correct placement of the shoulders; that they are open, down and 'falling apart'. It is important that the shoulder-blades should never be drawn together. Rather they should be opened away from one another so the back is quite flat. From this position the shoulders should not be taken further back until a much more advanced training is undertaken.

First Year

1. a. *Tempo 2/4.* Prepare in first with the arms in low position.

Bar 1. Lift both shoulders upward;

Bar 2. Return to normal.

After four times, rest and repeat.

Second Year

2. a. In the same manner and *tempo*, lift each shoulder separately and later alternately.

Third Year

3. a. Add a movement of each shoulder forward separately and later

alternately. Be sure that no other part of the body is affected by the movement of the shoulder.

Fourth Year

4. a.   *Tempo 4/4.*   With the arms in parallel second, palms upward, make circles, both *en dehors* and *en dedans*, small at first getting larger as the movement becomes free without affecting the rest of the body. It is important to observe the lengthening of the spine and its release upwards so correct posture can be maintained and the rib cage does not protrude.

Turns of the Waist: This is to add a new dimension to movement by isolating the upper body from the legs and pelvis. The exercises may be done either sitting or standing.

Second Year

2. a.   *Tempo 2/4.*   On four chords, prepare facing front in first position of the feet with the hands on the waist.

  Bar 1.   Turn the head and upper body from the waist as one unit, to face point 2. Look directly to point 2 so the shoulders and elbows point to 8 and 4. The legs and pelvis remain facing point 1;
  Bar 2.   Hold the position;
  Bar 3.   Return *en face*;
  Bar 4.   Hold.

Repeat three times to the right then four times to the left. Later alternate the directions.

Third Year

3. a.   *Tempo 4/4 or 3/4*   making two bars of 3/4 equal one of 4/4, do the exercise as in Second Year but allow the body to turn as far as possible while keeping the legs and pelvis *en face*. Add various arm movements and positions, such as from first position open the right arm to second with the right turn of the body while the left remains in first or, open the right arm to second and lift the left to third position. Make sure the head and eyes lead the turning movement. Later alternate the movement from side to side.

Fourth Year

4. a.   *Tempo 6/8.*   Prepare with a turn of the body to the right, the left arm in third and the right in second positions.

  Bar 1. 1,2,3,   Bend the body forward from the waist, turn it to the front and meet the arms in first position; keep the legs perpendicular;
  4,5,6,   Turn to the left and lift the body upright with the right arm in third and the left in second.

Repeat three times, rest and repeat.

Side Bends

Third Year

3. a. *Tempo 4/4.* Prepare standing in parallel or rotated first position in parallel low position.

Bar 1. Lead with the crown of the head in a circular movement of the body to the right side; allow the right hand to slide down the right leg; keep the face to the front;

Bar 2. Return to the upright position, leading with the crown of the head.

Repeat three times to the right then four to the left.

Note: The shoulders and head must remain in the correct relative position during the bend. The body should bend towards a point distant from the feet as if leaning over a barrel.

Fourth Year

4. a. *Tempo 4/4.* Stand in rotated first position and prepare the arms to parallel second.

Bar 1. Bend to the right side until the arms are in a diagonal line leading down to the right side. Keep the face to the front.

Bar 2. Return to the upright position.

Do to alternate sides from four to eight times.

Later, do the same with one arm in third and the other in *demi-seconde*. When this is mastered, the arm and body movement may be done with a simple waltz. The arms can change position through either first or third positions.

Hands and Fingers

The hands and fingers of a dancer are very expressive and it is through them that subtlety of feeling is shown. These exercises are to make the child more aware of these sensitive qualities.

First Year

1. a. *Tempo 2/4.* On four chords, prepare by kneeling on two knees and sitting back.

Bar 1. Place the palms of the hands on the knees;

Bar 2. Lift one hand and look into its palm;

Bar 3. Replace the hand on the knee;

Bar 4. Hold the position looking erect.

This is done four times with each hand and later both hands are lifted at the same time while alternating the glance.

Note: This can be done in various qualities, such as, firm on the knees and soft when lifted or the reverse.

1. b. *Tempo 4/4.* Standing or kneeling, prepare the right arm to parallel first then bend the elbow until the lower arm is perpendicular with the palm turned to the front.

Bar 1. Turn the palm to face inward one quarter turn;

Bar 2. Turn it to face its respective shoulder;

Bar 3.   Return to face inward;

Bar 4.   Return to the front.

After four times, on two additional chords, extend the arm to first and lower. Repeat with the left arm. Later use two arms together.

Second Year

2. a.   *Tempo 2/4.*   Stand in first position and prepare by lifting the arms to parallel first. Taking one bar for each movement, turn the palms to face each other, to the ceiling, to face each other and return to face the floor.

2. b.   *Tempo 4/4.*   Working with a partner, one child places her palm on the upturned palm of the other. Change positions by rolling the hands round each other. The purpose of this is to feel the hand and it can be done in different *tempi* with different qualities. (This can also be done with one's own hands.)

Third Year

3. a.   Alternate the movements of the hands in all the previous exercises and develop movements in opposition.

Fourth Year

4. a.   Develop movements of the hands through personal space, using different qualities and dynamics as the planes of the hand move through space, for example, in a figure of eight.

Fingers

First Year

1. a.   *Tempo 2/4.*   Prepare standing, sitting or kneeling. Lift the hands in front of the shoulders with the fingers spread open.

Bar 1.   Clench the hands;

Bar 2.   Shoot the fingers out fully extended.

Concentrate on one hand at a time and later both hands together.

The movement can be done in various directions and voice sounds can be used to heighten the expression.

1. b.   With the children counting aloud, from a clenched fist, open one finger at a time. One count to open and one to hold and think of the next move.

Second Year

2. a.   *Tempo 4/4.*   Commence with extended fingers, palms facing or turned away from the body;

Bar 1.   1,2,   Close the thumb and hold;

3,4,   Close the first finger and hold;

Bar 2.   Close the second then third fingers;

Bar 3.   1,2,   Close the little finger;

3,4,   Open the thumb then first finger;

Bar 4. 1–3, Open the other fingers;
           4, Hold.

Use one hand at a time until the exercise is mastered then use both hands together. Later start the movement from the little fingers. Try the exercise in unison and in opposition.

2. b. Choose the *tempo* suitable for double or multiple finger movements from an extended position to the palm and back to the open position. Use one finger at a time in varying qualities, for example, *legato* or *staccato*.

Third Year

3. a. *Tempo 4/4.* Standing, sitting, or kneeling, prepare with the arms in parallel first or second with the palms turned upward and the elbows relaxed.

Bar 1. One at a time, starting from the little one, roll the fingers into a fist as the wrist bends toward the body;

Bar 2. Unroll the fingers as the wrist bends as far as possible away from the body. Start from the thumb.

3. b. *Tempo 4/4.* Prepare as for 3. a.

Bar 1. Roll the fingers and wrists inward with more bend in the elbows;

Bar 2. Rotate the fists inwards, down, outwards and up;

Bar 3. Push out to full arm length opening the fingers but holding them together;

Bar 4. Turn the palms upward.

This exercise can be done in different *tempi* and with various qualities and dynamics.

Fourth Year

4. a. In this year, the teacher should draw on imagination and knowledge of hand movements and positions in ethnic dance, for example, Indian positions of the deer or peacock and the movements of picking and throwing flowers, harvesting and throwing seed, etc.

The children, of course, will investigate the possibilities of hand movements in their improvisations.

Circles of the Wrists

To music of the teacher's or children's choice, use timing which allows the child to register the beginning, the movement and the finish of the following exercises.

First Year

1. a. Shake the wrists in various directions and in circles.

Second Year

2. a. Draw circles on the floor with the fingertips using the wrists only. Later draw the circles in the air keeping the rest of the arm still. Make the circle clockwise and anti-clockwise.

Third Year
3. a.   Draw figure eights on the floor and in the air with the fingers and wrists, keeping the rest of the arm still. This can be done in first or second positions of the arms.

Fourth Year
4. a.   Draw figure eights in all the positions of the arms and in the movement patterns between them. Use as little of the rest of the arm in the figure eight as possible. Draw circles and figure eights in the same and in the opposite directions. Try different dynamics and qualities.

Arm Waves from Stroking Movements of the Hands

First Year
1. a.   Hold one hand up with the fingers stretched and the palm facing inward and stroke its palm with the palm of the other in a downward direction. Then stroke it upwards with the back of the hand. Start both stroking movements at the wrist of the working hand and go through the hand to the fingertips. Use various dynamics and qualities so as to develop sensitivity in the hands.

Second Year
2. a.   *Tempo 2/4.*   Place the wrists touching and the hands open in a flower shape.

Bar 1.   Going through the hand, place the palms together;
Bar 2.   Place the fingers together;
Bar 3.   Separate the wrists keeping the fingers together;
Bar 4.   Lift the arms until only the fingertips touch;
Bars 5–6.   Separate the fingers and open the hands into a parallel position;
Bars 7–8.   Place the wrists together.

Over the year gradually increase the speed of the movement until it is completed in two bars of 4/4.

Third Year
3. a.   Repeat 2. a. without touching the hands. Later the hand waves can be done in various positions and directions. Work the waves in the same direction with both hands and in opposition. Make the movement slow so as to feel the soft quality in the fingers.

Fourth Year
4. a.   Execute 2. a. starting by placing the elbows together and using the forearm in the exercise. Then extend the wave movement through the whole arm in all positions and directions in unison and in opposition. The waves should be small at first getting bigger with understanding of the correct quality.
Note: All these movements can be done in various positions and directions which gives scope for invention by the teacher and the student.

Control Exercises

These exercises analyse the mechanics of some basic classical dance exercises and prepare for them step by step.

Brushes Leading to Battement Tendu

The movement of the foot along the floor from a closed to an open position and its return, is a basic movement in the dance. It is the beginning and end of many steps which require the working leg to move away from the supporting leg and return to it with a sliding movement along the floor.

It teaches the exact directional movements to fourth positions *devant* and *derrière* and to the side to second position. When these directions are used in the following order; front, side, back and side, it is called *en croix*, in the shape of a cross. This exact directional understanding is essential in the dance.

During the study of this exercise the supporting leg and body are made strong while correct posture is controlled and made habitual. It also loosens the hip joint and encourages turn-out. It educates the working leg to extend fully from the toes through the insteps, ankles and knees and ensures that the calf muscles and thighs are well pulled up.

The movement may be long, smooth and sustained or quick and sharp. It is a light soft yet strong and later dynamic movement which slides or glides over the floor.

First Year

Teach a simple point of the foot to the front and the side in parallel positions. See that the foot and leg are correctly aligned and fully stretched in the required direction.

1. a.　*Tempo 2/4.*　Stand in parallel first. On four chords, prepare the arms as required by the teacher.

Bar 1.　Point the foot directly in front of the shoulder; hold the body and arms still;

Bar 2.　Return to first position;

Bars 3–4.　Hold the position with the arms and body still and well lifted; head erect.

Four times with each leg is sufficient. In the same manner and timing, point to the side.

Second Year

2. a.　*Tempo 2/4.*　Stand in first parallel and on four chords prepare the arms. Transfer the weight on to the supporting leg on the fourth chord.

Bar 1.　Taking the full two counts, slide the foot along the floor, and, without transferring the weight from the supporting leg which must carry the whole weight of the body, allow it to lift slightly from the floor. The toes, insteps, ankles and knees must be straight and the direction exactly in front of the working shoulder.

Bar 2.　Return the toe to the same point on the floor from which it was lifted and slide the foot back to first position. Make sure the sole

71

of the foot brushes or strokes the floor as this gives the correct quality to the movement and encourages the student to feel the floor.

Bars 3–4.   Transfer the weight back onto two feet and correct the posture. Four times with each leg is sufficient. In the same manner and timing, do the exercise to the side in parallel second.

2. b.   In the same manner and timing, the exercise is now done with the legs rotated about fifteen degrees from parallel first.

Third Year

3. a.   *Tempo 2/4.*   Repeat the exercises 2. a. and 2. b., without pauses; take one bar to complete one brush in either parallel or rotated positions. Make sure to keep the weight on the supporting leg throughout.

3. b.   *Tempo 4/4.*   Prepare in parallel first, arms in *bras bas*.

Bar 1.   1,   Brush out and hold the toe *on* the floor without lifting it;
              2,   Hold the point; think about the position;
              3,   Close;
              4,   Hold, think about posture.

After four times with each leg repeat in the same manner to parallel second.

3. c.   Exercise 3. b. is developed in a slightly rotated position of the feet to the front and to the side.

Note: Make sure that, when the leg brushes forward, the toe of the working foot stretches into the line of the heel so that the movement is directly forward. This also ensures that the shin muscles and those at the front of the foot complete the full stretch of the leg. To the side, make sure that the toe finishes the extension in a line with the heel of the supporting foot. When these directions are mastered, add brushes to the back directly behind the shoulder on the side of the working leg.

Maintain correct posture and see that the weight is transferred on to the supporting leg at the commencement of the movement and returns to two feet at the finish. Hold the body and arms well lifted and quite still without strain. The arm positions may be chosen at the discretion of the teacher.

When introducing the exercise in rotated positions, it is helpful to learn it at the *barre* and later take it to the centre.

Fourth Year

4. a.   Continue with the exercises for brushes in all directions, rotated and in parallel positions.

4. b.   Introduction to *battement tendu*.

Tempo 4/4.   Stand in first position facing the *barre*. On two chords place the hands on the *barre*.

Bar 1.   1,2,   Extend the working leg to forty-five degrees *en l'air à la seconde, derrière* or *devant*;
              3,4,   Flex the foot;
Bar 2.   Hold the flexed position increasing the rotation to the child's maximum;

Bar 3.   1,2,   Fully stretch the ankles, insteps and toes while keeping the turn-out held strongly;

3,4,   Place the toe on the floor in *seconde* or fourth *derrière* or *devant*;

Bar 4.   1,2,   Close into first position;

3,4,   Hold with the weight on both legs.

This exercise precedes *battement tendu* proper.

Battement Tendu

Teach facing the *barre* with two hands on it, first to the second position then to the fourth *derrière* and lastly to fourth *devant*. If the *barre* is too close to the wall to be able to extend the working foot in front when facing it, do the *battement tendu devant* side to the *barre* holding with one hand.

4. c.   *À la Seconde*

Tempo 4/4.   Stand in rotated first position, facing the *barre*. On two chords, place the hands on the *barre* directly in front of each shoulder and allow the elbows to be released downwards. Transfer the weight to the supporting leg.

Bar 1.   Going through the foot, slide the working leg out along the floor to second position;

Bar 2.   Hold the position with the big toe touching the floor and the toes, insteps and ankles fully stretched;

Bar 3.   Close the leg to first position going the reverse way through the foot;

Bar 4.   Hold the position.

Four times with each leg.

Note: Both legs must be fully pulled up in the calf muscles, the knees and the thighs. Keep maximum rotation as the leg extends. Lift the heel leaving the half *pointes* on the floor until half way to second position then continue to lift until only the tip of the big toe is on the floor. Take great care that the foot is not sickled or the toes pressed and turned under but are stretched straight and firmly down to the floor. There must be no weight on the working leg. During the extension to the second, the heel must be pressed forward and the toes held back with the outside muscles of the leg and foot so the foot can move in a direct line to second position opposite the heel of the supporting leg.

Close the leg lightly but firmly to the first position, drawing it along the same line as used in the extension. Lower the half toe then the heel. When going through the foot, the movement should be smooth and continuous with no stopping to interrupt it. See that both legs are straight in first position and that the heels, knees and thighs are touching.

4. d.   *To Fourth Derrière*

Teach this, facing the *barre*, in the same manner and timing as to the second.

Note: Transfer the weight on to the supporting leg and slide the working one back along the floor to fourth *derrière*. The toes lead the movement back coming into a direct line with the heel as the whole foot stretches. The heel remains opposite its position in first so that the line of the leg is directly behind the shoulder blade. Maximum rotation must be held in both legs and the body should be lifted and still. The pelvis must not tilt or move out of alignment. The shoulders are directly over the hips.

When closing, the heel leads the way forward while the toes are pressed back to maintain maximum turn-out as the foot meets the supporting heel in first position. All five toes must be on the floor as the foot is lowered through the *demi-pointe* so that it does not roll either forward or backward.

4. e.   *To Fourth Devant*

Teach this in the same manner and timing as for *seconde* and *derrière*, facing or with one hand on the *barre* and sideways to it.

Note: Transfer the weight to the supporting leg and slide the working one along the floor to fourth *devant*. The heel moves strongly forward and the toes are held back to maintain rotation. As the foot lifts through the *demi-pointe*, the toes fully stretch into line with the heel, not the heel into line with the toes. This is important as it trains the foot for its part in later springing steps and *relevés*. The tip of the big toe only remains on the floor.

When closing, the toes begin the movement backwards so the heel remains forward and the foot is in one line parallel with the supporting one. A fully rotated leg and foot return to first position, the toes and heel arriving into position at the same time. All five toes must be on the floor to prevent rolling.

General Notes: The body must be released upwards through the supporting leg, the pelvis and the upper body which are all held quiet and motionless. The hips must not twist or lift. The head should be held erect with no strain in the neck. The eyes look straight ahead as if into a mirror.

Towards the end of Fourth Year, the exercise may be done without pauses and in a slower *tempo* as this will strengthen and consolidate the movement.

Two *battement tendus* in each position are sufficient when introducing it *en croix*. When the exercise is executed without pauses, the weight may remain on the supporting leg throughout returning to both legs at the finish of the exercise.

Remember that the working leg must be rotated in the hip-socket as one unit and must be independent of the rest of the body. This should be easily understood as so many previous exercises have lead up to and prepared for this more advanced work.

Demi-Rond de Jambe

This is the introduction to exercises for round movements of the leg which join the points of the open positions of fourth *devant*, second and fourth *derrière* for *en dehors* or outward movements and the reverse for *en dedans* or inward movements. Introduce in the Fourth Year

En dehors

4. a.   *Tempo* 4/4.   Lie on the back in rotated first position of the feet and with the arms in second position.

> Bar 1.   1,2,   Extend the right leg, fully pointed to fourth *devant*;
>
> 3,4,   Carry, fully rotated, to second position;
>
> Bar 2.   1,2,   Close in first position;
>
> 3,4,   Hold.

Repeat three times then do with the left leg.

4. b.   *Tempo* 4/4.   Stand facing the *barre* in first position, prepare the arms with the breathing movement and then place them on the *barre*. ·

> Bar 1.   1,2,   *Battement tendu devant;*
>   3,4,   Draw a circle on the floor to second position;
> Bar 2.   1,2,   Close in first position;
>   3,4,   Hold.

Repeat three times, and repeat four times with the left leg.

4. c.   *Tempo 4/4.*   Lie on the stomach and do the movement from second to fourth *derrière* and later stand at the *barre* and add this movement to 4. b.

En dedans

4. d.   Lie on the stomach and do the movement in the same time but from fourth *derrière* to second. Make sure the hips remain on the floor and the rotation of the leg is maintained.

4. e.   Standing at the *barre*, reverse the movements of 4. b., that is, from fourth *derrière* to second and close.

4. f.   Make the movement from second to fourth *devant*, lying on the back then at the *barre*.

Note: The pelvis must be held level and still, the only movement being in the hip-socket. Rotation must be maintained throughout on BOTH legs.

Position of Cou-de-Pied

This position, in its variations, is used in many poses and steps and so has its place in the exercises. In this course, by slow stages, the student is lead up to an understanding of this very difficult position the final forms of which will be encountered in the study of classical dance.

Second Year

2. a.   *Tempo 4/4.*   Stand in parallel first position. On four chords prepare the arms.

> Bar 1.   Draw the right toe back along the supporting foot until the half point is resting on the floor beside the heel of the left foot with the knee and foot in parallel position.
> Bar 2.   Hold the position and register it;
> Bar 3.   Slide the right foot back into parallel first;
> Bar 4.   Hold the position thinking of the posture.

Repeat three times, rest then repeat with the left leg. When the position on the *demi-pointe* is fully understood, lift the working foot on to fully pointed toes level with the heel of the supporting leg.

Third Year

3. a.   In the same manner and timing, lift the working foot off the floor until the fully pointed toes are level with the ankle bone of the supporting leg.

Fourth Year

4. a.   *Devant.* In the same manner and timing, with rotated legs, place the working foot on the half point in third position in front of the supporting foot. Later use a fully pointed foot *par terre.*

4. b.   *Derrière.* Place on the half and later full point in third position at the back of the supporting leg.

4. c.   *En l'air.* From a rotated first position lift the fully pointed working foot to ankle height on the supporting leg with the toe touching the inside of the supporting ankle on the achilles tendon.

Note: Make sure that the working foot does not sickle. *Devant*: The big toe must be in a direct line with the shin and the knee while the heel is pressed well forward. *Derrière*: The heel touches the back of the supporting ankle and the toe is pressed back. See that the thigh is released in the hip–joint so it can rotate freely and be held in that position without strain.

Pas de Cheval
This exercise is a development of brushes together with *cou-de-pied* positions and introduces the movement of the foot for *pas de cheval* and later movements such as *développé*. It encourages the feeling in the feet so they become an instrument of expression as well as being functional platforms.

Second Year
2. a.   *Tempo 4/4.*   Stand in first position parallel. On four chords, prepare the arms and *dégagé* to fourth parallel *devant*.

Bar 1.   1,2,   Draw the sole of the right foot along the floor to the *cou-de-pied* position *par terre*;

3,4,   Hold the position;

Bar 2.   1,2,   Place the toes in the *cou-de-pied* position and lightly brush their tips with a fully stretched foot, along the floor to *pointe dégagé devant*;

3,4,   Hold the position correcting it and the posture.

Repeat three times and then repeat four times with the left leg.

Third Year
3. a.   *Tempo 4/4.*   On four chords, prepare as before.

Bar 1.   In the same manner as 2. a. draw the foot to *cou-de-pied par terre* and then lift it *en l'air*;

Bar 2. 1,2,3,   *Développé* the leg to the same height in fourth *devant* parallel;

4,   Place the toe on the floor in fourth position.

Execute four times with each leg. Hold the arms in the chosen position.

Fourth Year
4. a.   Repeat 3. facing the *barre* and using a rotated third position. Rotate both legs to the maximum of which the child is capable.

4. b.   When mastered to the front do the exercise to the side in a rotated second position.

Later the exercise should be taken to the centre.

Relevé Lent, Grand Battement and Développé
These exercises strengthen the leg and loosen the hip-joint. They add lightness and height and encourage suspension of the leg in the air.

1. a.   *Tempo 2/4.*   Lie on the back with the arms by the side of the body. On

four chords prepare by drawing the knees up keeping the soles of the feet flat on the floor.

Bar 1.   Holding the knees together in parallel position, stretch the right leg in the air without altering the position of the knee;

Bar 2.   Hold, try to point the foot;

Bar 3.   Replace the foot alongside the other;

Bar 4.   Hold correcting the position of the flat back on the floor.

Four times with each leg is sufficient.

Second Year

2. a.   *Relevé Lent*

Tempo 2/4.   Lie on the back with the arms by the side. On four chords, prepare by drawing up both knees and then stretching the right leg.

Bar 1.   Working in parallel positions, lift the right leg, fully stretched, to forty-five degrees or ninety degrees without lifting the hips from the floor;

Bar 2.   Hold the position stretching the leg and foot;

Bar 3.   Slowly lower to the floor;

Bar 4.   Hold, correcting the body placement.

Repeat three times then do four times with the left leg.

Note: Make sure that the full time of the bar is taken up with the lifting and lowering of the leg. Do not allow it to be thrown up and down in an uncontrolled manner.

2. b.   *Développé*

Tempo 4/4.   Lie on the back. On four chords, prepare by drawing up both knees, opening the arms to second and stretching the right leg on the floor in parallel position.

Bar 1.   1,2,   Draw up the right knee to *retiré* position parallel, the foot passing through the *cou-de-pied* position *par terre*;

        3,4,   Hold;

Bar 2.   1,2,   Unfold the right leg *en l'air* to forty-five degrees or ninety degrees to full stretch of the knee and foot;

        3,4,   Hold, thinking of the corrections to the posture and the leg;

Bar 3.   1,2,   Bend the knee with the foot pointed and replace in the *retiré* position;

        3,4,   Hold;

Bar 4.   1,2,   Stretch the right leg on the floor;

        3,4,   Hold making necessary corrections.

Repeat three times then repeat four times with the left leg.

Third Year

3. a.   *Relevé Lent* and *Grand Battement*

Tempo 2/4.   Lie on the back with both legs stretched in parallel. On four chords, prepare the arms to second position;

Bar 1.   Lift the working leg as high as possible with both hips on the floor;

Bar 2. Hold;

Bar 3. Lower;

Bar 4. Hold.

Execute four times with each leg. Later alternate the legs eight times in all.

3. b. *Développé*

Tempo 4/4. On four chords, prepare the arms to second and the legs stretched in parallel position.

Bar 1. 1,2,3,4, Draw up the working knee to parallel *retiré*;

Bar 2. 1,2,3,4, Slowly unfold the leg *en l'air*;

Bar 3. Hold;

Bar 4. 1,2,3,4, Slowly lower the straight leg.

Fourth Year

4. a. *Grand Battement*

Tempo 2/4. Lie on the back with both legs stretched in parallel and later rotated first position. On four chords, prepare the arms to second position.

Bar 1. Lift and hold;

Bar 2. Lower and hold.

Do four times with each leg. This can also be done to the second position lying on the back and, after studying *relevé lent* (4. c.) to the back, lying on the stomach to the back.

4. b. *Développé*

Tempo 4/4. Lie on the back in rotated first position with the arms in second and repeat exercise 3. b. maintaining maximum rotation throughout.

4. c. *Relevé Lent*

Tempo 4/4. Prepare as for 4. b.

Bar 1. 1,2,3, Slowly lift the working leg;

4, Hold;

Bar 2. 1, Hold;

2,3,4, Slowly lower.

Execute four times on each leg.

Lying on the stomach, this exercise can also be done *derrière*.

Note: The leg must work freely and independently. The legs must be fully stretched and the feet pointed in all the exercises. Use the inside muscles and those at the back of the leg only. Do not exert the thigh muscles. Use the hip-joint like a hinge. The hips must both be on the floor throughout all the progressions. The body should be held still and peacefully. The spine must be released and lengthened and no strain shown or felt.

Arm Waves

These exercises are to soften the lifting and lowering of the arms in extended positions such as in *arabesque*. They also add a useful movement to the repertoire for dances and improvisation.

Lifting and lowering

First Year

1. a. *Tempo* 4/4. Stand in parallel first.

Bar 1. Lift straight arms with clenched fists, palms down, to first;

Bar 2. Release the hands and allow the elbows to soften as the arms float down to arms low.

Reverse this with a soft lift, clench the fists and lower with a pressing feeling. It can also be done in the second position.

Note: Make sure the body is well lifted against the lowering of the arms. Use this exercise after doing 'fairy runs' explaining that it will help to use the arms better.

Second Year

2. a. *Tempo* 4/4. Prepare the feet in parallel first and the arms low.

Bar 1. 1,2, Lift the arms to parallel first leading with the back of the wrists and with softened elbows;

3, Bring the fingers into line with the wrists and arms;

4, Hold lightly;

Bar 2. 1, Soften the elbow as the arm begins to lower;

2, Soften the wrist as the arm lowers further;

3, Bring the fingers into line with the arm;

4, Hold the arms low position.

After four times, rest and repeat.

Third Year

3. a. *Tempo* 4/4 or 3/4. As for Second Year but now lift the arms to the height of third position. Alternate the arms in the movements up and down and use positions such as *arabesque* with one arm in first and the other in second.

Fourth Year

4. a. *Tempo* 3/4. Standing, walking, running, etc. Prepare on four chords.

Bar 1. Lift the arms to a high side V-position;

Bar 2. 1, Relax the elbow and lower it to shoulder level, slightly soften the wrist;

2, Soften the wrist further and press outwards and upwards in a circular movement;

3, Lift with the back of the wrist to complete the circle to the original position;

Bar 3. Repeat Bar 2;

Bar 4. Lower softly.

These waves can be done in all directions and at all heights.

Arm Swings

This movement encourages a rhythmic use of the arms which is free flowing yet controlled. It is easy to co-ordinate with rises and springs as it reinforces the rule that the arms are in *bras bas* in *plié* and lift as an active part of the spring or rise. It establishes the idea that the arm movements assist the work of the legs and body and must always be an integral part of any exercise or step.

First Year

1. a. *Tempo 6/8.* Stand in parallel first position, arms in low position. Prepare with the breathing movement to *demi-seconde*.

Bar 1. 1,2,3, Swing the arms down through low position;
        4,5,6, Swing them up to *demi-first*;
Bar 2. 1,2,3, Swing them in reverse pattern to low;
        4,5,6, Swing up in reverse pattern to *demi-seconde*.

The movement is continuous for eight to sixteen bars of music.

Note: The arms will fall naturally into a curved position in *demi-first*. Encourage this as it is an excellent introduction to the curved arm positions of classical dance. Be sure the arms stop in a correct position and at the same height on each swing.

Second Year

2. a. *Tempo 6/8.* Commence in first position parallel or rotated. Open the arms to *demi-seconde* with the breathing movement.

Bar 1. 1–3, Swing through *bras bas*;
        4–6, Swing up to classical first position;
Bar 2. 1–3, Reverse the swing pattern to second parallel.

Note: Insist on a correct first position and do not allow the second position to be too high. Use this movement with balances, rises or springs.

Third Year

3. a. *Tempo 4/4.* Prepare with the breathing movement to *demi-seconde*.

Bar 1. 1,2, *Demi-plié* lower the arms to *bras bas*;
        &, Spring and swing the arms to *demi-first*;
        3, *Demi-plié* and lower the arms to *bras bas*;
        4, Stretch the knees and swing the arms up to *demi-seconde*.

Use with divided rises and springs, skips and gallops, etc.

3. b. Swing the arms up to third position in the same manner and timing.

Fourth Year

4. a. *Tempo 4/4.* Commence in first position. Prepare with the breathing movement to *demi-seconde*.

Bar 1. 1,2, *Demi-plié* lower the arms to *bras bas*;
        &,3, Spring and land in *demi-plié*, swing the arms to *demi-first*;
        4, Stretch the knees and open the arms to *demi-seconde*;
Bar 2. &, *Allongé*;
        1,2,3,4, Rest or repeat the exercise.

Later use the third position. A bar's rest between the springs will allow the arms time to open slowly during that bar. In travelling steps the arms can be used one at a time so that the right does the movement on the first step and the left on the second.

Classical Arm Positions and Port de Bras

These exercises prepare the student for the understanding of the lifted and rotated position of the upper arm in classical dance, which allows the forearm to be free and without strain. They introduce the rounded positions of the arms and their transition from straight lines to curved and vice versa. This, in turn, leads to fluidity of arm movements and a free flowing feeling through the whole body.

Second Year

2. a. *Bras bas*

Tempo 4/4. Stand in first position, arms low.

Bar 1.		Open to *demi-seconde* position;
Bar 2.	1,2,	Hold the shoulder and upper arm still as the forearms curve toward each other;
	3,4,	Hold the elbow still as the forearms complete the oval position in front of the body. The palms will now face upwards;
Bar 3.	1,2,	Keeping the elbows still, leading with the fingers, open the forearms.
	3,4,	Complete the opening to *demi-seconde*;
Bar 4.		Lower softly to arms low.

2. b. First position

Tempo 4/4. Stand in first position, arms low.

Bar 1.		Lift the arms to parallel first;
Bar 2.		Draw the hands in on a straight line as they turn at the wrists until the palms face the body. The elbows curve and move outwards, keeping the same level, until the insides of the elbows are facing each other. In this position the upper arm is held still while the forearm is rotated to form one circular line with it.
Bar 3.		Hold the position, correcting and memorizing it;
Bar 4.	1,	*Allongé* by stretching in a slightly circular movement downwards, up and outwards to parallel first, do not allow the elbows to straighten fully inside the line of the shoulders, the insides of the elbows should always face one another.
	2,3,4,	Lower softly to low position.

2. c. *Port de bras*

Tempo 4/4. Stand in first position with the arms in *bras bas*. On four chords prepare with the breathing movement.

Bar 1.	Lift the arms to first position, look to one hand;
Bar 2.	Hold the position registering and correcting it;
Bar 3.	Lift to third position;
Bar 4.	Hold;
Bar 5.	Lower to first;
Bar 6.	Hold;
Bar 7.	Lower to *bras bas*;
Bar 8.	Hold and lift the eyes to look forward.

The exercise is done twice following the right hand with the eyes and twice following the left.

2. d.   Second Position

Tempo 4/4.   Stand in first position with the arms in *bras bas*. Prepare with the breathing movement.

Bar 1.		Lift the arms to parallel second position looking to one hand.
Bar 2.		Hold the upper arm still with the insides of the elbows facing front, rotate the forearm bringing the hands slightly forward as the palms turn to face one another, the insides of the elbows, wrists and palms are then in one line facing towards the centre of a large circle.
Bar 3.		Hold the position;
Bar 4.	1,2,	Maintain the upper arm position as the forearm makes the *allongé* movement to parallel second position, follow the movement with the eyes;
	3,	Lower to *demi-seconde*;
	4,	Complete the movement to *bras bas* with the forearms only.

Note: If three children, holding their arms in second position, make a circle with their fingers touching the elbows of the others, the circle will be approximately the size of the completed circle of second position.

2. e.   Third Position

Tempo 4/4.   Stand in first position with the arms in *bras bas*. Prepare with the breathing movement.

Bar 1.	Lift the arms to a high V halfway between second and first positions, with the palms turned outwards.
Bar 2.	Hold the upper arm still as the forearm makes a circular movement inward to third position with the palms facing the body, look into one hand;
Bar 3.	*Allongé*, maintaining the upper arm position, to the high V;
Bar 4.	Lower softly to *bras bas* following the hand with the head and eyes.

Four times look to the right hand and then four times to the left.

2. f.   Opening from First to Second Position

Tempo 4/4.   Stand in first position with the arms in *bras bas*. Prepare with the breathing movement.

Bar 1.	1,2,	Lift the right arm to first position, look at the right palm;
	3,4,	Hold the position making sure it is correct;
Bar 2.	1,2,	Hold the upper arm still and open the forearm, follow with the eyes;
	3,4,	Holding the arm in this position, open from the shoulders to second position;
Bar 3.		Hold, registering the correct position;
Bar 4.		*Allongé* and lower to *bras bas*.

Use the right arm then the left four times each.

When understood move both arms together, follow first the right arm and then the left.

Third Year

3. a.   Opening from Third Position
Tempo 4/4, 2/4 or 3/4.   Stand in first position with the arms in *bras bas*.
Prepare with the breathing movement.

Bars 1–2.		Lift the arms slowly to third position, look to the right hand;
Bar 3.	1,	Lift slightly the fingers then the forearm without altering the elbow position;
	2,4,	Keeping the shape of the arms, cut the air with the side of the arms and the little fingers as they open to second position;
Bar 4.		*Allongé* and lower to *bras bas*.

Note: To maintain the shape of the arms when opening, the upper arm will rotate slightly as it is lowered thus keeping the insides of the elbows facing the front.

Various combinations of arm positions may be taught in the centre, for example, one arm in second and the other in third or first or one arm in *demi-first* and the other in third.

Various combinations of arm movements may be taught at the *barre* using one arm and later, in the centre, using two.

Co-ordination
General Note: When isolation exercises have been studied and are understood, they should be combined in various ways for co-ordinating all parts of the body, especially the arms, head and legs. Remember it is the movement between positions and poses that is dancing, the positions are the punctuation so that the movement plus the pose makes a sentence or a phrase of movement.

Transference of Weight

The natural transference of weight from one foot to another is taken for granted yet is very often executed badly, as witnessed by the many people whose walk is ungainly and unsteady. Being conscious of the posture and the transference of the body as a whole from foot to foot, makes any locomotive movement more sure. The maintenance of balance by complete weight transference allows speed to be controlled and movement securely arrested. As the sure-footed animal seldom slips and falls, so the sure-footed dancer rarely injures himself in this way.

The full beauty of a dance pattern is shown only when the whole body moves through aerial space as well as floor space. When the body thrusts forward, sideways or backward, excitement is added to the beauty of the movement for both the audience and the dancer.

The exercises in this section are to enable the child to understand the various ways in which the weight can be transferred from one foot to the other and how to maintain balance during and after the transference. From the first year of study through to professionalism, it is essential to be able to change weight surely, either quickly or slowly. These exercises are designed to improve the performance of the natural action.

Walking
First Year
Should a child have difficulty in consciously swinging the arms in opposition to the legs when walking, crawling is the natural way to establish feeling for and understanding of this balancing action. It is also a lot of fun when 'being' animals or imaginary things.

1. a.   Crawling
Tempo 4/4.   Prepare by kneeling down on both knees and placing the hands on the floor.
   Bars 1–2.   Crawl;
   Bars 3–4.   Roll over and back on to all fours.
Make a game of it and crawl in all directions and floor patterns.

1. b.   Natural Walking
Stand in a big circle. Prepare with the outside foot pointed and the hands on the waist or holding the skirt. Walk in time to the music singly or holding hands with partners. Vary the speed and quality of the walk.

1. c.   Step
Tempo 2/4.   On four chords, prepare the right foot pointed in front and the arms holding the skirt or at the waist.
   Bar 1.   &,   Lift the foot slightly;
            1,   Step forward on to the right foot taking the weight of the upper body forward over the leg;
            2,   Close the left foot to the right in first position;
   Bar 2.   Stand still on two feet;
   Bars 3–4.   Prepare the right foot to repeat the step. Use the right leg then the left four times each. Later alternate right and left.

1. d.   Walking
Tempo 2/4.   Prepare the right foot in *dégagé devant* and the arms as desired.
   Bar 1.   &,   Lift the pointed foot a little;
            1,   Step forward through the foot, hold the arms in position;
            &,   Pass the left foot through parallel first position, point in fourth *devant* and lift it;
            2,   Step on to the left foot.
This can be done moving either forward or backward.
1. e.   This is to co-ordinate rhythm and movement.
Tempo 4/4.   Stand in first position. On four chords, lift the arms to parallel first, bend the elbows until the hands are opposite the shoulders with the palms turned towards each other ready for clapping.

Bars 1–2. Eight claps;
Bar 3. Place the hands on the hips, keeping the upper arm firmly held;
Bar 4. Prepare the right foot pointed in front;
Bars 5–6. Take eight steps forward;
Bar 7. Close the feet together and think about preparing to clap again.
Bar 8. Prepare the arms for repeating the figure.

This can be done forward or backward, in a circle or *en diagonale*.

Note: At this stage introduce the walking entrance to class, possibly in a circle. Stop, facing the centre of the circle where the teacher can stand, make a *révérence* and greet the teacher before commencing the lesson.

Second Year

2. a.   Walking
Tempo 4/4.   Prepare in *dégagé devant* and the arms as desired by the teacher.
Bar 1.   1,   Lift the pointed foot a little from the floor;
    2,   Step forward (or back);
    3,   Pass the other foot through the *cou-de-pied par terre*;
    4,   Point it in fourth *devant* (or *derrière*).

Continue in given floor pattern.

2. b.   *Tempo* 4/4.   Prepare with the right foot pointed in front and the arms in *demi-seconde*.
Bar 1.   &,   Lift the right foot a little;
    1,2,3,   Take three steps;
    4,   Pause on the right foot with the left in *cou-de-pied par terre*; close the arms to *bras bas*;
Bar 2. 1,2,3,   Continue the pause and open the arms with the breathing movement;
    4,   *Dégagé* the left foot *devant*.

Continue in a given floor pattern. Later do the exercise in a slightly rotated position of the feet.

Note: Make sure that the toe of the working foot is placed directly in line with the heel of the supporting foot so the walk is not in an ungainly open position. The feet should always be placed along one line on the floor.

2. c.   With Changes of Direction
Teach changes of direction on two or one foot before using them with walks (see Turning, p. 112). The change is done on the whole foot, very slightly lifting the weight from the heel and turning on the ball of one foot while the other leg is held in first, third or fifth position and is lifted very little as it swings with the turn of the body and the supporting leg. The following exercise is an example of a turn after a step.

Tempo 2/4.   Prepare facing point 2. On four chords prepare the arms and *dégagé* the right foot to point 2.
Bar 1.   Step forward on the right foot;
Bar 2.   Turn on the ball of the right foot to face front as the left is drawn into first position, close the arms to *bras bas*;

Bar 3.　Continue to turn on the ball of the right foot to face point 8 carrying the left in first position;

Bar 4.　*Dégagé* the left foot to point 8, lift the arms to *demi-first* and open them to *demi-seconde*.

Repeat three times. Later take eight steps in the diagonal direction before making the turn.

Third and Fourth Years

3. a.　Develop the smoothness and fluid quality of the walks. Add pauses and poses in *cou-de-pied* and *dégagés devant* and *derrière*.

3. b.　Add arm movements.

3. c.　Vary speed, rhythm and directions. See the following examples:

Poses *derrière* in *épaulement* directions

Tempo 4/4.　Prepare *effacé* with the right foot *dégagé devant*, make the breathing movement to *demi-seconde*.

Bar 1.　　　　　Lift the foot, *allongé* the arms;

　　　　1,　Step in the *effacé* direction and *dégagé* the left foot *derrière*, close the arms to *bras bas*;

　　2,3,4,　Lift the arms to pose *effacé*;

Bar 2.　1,2,　Hold the pose;

　　　　3,　Close the foot to first position and open the arms to *seconde*;

　　　　4,　*Dégagé devant croisé* with the left foot, *allongé* the arms;

Bar 3.　　1,　Step in the *croisé* direction on the left foot, arms to *bras bas*;

　　2,3,4,　Lift the arms to pose *croisé*;

Bar 4.　1,2,　Hold the pose;

　　　3,4,　Close and *dégagé* the right foot *effacé* and use the arms as before.

The exercise moves in a diagonal line across the studio. Later reverse the exercise.

Note: The same pose can be repeated *en diagonale* before alternating them.

Poses *devant* in *épaulement* directions

Tempo 4/4.　Prepare in *dégagé devant effacé*, the arms in *demi-seconde*.

Bar 1.　&,　Lift the foot, *allongé* the arms;

　　　　1,　Step in the *effacé* direction, arms to *bras bas*;

　　　　2,　Step in the *croisé* direction, lift the arms to *demi-first*;

　　　3,4,　*Battement passé* to *dégagé devant effacé*, open the arms to pose *effacé*;

Bar 2.　　　　　Hold the pose and prepare to repeat.

This can also start *croisé* and later the exercise can be reversed.

Alternatively to 3/4 *tempo*, use eight bars and take three steps to alternate the pose.

Note: Make sure the spine is released and the body well lifted as the whole weight is placed on one leg. See that the head and eyes are looking in the correct direction throughout the exercises.

Running

To be able to run lightly, swiftly and beautifully should be an aim of all dancers, great and small.

First Year

1. a. *Tempo* 2/4. Run on *demi-pointes* with very small steps, in time with the music. Use various floor patterns.
1. b. *Tempo* 2/4. Swedish runs with the feet well lifted behind the knees.
Note: Boys may prefer to concentrate on the Swedish runs being elves rather than fairies! Both kinds can run *sur place* or travel. Let the children work in partners in small folk dance patterns. Use arm waves for the small runs and hands at the waist for the Swedish ones.

Second Year

2. a. Long natural stride runs forward, using the arms naturally in opposition, are great fun!

Third Year

Introduce exercises to improve the runs.

3. a. *Tempo* 3/4. Prepare with *dégagé devant* and the arms as required.

Bar 1. &, Lift the working foot slightly;

1, Step forward into *demi-plié*;

2, Pass the other foot through *cou-de-pied par terre* in the *demi-plié*;

3, Stretch the supporting leg and brush the other to fourth *devant* slightly lifted from the floor.

Continue this in a floor pattern. Later move backward. After the introduction to the movement 'for *tombé*', (p. 88) add a small rise on the count &.

Fourth Year

4. a. Increase the speed and fluidity of the runs and hold the arms in various positions or use a simple *port de bras*.
4. b. Add a long jumping step (for *grand jeté en avant*). Do three runs and a long *jeté*. Hold the arms in first position for the runs and extend to second *arabesque* for the *jeté*, that is, the natural arm forward in opposition.

Tombé

Third Year

3. a. *Tempo* 4/4. Stand in third position of the feet with the right foot in front. Prepare with the breathing movement of the arms.

Bar 1. 1, *Dégagé* the right foot *devant*, lift the arms to first position;

2, Incline the body forward, leading with the chest, extend the right foot further and from a straight knee on the left leg, fall into a *demi-plié*, extend the arms to parallel first with *allongé*.

> 3,4,   Draw the feet together on straight knees in third position
> and curve the arms again to first position.

Tombé four times on each leg. When the exercise is understood, add a rise on
the count &, after the *dégagé devant*. Also move backwards and sideways with
the *tombé*.

Marching

First Year

1. a.   Teach natural marches lifting the knees in parallel. Lift the working
leg and place a fully pointed toe on the inside of the supporting knee. Allow
the arms to swing naturally in opposition. March on place and travelling.
Make sure to prepare and finish the exercise properly.

Second Year

2. a.   Add varying speeds for balance and control. For example, to 4/4 *tempo*,
one march to one bar then two to the next bar or, three marches and a pause
on the fourth count of the bar. Do the exercises on place and travelling in
directional patterns.

Note: To ensure that the working foot is fully pointed, lift first to the *cou-de-
pied* and then to knee height holding the foot fully stretched.

2. b.   Introduce changes of direction and turning.

Tempo 4/4.   Stand in parallel first facing point 8. Prepare the arms.

> Bar 1.   1,   Turn to point 2 on the left foot, releasing the heel slightly
> and turning on the ball of the foot while the right is held
> in parallel first lifted sufficiently to allow the turn to be
> smooth;
>
> 2,   Lift the right knee;
>
> 3,4,   Two marches *sur place*;
>
> Bar 2.   1,2,   Two marches *sur place*;
>
> 3,4,   Close in parallel first and pause.

Continue making a quarter turn on each two bars of music. Hold the arms in a
position or move them through various parallel positions. This can, of course,
be done from *en face* to points 3, 5 and 7. Make the turn to the right then to the
left. Finish with the feet together.

Note: Make sure the turn is a right angle and that the shoulders turn at the
same time as and directly over the hips. The head and eyes should be used as in
the Isolation exercises to turn and focus with each quarter turn.

Third Year

3. a.   *Tempo 4/4.*   Stand in parallel first facing point 1. Prepare the arms
and lift the right leg to parallel *retiré*.

> Bar 1.   1,   Turn on the ball of the left foot and step on to the right leg
> making a quarter turn to point 3. Lift the left knee;
>
> 2,3,4,   March left, right, left;
>
> Bars 2–4.   Repeat turning to points 5, 7 and 1.

Turn to the right then to the left. Later travel on the three marches.

Fourth Year

4. a.   Now keep the thigh of the working leg horizontal and the lower leg perpendicular. Finish in a pose on one leg.

4. b.   Introduce marching on *demi-pointe* and in *demi-plié*.

4. c.   March with the working leg extended in front with a fully pointed foot.

Skipping

First Year

1. a.   *Tempo* 2/4 or 6/8.   Do natural skips in a circle or *en diagonale*. Place the hands at the waist or hold the skirt.

1. b.   *Tempo* 3/4.   Prepare the right foot pointed in front and the hands at the waist.

Bar 1.	1,	Step on to the right foot and lift the left to parallel *retiré*, hold the arm position;
	2,3,	Hop on the right leg holding the left, the body and arms still;
Bar 2.	1,	Step on the left leg;
	2,3,	Prepare the right leg again in *dégagé devant*.

Repeat three times then execute the exercise four times starting with the left.

Note: This exercise will help those children who have the common difficulty of being able to skip on one leg only, because the concentration can be on the weaker leg.

Second Year

2. a.   *Tempo* 6/8.   Prepare with the right leg in *dégagé devant* and the arms as set by the teacher.

Bar 1.	&,	Lift the right foot a little and hop on the left;
	1,	Step on to the right leg, lift the left to parallel *retiré*;
	2,	Hop on the right;
	3,	Spring and land in *demi-plié* in parallel first;
	4,5,	Stretch the knees;
	6,	*Dégagé* the right leg in preparation.

Repeat three times on the right then four times on the left. Later alternate the legs. Aim for a high spring from the jumping foot and hold the one at the knee well stretched. The body must be still and show no effort or reflected movement.

Third Year

3. a.   To improve the height and lightness of the spring, combine a skip with another step.

Tempo 4/4.   Prepare the right leg *dégagé devant* and the arms in *bras bas*.

Bar 1.	&.	Hop on the left leg, make the breathing movement of the arms;
	1,	Step on the right leg, lift the left to parallel *retiré*, close the arms to *bras bas*;

&,   Spring on the right leg, lift the arms to first position;

2,   Step onto the left leg, hold the arms in first position;

&,3,   *Pas de chat* gallop finishing with two feet together in parallel first, open the arms to *demi-seconde*;

4,   Spring in first, *allongé* the arms in *demi-seconde*.

Repeat three times then four times starting with the left. Later alternate the legs.

Note: The body should be well lifted and show no reflected movement. The arms must move freely and smoothly in co-ordination with the leg movements. The head and eyes should follow one hand, usually on the side of the commencing foot.

Fourth Year

4. a.   Teach high-flying skips with the working foot at the knee of the supporting leg and both feet fully stretched. Swing the arms into second *arabesque* which is the natural arm in opposition. Look in the direction of travelling and hold the head high. Execute the step on the same leg with one or three running steps between the springs. This introduces a really high jump and a feeling of flying through the air. Encourage this quality and allow no strain or tension in the arms or body.

4. b.   In rotated positions of both the working and supporting legs, skip with the lifted leg in a small *attitude devant* or *derrière*. The working thigh must be in direct line with the shoulder and not be over-crossed nor too open. The arms are held still or make a simple *port de bras* and the head and eyes usually look to the lifted foot.

Tempo 6/8.   Prepare in *dégagé devant*, arms in *demi-seconde*.

Bar 1.   &,   Lift the foot, *allongé* the arms;

           1,2,3,   Skip, swing the arms to *bras bas*;

           4,5,6,   Skip, lift the arms to first position;

Bar 2. 1,2,3,   Skip, lift the arms to third position.

           4,5,6,   Skip, open the arms to second position.

Note: In the Fourth Year, this type of exercise for co-ordination and the smooth transition of the arms is very valuable.

Gallops

There are two kinds of gallops taught during this four year course.

1. The *pas de chat* gallop which moves forward.

2. The gallop in fifth position of the feet which moves forward, sideways and backward.

First Year

1. a.   Allow the children to gallop round the room with the *pas de chat* gallop lifting the knees and holding the body and arms as still as possible. Then give the exercise to improve the execution.

1. b.   *Pas de Chat* Gallop
Tempo 2/4.   Stand in parallel first and prepare the arms to *demi-seconde.*
>Bar 1.   1,   Lift the right knee to parallel *retiré;*
>   2,   Replace in first position;
>Bar 2.   Lift and replace the left leg;
>Bar 3.   *Demi-plié* on both legs;
>Bar 4.   Stretch the knees.

1. c.   *Tempo 2/4.*   Prepare with the right foot pointed in front and the hands at the waist;
>Bar 1.   1,   Step on the right leg and lift the left knee;
>   &,2,   Spring lifting the right knee and land on the left, place the right foot in parallel first *demi-plié;*
>Bar 2.   Stretch the knees and prepare the right foot again in *dégagé.*

Four times with each leg is sufficient. If thought necessary, rest then repeat.

Second Year

2. a.   *Pas de chat* Gallop
Tempo 2/4.   Prepare in *dégagé devant* with the arms in *demi-seconde.*
>Bar 1.   1,   Step on to the right leg;
>   &,2,   One *pas de chat* gallop;
>Bar 2.   Two *pas de chat* gallops;
>Bar 3.   &,1,   One gallop, close in first *demi-plié;*
>   2,   Deepen the *demi-plié;*
>Bar 4.   Stretch the knees and *dégagé* the right leg *devant.*

Repeat three times then use the left. Later, alternate the legs.

2. b.   Side Gallop
Tempo 2/4.   Prepare with the right foot *dégagé à la seconde* and hold the skirts.
>Bar 1.   &,   Lift the right foot to the side;
>   1,   Step onto the right foot, spring, bringing the left leg to the right in first position in the air;
>   &,   Land on the left leg in *demi-plié* and extend the right to the side;
>   2,   One gallop sideways.
>Bar 2.   1,2,   Two gallops sideways.

Make a floor pattern, with partners or solo. Travel to the right then to the left.

Note: The feet must be fully stretched in the first position *en l'air* as this step is the preparation for gallops in fifth position.

Third Year

3. a.   *Pas de Chat* Gallops
Do the *pas de chat* gallop without preparation and without a step to commence, that is, from a standing start. Use a simple arm movement.
Tempo 4/4.   Prepare the arms.

Bar 1.   1,2,   *Demi-plié* in parallel first position, lower the arms to *bras bas*;

&.3,   Spring into the *pas de chat*, lift the arms to third position;

4,   Stretch both knees and open the arms to second position then *allongé* in preparation for the next step.

After four times with each leg alternate them.

3. b.   Gallops in fifth position

Sit on the floor with the legs in a rotated first position and the fingertips on the floor in second position. Hold the body and head erect and released upwards.

Tempo 4/4.   Place the feet in fifth position and hold for six counts then return to first for two. Practise with one foot in front four times then with the other, later alternate the feet.

3. c.   *Tempo 4/4.*   Lie on the stomach and later on the back. Place the legs in fifth position and the arms in second position.

Bar 1.   1,   Lift the legs in fifth a little from the floor;

2,   Open to a small fourth;

3,   Draw the legs together in fifth position;

4,   Lower to the floor.

This should be done no more than four times with each foot in front.

Note: The legs and feet must be fully stretched and the body held still.

3. d.   *Tempo 4/4.*   Stand in third position sideways at the *barre*. Prepare by *dégagé devant* in *demi-plié*, lift the arm to first position.

Bar 1.   1,2,   *Tombé* forward to fourth position *demi-plié* on the front leg, hold the arm in first position;

3,   Draw the back foot into fifth position on the *demi-pointes*, hold the arm position;

4,   *Coupé* under to *demi-plié* and extend the working leg in preparation for the following step.

This can be done forwards, sideways and backwards. When mastered, other arm positions and movements may be used.

Fourth Year

4. a.   Gallops in Fifth Position

Tempo 2/4.   Stand in third position in the centre. Prepare with *dégagé devant* on *demi-plié*, open the arms to *demi-seconde*.

Bar 1.   1,   *Tombé* into fourth position, hold the arm;

&,   Spring into fifth position travelling forward, hold the arm;

2,   *Coupé* under and extend the front foot; .

Bar 2.   Repeat.

This travels forwards, sideways and backwards. When mastered add arm movements. It is helpful to teach this exercise at the *barre* before transferring it to the centre.

4. b.   *Tempo 2/4.*   Prepare with *dégagé devant* and the arms in *demi-seconde*.

Bar 1.   1,   *Tombé* forward, lower the arms to *bras bas*;

&,   Draw the back foot into fifth with a spring travelling forward, lift the arms to first position, *coupé* under;

	2,	*Tombé* and open the arms to *demi-seconde*;
Bar 2.		Repeat bar 1, but carry the arms in *demi-seconde*;
Bar 3.		Repeat using the arms as in bar 1.;
Bar 4.		Repeat bar 2.

Coupé

A *coupé* cuts the weight from one foot to the other without travelling. It is a joining movement and is used with many steps. It can be done in a rise, with a spring or in *demi-plié*. It is important that the dancer fully understands the various ways in which the weight can be changed in fifth position 'under' or 'over', that is, on to the back foot or on to the front one.

First Year
1. a.   Use any step that changes the weight from one foot to the other without travelling, for example, marching or running *sur place*.

Second Year
2. a.   Repeat the same exercises now on *demi-pointe* in first position, in *demi-plié* or one leg in *demi-plié* and the other on *demi-pointe*. Lift the working foot to the parallel *cou-de-pied* position. Make sure there is no movement away from the spot. Hold the arms in a position or use a simple *port de bras*.

Third Year
3. a.   The same exercises on *demi-pointe* as in second year are now in a rotated third position of the feet. Lift the working foot to the *cou-de-pied* position *devant* or *derrière en l'air* with fully stretched insteps and toes.

3. b.   *Tempo 4/4*.   Prepare by lifting the right foot to *cou-de-pied* position either in parallel or rotated. Open the arms to *demi-seconde*.

Bar 1.	1,	*Coupé* on to the right leg in *demi-plié*, close the arms to *bras bas*;
	&,2,	Stage *assemblé* or *glissade*, etc., lift the arms to *demi-first*;
	3,	Stretch the knees and open the arms to *demi-seconde*;
	4,	Lift the working foot to *cou-de-pied* position.

Repeat three times then four times with the left.

Note: When the working leg is lifted in front the *coupé* is *over*. When it is lifted at the back, the *coupé* is *under*. Do the exercise both ways with the chosen step travelling forwards, sideways or backwards.

Fourth Year
4. a.   *Tempo 4/4*.   Prepare by *dégagé devant* with the arms in *demi-seconde*.

Bar 1.	1,	Draw the right foot into fifth position on the *demi-pointes*, close the arms to *bras bas*;
	2,	*Coupé* over onto the right leg, lift the left to *cou-de-pied* position *derrière*, hold the *bras bas*;
	3,4,	Extend the left leg to *dégagé derrière* and open the arms to *demi-seconde*;
Bar 2.		Repeat with the *coupé* under on to the left leg.

After four times, repeat with the left foot in front. The exercise can also be done extending the leg from fifth *demi-pointe* as the *coupé* is executed on count 2.

4. b.　Add a *demi-plié* on the *coupé* in 4. a.

4. c.　Spring *coupé*. Prepare by doing 4. b. without the extension of the working leg and feel a high lift of the body in the fifth *demi-pointe* then add the spring in fifth.

Tempo 4/4.　Prepare in third position. On two chords lift the front foot to *cou-de-pied devant* and open the arms to *demi-seconde*.

Bar 1.　&,1,　*Demi-plié*, close the arms to *bras bas*;

&,　Spring into fifth position *en l'air*, hold the arms still;

2,　Land in *demi-plié* on the front leg (*coupé* over) and with back foot, well pointed, carefully placed *sur le cou-de-pied derrière*;

&,3,4,　*Coupé* under and over, hold the arms still;

Bar 2.　1,2,　Place the working foot in *demi-plié* in third position;

3,4,　Stretch the knees and lift the front foot.

Do the exercise twice only with each foot in front and later start with *coupé* under. It is helpful to prepare this exercise at the *barre*, holding it lightly with both hands.

Note: Take great care of the placement of the working foot *en l'air*. Do not allow any disturbance of the body or lifting of the shoulders during the spring.

Chassé

A *chassé* is a joining step in which the weight is transferred from a closed to an open position in *demi-plié*. The working foot remains fully on the floor and the *plié* maintains the same depth throughout the movement. *Chassés* travel in all directions. The weight of the body may be returned to the supporting leg or be transferred through on to the working leg.

First Year

1. a.　*Tempo 4/4.*　Stand in parallel first position and prepare the arms as required.

Bar 1.　1,2,　*Demi-plié*;

3,4,　Slide the right foot forward in *demi-plié* to fourth position;

Bar 2.　1,2,　Place the left foot into parallel first in *demi-plié*;

3,4,　Stretch the knees.

Four times with each foot.

Second Year

2. a.　*Tempo 4/4.*　Stand in rotated first position. Prepare with the breathing movement of the arms.

Bar 1.　1,2,　*Demi-plié*, hold the arms in *bras bas*;

3,4,　Slide the right foot, on the whole foot, into fourth *devant* in *demi-plié*;

Bar 2.　1,2,　Slide the right foot back to first *demi-plié*;

3,4,　Stretch the knees.

Four times with each leg. Later add the movement to the back and the side.
Note: Make sure the weight is evenly placed in the open position.

Third Year

3. a.   Do the same exercise as second year in rotated third position and use the arms. From *demi-seconde* close into *bras bas* on the first *demi-plié* and open them to *demi-seconde* as the knees stretch.

3. b.   *Tempo 4/4.*   Stand in third position of the feet and prepare the arms to *demi-seconde*.

Bar 1.   1,2,   *Demi-plié* and close the arms to *bras bas*;

3,4,   Slide forward into fourth position *demi-plié*, hold the *bras bas*;

Bar 2.   1,2,   Transfer the weight to the front leg in *demi-plié*, lift the arms to *demi-first*;

3,4,   Close the back leg, with a stretched foot, to the front one as the.front knee stretches, open the arms to *demi-seconde*.

Four times with each leg. The exercise is also to fourth *derrière* and to the second position.

Note: See that the shoulders move directly over the working leg on the transference.

Temps Lié

A *temps Lié* is a step in its own right but can also act as a joining step. In it the weight is transferred from a *demi-plié* in a closed position through a fully pointed working foot extended in the required direction then transferred through *demi-plié* or onto a straight leg. It is a very beautiful way of changing the weight to one leg and when done on to a straight leg, prepares for the *piqué* or *posé* movement. The quality is continuous and flowing.

Third Year

3. a.   *Tempo 4/4.*   Stand in third position. Prepare with *dégagé devant* and the arms in *demi-seconde*.

Bar 1.   1,2,   *Demi-plié* on the supporting leg, *allongé* the arms;

3,4,   Step into *demi-plié* in fourth position, close the arms to *bras bas*;

Bar 2.   1,2,   Transfer the weight to the front foot and stretch both legs; open the arms to *demi-seconde*;

3,   Close in third *derrière* and hold the arms in *demi-seconde*;

4,   *Dégagé devant*.

Four times with each leg. Later add the movement to the back and the side.

Fourth Year

4. a.   *Tempo 4/4.*   Stand in third or fifth position and prepare the arms to *demi-seconde*. *Allongé* on the count &.

Bar 1.   1,2,   *Demi-plié*, lower the arms to *bras bas*;

3,4,   *Dégagé devant* in *demi-plié*, lift the arms to *demi-first*;

Bar 2. 1, Place the foot down in *demi-plié* in fourth position, hold the arms;

2, Transfer the weight to the front foot and stretch the knee, also stretch the back foot in *dégagé derrière*, open the arms to *demi-seconde*;

3, Hold the pose;

4, Close in third or fifth position of the feet and hold the arms in *demi-seconde*.

The exercise also travels backwards and sideways.

Note: Release the spine throughout and carry the shoulders directly over the hips.

Prances

These are to change the weight in the air and to encourage lightness in movement and springs.

First Year

Introduce these towards the end of the year when platform and rising exercises have been mastered.

1. a. *Tempo 2/4*. Stand in parallel first and prepare the arms holding the skirt.

Bar 1. Lift the right foot to the *demi-pointe*;

Bar 2. Rise on to both *demi-pointes*;

Bar 3. Lower the right heel;

Bar 4. Lower the left heel.

Four times with each foot.

Note: Be sure to encourage the feeling of lifting the body as for a spring.

Second Year

2. a. *Tempo 4/4*. Stand in parallel first and prepare the arms. Place the right foot on the *demi-pointe*.

Bar 1. 1, Rise on both *demi-pointes*;

2, Lower the right heel;

3, Rise on both *demi-pointes*;

4, Lower the left heel.

Four times with each foot.

Third Year

3. a. *Tempo 4/4*. Stand in parallel first and prepare the arms.

Bar 1. 1, Rise on both *demi-pointes*;

2, Lower the right heel and lift the left knee to parallel *retiré*;

3, Rise on the right and replace the left on *demi-pointe*;

4, Lower the left heel and lift the right knee.

Four times commencing with each leg.

3. b. *Tempo 4/4*. Prepare as before.

Bar 1. 1, Lift the right knee on a *demi-plié* on the left leg;

&,2, Change feet in the air with a light spring, land in *demi-plié* on the right with the left knee lifted;

3, Hold the *demi-plié* on the right and close the left into *demi-plié*;

4, Stretch the knees.

As usual, four times on each leg is sufficient.

Fourth Year

4. a. *Tempo 4/4.* Prepare in *demi-plié* with the working leg in parallel *retiré*. Hold the arms in *demi-seconde*.

Bar 1.   1,   Spring, changing feet in the air;

        &,2,3,4,   Repeat three times;

Bar 2.   1,   Place the working leg in *demi-plié* with the supporting one;

        2,3,   Stretch the knees;

        4,   Prepare as before.

Repeat three times, rest and do four times commencing with the other leg. This is done *sur place en face* then with quarter turns on each two bars of music.

4. b.   The step now travels in various floor patterns with arm movements and when strong enough, without the pauses.

Note: See that the feet are well stretched under the body in the air and that the body is balanced and carried smoothly without strain. There must be no reflected movement in the body or arms.

Falling

To make full use of the levels in space, the placement and movement of the body at floor level must not be neglected. A movement can lead slowly down to a resting place on the floor or can commence an upward movement line from it. Falling swiftly can be an exciting part of an aerial pattern with considerable dramatic overtones. When a dancer falls he does not hurt himself because he knows HOW to fall. Children frequently fall and often injure themselves, sometimes badly, so it is useful for them, too, to know how to fall.

The first principle of falling is that the body must relax. This allows the joints to give freely and the body to find its way on to the better padded parts such as the thigh and the buttock. At all cost, landing on bone must be avoided. The knees and the coccyx are the most vulnerable parts and landing on either can cause very painful injuries. The body should fold up and roll to minimize the shock of the fall. The following is an example of one way to fall.

First Year

1. a. *Tempo 2/4.* Prepare kneeling up on two knees. Lift the arms to parallel third position.

Bar 1.   Sit back on two knees, allow the elbows and wrists to relax and fall on to the knees while the head and upper spine curl forward;

Bar 2.   Let the arms fall to the floor round the knees as the hips roll onto the right thigh, the weight of the head and shoulders moving in the opposite direction to control the fall;

Bar 3.   Continue rolling through the body on to the right shoulder;

Bar 4.   Roll the upper body on to the back of the shoulders leaving the knees bent and the legs lying on the side of the thigh.

Second Year

2. a.   *Tempo 2/4.*   Commence kneeling on the right knee with the arms in third position.

Bar 1.   1,   Place the left knee in the kneeling position as the body folds up as before;

2,   Roll on to the right thigh as before;

Bar 2.   Complete the fall.

Third Year

3. a.   *Tempo 4/4.*   Stand in parallel first with the arms in parallel third.

Bar 1.   1,2,   Kneel placing the weight on the instep of the right foot (to keep the knee from hitting the floor);

3,4,   Complete the fall.

Note: As the fall becomes faster, the right arm can be used to break the fall. See that the wrist and elbow relax immediately on contact with the floor.

Fourth Year

4. a.   *Tempo 4/4.*   Stand in parallel or rotated first. Prepare with the breathing movement.

Bar 1.   1,2,   *Demi-plié*, close the arms to *bras bas*;

&,   Spring from two feet, lift the arms to third;

3,   Land on the left leg in *demi-plié*, place the right instep on the floor and lower until the knee almost touches the floor;

&,   Break the fall with the right arm as the body rolls on to the thigh;

4,   Roll through the body to any finishing position desired.

Note: It is useful for children to do simple somersaults and other rolling movements on the floor. Encourage the children to experiment with various ways to fall, especially in their improvisations when the fall can be used expressively.

Balance and Line

It is essential that the body be well balanced both when stationary or in movement, on the floor or in the air. These exercises are in two groups, balance in place and balance in and after movement.

First Year

1. a.   Run and stop when the teacher stops the music. Stop in a pose like a statue or just freeze the movement. Let the child choose the pose.

1. b.   Run, fall down, roll over, get up and stand still. (Avoid falling on the knee.)

1. c.   Rise on the *demi-pointes* and balance with the arms in a chosen position.

Second Year

2. a.   Take three walking steps and balance on one leg with the other in *cou-de-pied* position or in parallel *retiré*. Hold the arms still in a chosen position.

2. b.   Using slow marches *sur place* step on the first count and balance on one leg for three counts. Swing the arms in opposition and hold during the balance.

2. c.   Rise on the *demi-pointes* with various arm movements.

Third Year

3. a.   *Tempo 6/8.*   Prepare with *dégagé devant* and the arms in *demi-seconde*.

Bar 1.   Six little running steps forward, lower the arms to *bras bas*;

Bar 2. 1,2,3,   Step forward into *demi-plié*, lift the arms to *demi-first* position;

4,5,6,   Stage *assemblé* forward, hold the first position of the arms;

Bar 3.   Rise on the *demi-pointes*, open the arms to *demi-seconde*;

Bar 4. 1,2,3,   Lower the heels;

4,5,6,   *Dégagé devant*.

This can be done *en diagonale* or in a floor pattern using the same foot to commence and later using alternate feet.

3. b.   *Tempo 6/8.*   Prepare *dégagé devant* and the arms to *demi-seconde*;

Bar 1.   Six running steps, closing the arms slowly to *bras bas*;

Bar 2. 1,2,3,4,5,   Step into a pose on one foot and balance;

6,   *Coupé* under and *dégagé devant* in preparation for the repeat.

3. c.   With two hands on the *barre*, rise on one leg, take the hands off the *barre* and balance with the arms in first position.

Fourth Year

4. a.   Balance on one leg from a spring.

Tempo 4/4.   Prepare in *dégagé devant* and the arms in *demi-seconde*;

Bar 1. 1,2,   Take two steps and lower the arms to *bras bas*;

&,3,   *Jeté* forward in parallel or rotated position, land in *demi-plié*, lift the arms to *demi-first* position with the spring;

4,   Hold the *demi-plié* and the arms;

Bar 2. 1,2,3,   Stretch the supporting knee and open the arms to *demi-seconde*;

4,   *Dégagé* the working leg *devant* for the repeat of the step.

Note: The exercise should be done in all *épaulement* directions, forward, sideways and backwards where possible.

4. b.   Balance after turning.

Tempo 4/4.   Prepare with a rise on *demi-pointes* and the arms in *demi-first*.

Bar 1.   Turn twice on two feet spotting to the front with the head and eyes;

Bar 2. 1,2,   Step into a pose;

3,4,   Balance;

Bar 3.   Balance;

Bar 4. 1,2,   Stand in first position with the arms in *bras bas*;

3,4,   Rise in the *demi-pointes* and lift the arms to *demi-first*.

4. c.   Balance on one leg.

Tempo 6/8.   Prepare in *dégagé devant* and the arms in second position.

Bar 1. &,1,2,3,4,5,6,   Two skips, swing the arms to first on the first skip and reverse to second on the second skip.

Bar 2.   1,2,3,   Step and rise on one leg on *demi-pointe* swing the arms through *bras bas* to first or third position;

4,5,   Balance and open the arms to second position;

6,   *Demi-plié* on the supporting leg.

Note: In improvisations encourage balance on various parts of the body and in group patterns or with partners.

Directional Poses

A pose is a harmonious picture composed of the head, arms, body and legs. The eyes add life and individuality and their use in performance creates the magic of a true artist.

The basic directional poses are *croisé* (crossed), *effacé* (shaded), and *écarté* (thrown open). These require an understanding of *épaulement* directions which are called by the same names. Here it is helpful to relate the points of the room or stage to a small individual square round each dancer and use their directional names. For example, with the right foot in front, point 8 is *croisé*, and *écarté devant*; Point 2 is *effacé* and *écarté derrière*; with the left foot in front point 2 is *croisé* and *effacé devant* and point 8 is *effacé* and *écarté derrière*. The early use of *épaulement* directions in a simple form makes sure the young student will show dimension in dancing and not appear like a cardboard replica of a dancer.

Croisé

First Year

1. a.   *Tempo 4/4.*   Stand in parallel first position facing point 8. Prepare the arms to parallel *demi-seconde* position.

Bar 1.   1,2,   Close the arms to low position;

3,4,   Lift the left arm to parallel *demi-first* and the right to *demi-seconde*, look to the left hand;

Bar 2.   1,2,   *Dégagé* the right leg to point 8, hold the positions of the arms and head;

3,4,   Hold, thinking of the position;

Bar 3.   1,2,   Close the leg to first;

3,4,   Close the arms following the front hand with the head and eyes;

Bar 4.   1,2,   Pause;

3,4,   Prepare to repeat the pose.

Point the left leg facing point 2.

Second Year

2. a.   *Tempo 4/4.*   Stand in a slightly rotated first position of the feet facing point 8. Prepare the arms to *demi-seconde*.

Bar 1. 1,2, Close the arms to *bras bas*, follow the right hand with the head;

3,4, *Dégagé* the right leg *devant*, lift the left arm to parallel *demi-first* and the right to parallel *demi-seconde*, look to the left hand;

Bar 2. 1,2, Curve the left arm, look to the palm;

3,4, Curve the right arm and look to its palm;

Bar 3. Hold the pose;

Bar 4. 1,2, *Allongé* the arms looking to the left hand;

3,4, Close the arms and leg, follow the left hand to *bras bas* and then look up to point 1. With the left leg face point 2.

Third Year

3. a. Exercise 2. a. is executed in the same manner and timing but both arms curve at the same time and the pose is held two counts longer.

3. b. Exercise 3. a. adds the *dégagé derrière*. With the right foot *dégagé* to the back to point 6 while facing point 2. With the left in *dégagé* to the back to point 4 while facing point 8.

Notes: Be sure the *dégagés* point in exactly the correct direction of the student's individual square, that is, *devant* to points 8 and 2 and *derrière* to points 6 and 4. See that the line of the body is straight with no twisting of the hips or shoulders and that the feeling for the line passing through the head, arms, body and legs is understood and experienced. In *épaulement* directions the back of the shoulders should not be visible to any part of the audience.

Fourth Year

4. a. *Tempo 4/4.* Stand facing point 8 with the right foot in front in *croisé* third position. Prepare with the breathing movement of the arms, follow the right hand with the head and eyes.

Bar 1. 1,2, *Dégagé* the right foot *devant*, lift the arms to *demi-first*, look to the right palm;

3,4, Open the right arm to *demi-seconde*, follow it with the head and eyes, leave the left arm in *demi-first*;

Bar 2. Hold the position;

Bar 3. 1,2, Open the left arm to *demi-seconde* following it with the head and eyes;

3,4, Turn the head and eyes to look at the right hand;

Bar 4. 1, *Allongé* both arms;

2,3, Close the leg and arms. Follow the right arm to *bras bas*;

4, Look up to point 1.

Also do this exercise with *dégagé derrière*. When mastered with the arms in *demi* positions, lift them to normal first and second.

Effacé
All Years

Use the same exercises in each year as for *croisé* and in the same manner and timing.

The position *effacé*: Face point 2 with the right leg in front for *effacé devant*. Face point 2 with the left leg to the back for *effacé derrière*. For both *devant* and *derrière*, the left arm is in *demi-first* and the right in *demi-seconde*. The head is turned to point 1. The feet and arms are reversed when facing point 8.

Écarté

Fourth Year

Devant: Face point 8 with the right foot in front in third position. Repeat exercise 4. a. for *croisé* but with the right leg in *dégagé* to the second position. The right arm is in *demi-first* and the left in *demi-seconde*. The head and eyes turn to point 1.
Derrière: Face point 8 with the right foot in front in third position. *Dégagé* the left foot to the second. The left arm is in *demi-first* and the right in *demi-seconde*. The head and eyes look to point 1. The feet and arms are reversed when facing point 2.
Note: With the head and eyes, always follow the arm which opens from first to second before closing then finish looking to the front.

Arabesques

An *arabesque* is a long, clear, flowing line running through the arms, head, body and legs. It is an amalgamation of positions of the arms, head, body and legs, the individual placement of which has been prepared in previous exercises in the training. *Arabesques* vary in the height of the leg in the air and in the use of the arms. In this course, the first three *arabesques* will be taught *par terre* only, commencing in the third year of training.

The harmony with which the parts of the body are joined together into the line of an *arabesque* shows the degree of artistry of the dancer and the use of the eyes in the clear out-going line of the pose, gives life and individual expression to its use in the dance. The expressive and aesthetic qualities of this beautiful pose should be stressed from the beginning.

Third Year

3. a.   First *Arabesque*
Tempò 4/4.   Commence facing point 3 in third position of the feet with the right foot in front. Prepare with the breathing movement.

Bar 1.   1,2,   Lift the arms to first position, look to the palm of the left hand;

3,4,   *Dégagé* the left leg to fourth *derrière* (point 7), hold the position of the arms and head;

Bar 2.   1,2,   *Allongé* the arms as the right extends directly to the front of its shoulder at shoulder level (point 3), open the left arm to second position, both palms are turned to the floor, the elbows are softened but are not allowed to drop towards the floor; follow the right hand as it extends and look beyond the fingers into the distance.

3,4,   Hold the pose;

Bar 3.   Continue to hold the pose thinking of all its aspects;
Bar 4.   1,2,   Close the leg into third position and the arms to *bras bas*;
          3,4,   Hold the position.

Repeat the exercise facing point 7 with the left foot in front.

Note: Remember the points of the room. Now refer to the equivalent directions of the dancers own small square of personal space.

3. b.   Third *Arabesque*

Exercise 3. b. for pose *croisé derrière* holds the position before the arms curve into first and second positions to make the line of third *arabesque*. The arms are at the normal height of these positions and the head and eyes look along and beyond the arm in first position.

Notes: Make sure that the spine is released and the weight is placed directly over the supporting leg. The back is upright and the line flows through from the fingers to the fully pointed toe of the working foot.

Fourth Year

Second *Arabesque*

This *arabesque* is like the first but has the opposite arm forward from the supporting leg. Combine it with the following exercise for first *arabesque*.

4. a.   *Tempo 4/4.*   Commence as for exercise 3. a.
    Bar 1.   1,2,   *Dégagé* the left leg *derrière*, lift the arms to first position, look to the left hand;
              3,4,   *Allongé* the arms, to first *arabesque*, look along the right arm;
    Bar 2.   Hold the pose releasing the spine and lengthening forward and upward;
    Bar 3.   1,2,   Meet the arms in first position, look to the left hand;
              3,4,   Extend the left arm to first and the right to second with the *allongé* movement to second *arabesque*; Look over the left shoulder to the audience;
    Bar 4.   Hold the pose.

On four additional chords, curve the arms, open the left arm to second following it with the head and eyes, *allongé* both arms and close them to *bras bas* and the leg into third position *derrière*. Repeat, facing point 7 with the opposite legs and arms.

Elevation

Elevation in springing steps adds the dimension of height to the aerial dance pattern. There are numerous qualities which can be expressed through elevation. Springing steps can be soft and floating or strong and dynamic according to the desire of the choreographer or the dancer. Terms like slow and quick, elastic and continuous, joining and blending, dynamic and purposeful have individual qualities and character which must be drawn into the range of expression in springing steps.

The musical accompaniment plays an important part in the training of springs. It should give the quality of the step and mirror the energy required to execute it. A good lively upbeat helps to revive flagging energy!

Quality will be studied in its own section but should be experienced in all exercises and steps of elevation.

The technique of jumping requires a strong basic training of the legs, body and arms. The posture must be held in the air as firmly as when standing so that a complete and easily recognizable picture is seen IN THE AIR. Too often the pose is achieved only after the dancer has alighted from the spring. To achieve the effect of the correct pose in the air, each part of the body has to play an important role.

The Legs: Because the jump depends on the strength and elasticity of the muscles and the stamina of the tendons and joints, the teacher must see that control and understanding have been achieved through the basic exercises for the legs. The muscles must be well trained in the strong push off from the *demi-plié* before the body is 'torn off' the floor into the air. This is achieved by the controlled development of strength in the foot and toes, the achilles tendon, the knee and the thigh. The simultaneous stretching of the muscles and tendons, together with the straightening of the joints, activates the upward thrust of the jump from the floor and fixes the position of the body in the air.

In landing, the weight of the body must be caught and controlled in the soft alighting into *demi-plié* without relaxing all the leg muscles. In this way the elastic movement is continued in the landing and in the final stretching of the knee after the jump.

When leaving the floor in a jump, the knees stretch, the heels lift and lastly the toes are 'torn off' the floor. When alighting, the tips of the toes touch the floor first followed by the balls of the feet and the heels then the knees and ankles bend in the *demi-plié*. Before taking springs to the centre, it is recommended to teach them at the *barre* in the divided manner until the student understands what is required.

The Body: The body must have undergone the basic training for posture and be strong enough to hold the required pose in the air. In springs which do not travel, the thrust must be directly upwards and the landing on exactly the same vertical plane. In travelling steps the spring is both upwards and in the direction of travel. This means that the posture must be held while moving through the air and requires great control.

The Arms: The arms actively assist the jump by leading the spring upwards and helping to keep the balance in the pose at the height of the spring. They also act as a parachute on the way down and, in this way, help to soften the landing.

The Head and Eyes: The direction of the 'glance' of the eyes and the position of the head at the climax of the jump adds necessary expression to the technique and gives individual artistry to the step.

The following exercises are to teach the basic principles of jumps and cover springs from two to two feet, from two feet to one foot, from one to the other and from one to two as well as those on one foot.

Temps Levé Sauté
This is the basic jump for all *allégro*. It connects the very important *demi-plié* with a stretch in the air on which all *allégro* is built. The elastic *plié* and a light, flying and energetic jump followed by a soft alighting is introduced in these springs. The jump can be from two to two feet or on one foot. The character is strong and energetic and lifted on the upbeat.

First Year
1. a.   Use natural bouncing springs on two feet in parallel first or second positions. Hold the arms still and keep the body calm and free from strain.

Second Year
2. a.   Spring naturally in slightly rotated first and second positions in various rhythms, such as four *sautés*, and pause for four counts. Hold the arms still and the body peaceful.
2. b.   Repeat, with co-ordination of the arms.
Tempo 4/4.   Stand in parallel or rotated first position. Prepare with a deep breath and open the arms to parallel *demi-seconde*.

> Bar 1.   1,   *Demi-plié*, swing the arms down to *bras bas*;
> &,   Stretch the knees, swing the arms up to first position;
> 2,   *Demi-plié*, swing the arms in reverse to *bras bas*;
> &,   Stretch the knees, swing the arms to *demi-seconde*;
> 3,   *Demi-plié*, swing the arms to *bras bas*;
> &,   Spring, lift the arms to first position at the height of the jump;
> 4,   Land in *demi-plié*, swing the arms down in reverse *bras bas*;
> &,   Stretch the knees and swing the arms to *demi-seconde*.

After four times, rest and repeat.
2. c.   *Sauté* on one foot.
Tempo 3/4.   Slow mazurka. Prepare in *dégagé devant* with the arms at the waist.

> Bar 1.   &.   Lift the working foot a little;
> 1,   Step into *demi-plié*;
> &,2,   Spring on one foot with the other in *retiré* parallel;
> &,3,   Repeat the spring;
> Bar 2.   1,   Place the working foot in *demi-plié* in first position;
> 2,   Stretch the knees;
> 3,   *Dégagé* the same working foot in preparation for repeating the step.

Four times on each leg is sufficient.

Third Year
3. a.   *Sauté* on two feet
Tempo 4/4.   Prepare in rotated first or second position. Breathe deeply and open the arms to *demi-seconde*, palms down.

> Bar 1.   1,2,   *Demi-plié*, lower the arms to *bras bas*;
> &,   Spring, lift the arms to first position;

3,   Land in *demi-plié*, lower the arms to *bras bas*;

4,   Stretch the knees and swing the arms to *demi-seconde*.

After four times, rest and repeat.

3. b.   *Sauté* on one leg

Tempo 3/4.   Slow mazurka. Prepare in *dégagé devant* and the arms to *demi-seconde*.

Bar 1.	&,	Small spring on the supporting leg lifting the working one a little from the floor;
	1,	Step into *demi-plié*, close the arms to *bras bas*;
	&,2,	Spring in parallel *retiré*, lift the arms to first position;
	&,3,	Repeat the spring holding the arms in first;
Bar 2.	&,1,2,3,	Three skips, open the arms slowly to second position, follow one hand with the head and eyes.

Four times on each leg is sufficient. Rest then repeat.

Fourth Year

4. a.   *Sauté* on two feet

Tempo 4/4.   Prepare in first or second position with the arms in *allongé demi-seconde*. Breathe deeply.

Bar 1.	1,2,	*Demi-plié*, lower the arms to *bras bas*;
	&,3-4,	Two springs, lift the arms to *demi-first* and hold;
Bar 2.	&,1,	Spring holding the arms;
	2,3,	Slowly stretch, open the arms to *demi-seconde*;
	4,	Pause and *allongé* the arms.

After four times, rest and repeat.

4. b.   *Sauté* on one foot

Tempo 3/4.   Slow mazurka. Prepare as for 3. b.

Bar 1.		Do as for 3. b. in rotated *retiré*;
Bar 2.	&,1,	Spring and land on two feet in third position, hold the arms;
	2,3,	Stretch and prepare the *dégagé* and the arms.

Repeat four times on each leg.

Teach this facing the *barre* with a *demi-plié* on the count of 1, until sufficient strength is gained to execute it in the centre.

Note: All springs on one foot are very difficult and should be done at the *barre* until the body is held straight and calm and shows no reflection of the effort required to execute the jump.

Assemblé

An *assemblé* is a jump in which the legs are gathered together in the air and which lands on two feet. In its finished form it also commences from two feet but in the preparatory 'stage' version it is allowed to step into the jump. This encourages the feeling of flight into the air with the lightness essential in springing steps.

First Year

1. a.   *Tempo 2/4.*   Prepare in parallel first position of the feet with the arms in *demi-seconde* or holding the skirt or at the waist.

Bar 1.   &,1,   Extend the right foot and step forward into a *demi-plié*;

&,2,   Jump landing in *demi-plié* in parallel first, hold the arm position;

Bar 2.   Stretch the knees.

Travel by stepping forwards, sideways and backwards four times with each leg.

Note: As in all jumps, the height of the spring is on the & beat.

Second Year

2. a.   *Tempo 2/4.*   Prepare in slightly rotated first position, open the arms with the breathing movement.

Bar 1.   &,   Extend and lift the right foot, *allongé* the arms;

1,   Step into *demi-plié*, swing the arms to *bras bas*;

&,   Spring bringing both feet together in the air, swing the arms to *demi-first*;

2,   Land in *demi-plié* in first position, hold the arms in first;

Bar 2.   &,   Deepen the *demi-plié*, swing the arms to *bras bas* with the reverse movement;

1,2,   Stretch the knees, swing the arms to *allongé demi-seconde*.

Travel forwards, sideways and backwards four times with each leg.

Third Year

3. a.   *Tempo 4/4.*   Prepare with *dégagé devant* and the arms open with the breathing movement.

Bar 1.   &,   Lift the extended foot strongly pointed;

1,   Step into *demi-plié*, swing the arms to *bras bas*;

&,   Swish the working leg through *demi-plié* in first position and extend it, spring and join the other leg to it in first in the air, swing the arms up to first position;

2,   Land in *demi-plié* in first, hold the arms in first;

&,   Deepen the *demi-plié*, swing the arms to *bras bas*;

3,4,   Stretch the knees and swing the arms to *demi-seconde allongé*.

Execute four times on each leg and when mastered forward add the step moving backwards.

Fourth Year

4. a.   *Tempo 2/4.*   Prepare in *dégagé devant* and open the arms with the breathing movement.

Bar 1.   &,   Lift the working leg slightly from the floor, *allongé* the arms;

1,   Step into *demi-plié*, lower the arms to *bras bas*;

&,   Swish the other leg through *demi-plié* in first and extend it, spring and gather the feet together in first position in the air, and lift the arms to first position;

    2,   Land in *demi-plié* in first, hold the arms in first;

Bar 2.   &,   Deepen the *demi-plié* and begin to open the arms to second;

    1,   Stretch the knees, open the arms to second;

    2,   Prepare with *dégagé* and hold the arms.

Perform four times with each leg and when mastered add the backward direction.

4. b.   *Coupé Assemblé*

Tempo 4/4.   Prepare with the right foot in the *cou-de-pied* position *derrière par terre* and open the arms with the breathing movement.

Bar 1.   1,   *Coupé* into *demi-plié* on the right leg, extend the left to the second position *en l'air*, lower the arms to *bras bas* and look into the left hand;

    &,   Spring, joining the left leg to the right directly under the body in third position *devant* lift the arms to first position;

    2,   Land in *demi-plié* in third position, hold the arms in first;

    &,   Deepen the *demi-plié* and begin to open the arms to second;

    3,   Stretch the knees, open the arms to second following the left hand.

    4,   Prepare to repeat the step.

Work up to four times with each leg.

Note: This *assemblé* can be done with the extension in all directions, forward, sideways and backward. It can also alternate feet to the second by closing the third position *derrière*. Remember this *assemblé* does not travel from the place of commencement. When mastered the use of the arms may be varied.

Sissonne Simple

A *sissone simple* is a spring from two feet landing on one. Commence teaching it in the Third Year only as it is very difficult to hold the balance when alighting on one leg.

Third Year

3. a.   *Tempo 4/4.*   Prepare in rotated first position and open the arms with the breathing movement.

Bar 1.   1,2,   *Demi-plié*, lower the arms to *bras bas*;

    &,   Spring from two feet to first position in the air with fully stretched feet and legs, lift the arms to first position;

    3,   Land in *demi-plié* on the right leg with the left in the *cou-de-pied* position *devant* or *derrière*, hold the arms in first;

    4,   Close the left leg into *demi-plié* in first position, arms in first;

Bar 2.   1,2,   Stretch the knees and open the arms to second following the left arm with the head and eyes;

    3,4,   Hold the position and prepare to repeat.

Perform four times with each leg.

Fourth Year

4. a. Repeat 3. a. but on &,4, in bar 1, spring into first position in the air and land in *demi-plié* in first position. Hold the arms in first position during the *petit assemblé* which is a jump closing from an open position. Use bar 2 to stretch the knees and open the arms to second position. Later work in third position.

Petit Jeté

A *petit jeté* is a spring from one leg to the other. However, it may be commenced from two feet when done in a series. It may travel or stay *sur place*. Introduce this step in the Third Year when the exercises for prances have given the feeling of lifting the body lightly into the air from one foot. Introduce at the *barre* then take to the centre.

Third Year

3. a. *Tempo 4/4.* Use four chords for preparation; On the first two, open the arms to *demi-seconde* and *allongé*. On the second two chords, *demi-plié* in first position and lower the arms to *bras bas*;

Bar 1. &,1, Spring as for *sissone simple*, landing with the working foot in the *cou-de-pied derrière*, hold the arms in *bras bas*;

&,2, Spring, changing the feet in the air, hold the arms;

&,3, Spring, changing the feet;

4, Close the working foot in *demi-plié* in first position, hold the *bras bas*;

Bar 2. 1,2, Stretch the knees and open the arms to *demi-seconde*;

3,4, *Demi-plié*, close the arms to *bras bas*.

Execute twice with each leg.

Fourth Year

4. a. Repeat 3. a. but commence in third and close into third position with a *petit assemblé* on count 4, in bar 1 then repeat the whole in bar 2 without a pause. Gradually increase the number of bars to four but be sure the student does not tire as this destroys rather than builds stamina. The head may incline slightly over the supporting leg in the *jetés* and be held upright on the *petit assemblé*. The exercise can be done with the working foot *devant* or *derrière* and it must be placed and held correctly in the *cou-de-pied* position.

Échappé Sauté

An *échappé* is an equal escaping of both feet from a closed to an open position. There are many kinds of *échappés* but in this course the preparation is for the simple *échappé sauté* to second position. Teach it firstly at the *barre*.

Third Year

3. a. *Tempo 4/4.* Prepare in first position and open the arms with the breath.

Bar 1. 1,2, *Demi-plié*, close the arms to *bras bas*;

&,3, Spring and land in second position in *demi-plié*, open the arms to *demi-seconde* with the breathing movement;

4, Stretch the knees, hold the arms in *demi-seconde*;

Bar 2. 1,2, *Demi-plié* in second, *allongé* the arms;

   &,3, Spring and return to first, close the arms to *bras bas*;

   4, Stretch the knees and prepare the arms with the breathing movement.

After four times, rest and repeat.

Note: Remember that when the foot points, the toe comes under the heel, not the heel moving out to the toe. When jumping the same rule applies and the toes snatch under the heels as they leave the floor. This gives height to the spring and avoids the legs shooting out past the second position in a *échappé sauté*.

Fourth Year

4. a. *Tempo 4/4.* Use the legs as for 3. a. and add the use of the arms as follows:

Bar 1. 1,2, Close to *bras bas*;

   &,3, Lift the arms to *demi-first* position;

   4, Open to *demi-seconde*;

Bar 2. 1,2, Slowly *allongé*;

   &, Hold in *seconde*;

   3, Close to *bras bas*;

   4, Breathing movement.

When mastered use third position of the feet changing on the closing (*changé*) or without changing (*sans changé*).

Turning

Turning is an element of the dance. It adds variety and dimension to movement and can be used as an essential part of a step or as a decoration to embroider others. It may be a quick turn or a slow rotation, done in one movement or divided into quarters or halves of a complete revolution. The head may be used with a whipping movement during the turn or may lead or follow in the direction of the turn. These exercises are designed to give an understanding of the principles of turning and to encourage freedom and security in turning steps. Exercises for the whipping movement of the head should have been studied in the Isolation section before adding it to the turn itself.

First Year

1. a. Turning on two feet with small steps

Tempo 4/4. Prepare with a rise on *demi-pointes* in first position and lift the arms to *demi-first*, look *en face*.

Bar 1.   Turn with small steps to point 3, hold the first position of the arms and turn the head with the body;

Bar 2. 1,2, Lower the heels and the arms to low position;

   3,4, Rise on the *demi-pointes* and lift the arms to *demi-first*;

Bars 3–8. In the same manner continue turning to the right with quarter turns returning to point 1.

Make two revolutions in each direction. Later turn with half then full turns.

1. b. Quarter Turns by swivel on one foot

Tempo 4/4. Prepare in parallel *seconde* position of the feet and arms.

Bar 1. 1,2, Rise a little on the *demi-pointes*, hold the arms in *seconde*;

3,4, Swivel on the right foot to face point 3 being sure to take the left leg, the body, arms and head and eyes in position during the turn;

Bar 2. 1,2, Lower the heels and the arms to low position;

3,4, Hold;

Bar 3. 1,2, Rise on the *demi-pointes* and lift the arms to parallel *seconde*;

3,4, Return to face point 1 on the right leg in the same manner;

Bar 4. Lower the heels and prepare to repeat.

Turn four times to the right then four times to the left.

Note: Make sure the balance is held at the end of the turn after the body turns as one unit.

Second Year

2. a. Head Leading the Body

Turns as in exercise 2. b. in Marching (p. 89) should have been studied before introducing the following exercise.

Tempo 4/4. Stand in parallel or slightly rotated first position and prepare the arms to *demi-first*.

Bar 1. 1, Turn the head and eyes to point 3. Hold the position of the body and arms facing point 1;

2, Swivel on the right toes turning the body and arms in first position to point 3;

3, Rise on the *demi-pointes*, hold the arm position;

4, Lower the heels and hold the first position of the arms;

Bars 2–4. Repeat turning to points 5, 7 and 1.

Rotate four times to each direction.

Note: Reach this speed of execution slowly. First take one bar for each movement then half a bar and finally one beat of the bar as above.

2. b. Half Turns

Exercise 2. a. is now done with half turns, the first to the right then reverse and return to point 1. to the left. Later make both turns in the same direction.

Note: Make sure that the head turns freely and independently before the body and arms move.

2. c. Full Turns with Small Steps

Turn with small steps *sur place* without the use of the head. Hold the arms in first position and look over the leading shoulder. Later, hold the leading arm in *demi-first* and the other in *demi-seconde*, still looking over the leading shoulder. Several turns can be done in this way.

Third Year

3. a.   Half Turns

Tempo 4/4.   Prepare in rotated first position and lift the arms to *demi-first*.
Bar 1.   1,   Turn the head and eyes to point 5;
    2,   Rise and turn in first to face point 5;
    3,   Balance;
    4,   Lower the heels;
Bar 2.   Complete the turn in the same manner and in the same direction.

3. b.   Quarter Turns with Arms, Leaving the Head

Tempo 4/4.   Prepare in first position of the feet and arms in *demi-seconde*.
Bar 1.   &,   *Allongé* and lower the arms to *bras bas*;
    1,   Rise on the *demi-pointes*, lift the arms to *demi-first* through *bras bas*;
    2,   Turn the body and arms to point 3, leave the head to point 1;
    3,   Turn the head and eyes to point 3;
    4,   Lower the heels and open the arms to *demi-seconde*;
Bars 2–4.   Complete the turn by quarters in the same direction.

3. c.   Half Turns with Head Leading

Tempo 2/4.   Prepare in first position of the feet and arms and turn the head and eyes over the left shoulder to point 7.
Bar 1.   Make a half turn with the head and eyes to point 3, that is, over the right shoulder;
Bar 2.   On two feet, turn the body to face point 5, carry the arms in first position and leave the head looking to point 3;
Bar 3.   Turn the head and eyes to point 7;
Bar 4.   Turn the body and arms to point 1. leave the head looking to point 7.

At first this is done with the turn on the first count and hold still on the second. Later, eliminate the pause and complete the turn in two bars.

3. d.   Turns with Small Steps

With small steps on the *demi-pointes*, turn on the spot with the arms in third position and the head looking over the leading shoulder or hold one arm in third and the other in second travelling towards the lifted arm. Multiple turns can be made in this manner.

Note: Take care to hold correct posture and position of the arms during the turns and do not allow the arms or body to sink or the shoulders to lift.

Full Turns

Fourth Year

4. a.   Quarter Turns, Leading with then Leaving the Head

Tempo 4/4.   Prepare as for exercise 3. b.
Bars 1–2.   Execute as 3. b.;

Bar 3.	1,	Rise on *demi-pointes*;
	2,	Turn the head to point 7;
	3,	Turn the body to point 7;
	4,	Lower the heels and open the arms to *demi-seconde*;
Bar 4.		Repeat bar 3 to complete the turn to point 1.

Rotate four times to the right and left.

En dehors and *en dedans*

The understanding of *en dehors* and *en dedans* is introduced. This is simply stated by the explanation that when the turn is to the right on the right leg it is *en dedans*. When it is to the right on the left leg it is *en dehors*. The turn to the left on the left leg is *en dedans* and on the right is *en dehors*.

4. b.   *En dehors*
Tempo 4/4.   Prepare in parallel first position of the feet, open the arms to *demi-seconde*.

Bar 1.	&,	*Allongé*;
	1,	*Demi-plié*, lower the arms to *bras bas*, look *en face*;
	2,	Rise on the ball of the left foot, lift the right to parallel *retiré* and the arms to *demi-first*. Make one complete turn to the right. The head is the last to leave point 1 and the first to return to it;
	3,	Close in *demi-plié* in first *en face*, hold the arms in *demi-first*;
	4,	Stretch the knees and open the arms to *demi-seconde*.

Turn in both directions four times each. At first, pause for one bar before repeating the turn, and later, eliminate the pauses if possible.
Note: It is most important not to allow the shoulders to swing away from facing directly to the front in the preparation for the turn.

4. b.   *En dedans*
Tempo 4/4.   In the same manner and timing, turn to the right on the right leg and to the left on the left.

4. c.   With Small Steps and the Use of the Head
Tempo 4/4.   Prepare with a rise on *demi-pointes* in first or third position and the arms in *demi-first*.

Bar 1.		*Bourrée*, turning as far as possible to the right leaving the head and eyes to point 1;
Bar 2.	1,	Whip the head and eyes to the right to point 1 as the body continues the turn, hold the arms directly in front of the body in first position;
	2,3,4,	Complete the turn of the body with small steps to face front.

At first, pause for two bars before repeating the turn and later eliminate the pause. When mastered in the divided manner do the exercise in even *tempo* without pauses. The arms can then be varied as long as they do not disturb the correct placement of the whole body.

4. d.   Using Different Levels
Add levels to the *bourrée* turns but without the use of the whipping movement

of the head. Later turn in spirals or any inventive shape.

Note: Remember that every exercise must be executed an equal number of times to the right and to the left. Encourage the use of turns on one foot or on various parts of the body and in poses during the Improvisation section of the lesson.

Exercises and Steps Turning

Third Year

From the Third Year, when the basic movements in exercises such as brushes and *battement tendus* and steps such as waltzes, triplets, spring points, *petit jetés* and various springs in *allégro* are understood and executed correctly, introduce the element of turning. At first, turn one quarter followed by a pause until the circle is complete. Then divide the circle into quarters without the pauses. Later turn with half a turn and a pause and then without the pause.

Make sure the whole body turns as one unit and in complete alignment facing the new direction after the turn and before the next one. Look positively to the direction in which the body is facing at the time. The eyes must focus on a definite point at eye level. Do not allow the student to stare blankly but be very alert with a clear and defined vision.

The ability to turn quickly and surely in any given direction is essential in dancing both from a technical and aesthetic point of view. If the young student is used to turning the body on two feet, pirouettes will not be a nightmare but a thrill when the time comes to learn academic turns on one foot.

Rhythm and quality

Part III

Qualities of Dance

Music and the Awareness of Time

The following exercises are used before teaching a new movement or step so that the required time, rhythm and quality are assimilated before translating them into movement. Some exercises can be done sitting and others standing or moving. See that correct lifted posture is maintained at all times.

Common Time

Tempo 4/4. There are four crotchets in 4/4 time. It is a marching and skipping time and is also that of the lively gavotte.

First Year

To establish the feeling for even beats and to co-ordinate sound and movement, these exercises introduce note values.

The crotchet which approximates to the heart-beat, is the basic measurement used in musical time signatures.

1.a. *Tempo 4/4.*
Bars 1–2. The teacher counts aloud from one to eight;
Bars 3–4. The children count aloud from one to eight.
Later alternate between two groups of children. Later still, one group counts from one to four and the other from five to eight.

1.b. Count aloud to a strong clear march and later alternate counting aloud with silent counting.

1.c. Do the same clapping the hands, hitting the floor or any other surface that makes an interesting sound. To measure the exact length of the crotchet beat, prepare by extending the arms to parallel first, bend the elbows and bring the hands opposite the shoulders with the palms facing. Clap in the centre of the body then, on the intermediate pulse of &, open the hands again to opposite the shoulders.

1.d. Repeat the previous exercises stamping *sur place* (on the spot) and then walking in free space or in a set floor pattern. As it is very difficult to anticipate the change of weight so as to step exactly on the beat, careful preparation must give sufficient time for the thinking process to ensure precision (see Preparations, p. 44).

1.e. Combine counting with clapping, stamping or marching *sur place* with silence and stillness.

1.f. Combine clapping with stamping or walking in free space or in a set pattern with stillness and silence.

When these exercises are understood, reduce the time to one-bar phrases of 4/4.

The minim is twice the length of the crotchet and there are two in one bar of 4/4.

1.a.   Prepare the arms by lifting to parallel first, keep the elbows at the same height, turn and place the palms together so that the elbows are bent slightly outwards making a first position.

Bar 1.   1, &,   Clap and open the arms on the same level until the hands are opposite the shoulders with the palms facing the body;

    2,   Hold the open position;

    3, &,   Repeat the clap and opening;

    4,   Hold.

This can be done with one group clapping minims and another crotchets. The teacher or the children can invent many variations combining counts, claps, bangs, stamps and walks. Add silence and stillness in poses. Adapt the exercises for crotchets to the time of minims.

The semibreve is the whole note and is four times the length of the crotchet. There is one semibreve in one bar of 4/4 time.

1.a.   Count aloud only the first beat of the bar and hold a singing tone through the length of the note. Softly clapping or banging the crotchets will help maintain the correct length of the semibreve but try, ultimately, to keep the time with silent counting.

1.b.   Prepare the arms as for clapping mimims.

Bar 1.   1,   Clap and open the arms;

    2,   Reach the point opposite the shoulders;

    3,   Open half way to second position;

    4,   Open to second position.

If this is done correctly, it will be found that the arms are now in a curved and well-supported classical second position and so this has become an exercise for arms as well as for time.

Adapt the previous exercises for the semibreve and invent more.

The quaver is half the length of the crotchet and there are eight in one bar of 4/4.

1.a.   Do the counting exercises in two bar sections so that A counts from one to eight twice then B uses the next two bars.

1.b.   Prepare the hands as for clapping crotchets and repeat the clapping exercises opening the hands only as far as the sides of the neck so the sound is half the length of a crotchet.

1.c.   Combine small runs on the beat with counting and clapping, in groups and in free or set floor patterns.

Second Year

The semiquaver is a quarter the length of the crotchet and there are sixteen in one bar of 4/4 time.

2.a.   Apply the previous exercises to this speed and invent more.

Rhythmic Patterns

First Year
Rhythm in Bars

With the four note values in the first year study, many interesting games can be invented working in groups which use different notes in successive or simultaneous bars. By this method a thorough understanding of time will be gained and a regular beat can be maintained over a reasonable period. Simple form can be taught in this way by, say, A using two bars of minims followed by B using two bars of quavers which, when repeated, makes Binary form.

1.a.   *Tempo* 4/4. Prepare the arms and the feet for clapping and walking.
Bar 1.   Clap four crotchets or walk four steps;
Bar 2.   Clap one semibreve or step and hold a pose.
1.b.
Bar 1.   Group A claps and walks four crotchets while group B holds a pose;
Bar 2.   Reverse the roles.
1.c.
Bar 1.   1, 2, 3, 4,   March four lifted march steps (four crotchets);
Bar 2.   &, 1, 2, 3, 4, Four skips (eight quavers).

Second Year

Accent and Rhythm within the Bar

When note values are established, rhythms can be made by using two or more different notes in one bar. Where the accent falls determines the character of the rhythm and controls the phrasing.
Example:
a.   *Tempo* 4/4. Two crotchets and one minim.
b.   *Tempo* 4/4. Four quavers and two crotchets.
Words can be used to make rhythms and also direct the movement to be made as;
a.   could be Walk/walk/bend-stretch,
b.   could be Run/run/run/run/step/jump.
Develop such ideas when inventing instructive exercises.
2.a.   Combine different note values to make rhythmic patterns, for example:
Clap or walk one minim and two crotchets. At first clap and open on 1, &, and hold for 2, &, then clap 3, 4. Later try to open the hands for the minim at a slower pace so the movement takes the same length of time as the sound of the note.
2.b.   In groups: A claps the first minim, B claps three quavers and rests the fourth. Extend this to walks, runs, skips or any appropriate movement in personal or general space. Use ideas to express such things as robots or animals.
2.c.   *Rests.* Clap or walk the first three crotchets in a bar, opening the hands on the & counts then hold open for 4, &. This is the equivalent of a rest in music and has the same value as the note it replaces. Vary the placement of the rest by holding the second and then the third beats. By the end of the year,

interesting percussive compositions can be made with claps, bangs, words or voice sounds with the children acting as the orchestra.

Third Year

Note Values
3.a.   *Tempo 4/4.* Prepare the arms for clapping and extend the foot to *pointe dégagé.*

Bars 1–2.   Walk and clap each crotchet;
Bar 3.   Walk and clap two minims;
Bar 4.   Step and hold a pose for one semibreve.

Vary this basic idea as much as possible so the children can move quickly and stop securely or change speed without faltering.

Accent and Dynamics
3.b.   Vary the accent, placing it now on the second beat and then on the third and later on the fourth. Set the musical pattern and ask the children to mirror it in movement or ask one child to demonstrate a pattern and the others to say where the accent falls. First do the exercise with claps and walks and then with dance steps.

Bar 1.   1,   *Chassé*, in words 'slide' or '*chassé*';
         2,   Step 'behind' or '*pas*';
         3,   Step 'side' or '*de*';
         4,   Step 'front' or '*bourrée*'

Make a strong dynamic movement on the accented count of 1, and make the three steps of the *pas de bourrée* very light so obtaining the real quality of this little running step.

Add:

Bar 2   1,   'Step';
         2,   'Step';
         &, 3, 'Assemblé';
         4,   'Stretch'.

Make the two steps light then accent the spring on the *assemblé*. Each bar can be a separate exercise before running them together.

Speed
3.c.   Speed up the *enchaînement* into one bar of 4/4 *tempo.*

Bar 1.   1,   *Chassé*;
         &, a, 2, *Pas de bourrée*;
         3,   *Assemblé*;
         &, 4,   Land and stretch.

With doubling the speed of the small introductory, preparatory or joining steps and placing the accents correctly, the *enchaînement* is properly phrased and will flow easily thus making dance sense.

Fourth Year

Words, Music and Movement

4.a.   Continue with the word, music and movement patterns in this year but these will now be mainly in Improvization where the children's imagination and inventiveness can be trained to work within artistic limits set by these patterns. However, patterns set by the teacher greatly assist in phrasing movement.

Bar 1. &, 1, &, 2, &, 'Skip, skip';
      3, &,   'Run, run';
      4,   'Pose';
Bar 2. &, 1, 2, 3, &, 'Wave, wave, wave';
      4,   'Prepare'.

4.b.   With a thorough knowledge of note values, the student should now understand that:

Simple time means that one movement equals one pulse.

Half time means that one movement equals two pulses.

Double time means that two movements equal one pulse.

Invent movements accordingly.

Changing Accent

4.c.   In this year the student should be able to change the accent in a four-bar phrase thus:

1, 2, 3, 4/1, *2*, 3, 4/1, 2, *3*, 4/1, 2, 3, *4*. with claps, walks, runs and simple movements.

4.d.   The change of accent to achieve a syncopated beat is very useful for more advanced exercises and if understood in simple form will greatly help the student as he progresses.

Bar 1. 1,   Clap;
      &, 2, 3, 4, &, Open the hands on the & counts and clap on the next three beats;
Bar 2. 1,   Open the hands;
      &, 2, 3, 4, &, Clap on the & beats and open on the counts.

Later hold the hands together on the fourth beat of the first bar and open on the first beat of the second bar then hold the fourth beat open.

Three-Quarter Time

Three crotchets in one bar, with varying accents, make the basis for several dance forms such as the minuet, waltz and the mazurka which will be introduced in this course. The previous counting, clapping and walking exercises can all be adapted to 3/4 time but other interesting things can be done to experience the particular rocking or swaying rhythm of this *tempo*, for example, simple beating time; down, out, up. When the accent is evenly placed on each beat the rhythm is that of a minuet. When the first beat is accented it is a waltz. The mazurka will be explained later.

1.a.   *Waltz Rhythm*
Tempo 3/4. Prepare the arms to parallel first with the fists clenched.
Bar 1.   1,   Make a strong downward movement of the wrists and arms;
       2, 3,   Release the wrists and allow the arms to float softly up to parallel first.
(See exercise for arm waves, p. 78.)
   Later add a *demi-plié* in parallel first on the count of 1, and rise on 2, 3.

1.b.   *Circular Movement*
Bar 1.   1,   From opposite the chest, clap the hands with an upward movement;
       2, 3,   Using the impetus of the clap, allow the hands to fall softly in a downward circular movement ready to clap again on the first beat of the following bar.
Reverse the clap downward and the circle upward when the wrists must move freely on the outward circle.

1.c.   *Rocking Boat*
Sit with the soles of the feet together and hold the ankles or knees. Be a boat with a tall straight mast rocking from side to side in time with the music. The sea is calm and peaceful so the rocking will be small and quiet. A storm gets up and the sea becomes rough and wild so with the use of more energy, the rocking will become stronger to mirror the feeling of the music. The storm passes and once more the sea is calm.

1.d.   *Swing on Knees*
Bar 1.   Sitting on two knees, swing the arms foward in parallel as the body rises on to the knees;
Bar 2.   Swing the arms down and back as the body sits and bends forward.

1.e.   *Waltz Rhythm*
Words can help with walking on the spot in waltz rhythm as; down/up/up and so on. Use words for all kinds of games and exercises.

Second Year

2.a.   *Rocking Boat*
In a progression of the rocking boat exercise, make a strong swing over on the first beat then place one hand on the floor and stretch the other out to parallel second on the second and third beats.

2.b.   *Figure Eight*
Draw a figure eight with the tips of the fingers on the floor taking one bar for half the figure. Cross the eight at the same spot on the floor each time and see that it corresponds with the accent on the first beat of the bar. Allow the wrist to turn naturally during the movement so that when the figure is understood, it can be drawn in the air and the wrist will turn so that on the first beat down and across, the palm is turned downward. On the second and third beats, it turns outward as it makes the upward movement. On the second bar, the back of the wrist crosses the centre and the palm faces inward on the way up. Make

the figure small at first then gradually increase the size until the whole arm becomes involved in the movement. Later incorporate a change of weight so the body sways with the figure eight.

2.c.   *Amalgamated Exercises*

Amalgamate exercises in 3/4 time, for example:
Do three swings on the knees as in First Year 1.d. then prepare for the Table Back exercise (try to 'go through' the hands lightly as the body falls on to them). Do the cat stretch for eight bars.

Third Year

3.a.   *Rocking Boat*

Develop the rocking boat exercise by lifting on to one knee, bend and look over the low shoulder and curve the lifted arm.

3.b.   *Figure Eight*

Develop the figure of eight first on the straight and then on the diagonal cross.

3.c.   On the horizontal, make a figure of eight with both arms crossing in the centre of the body at the height of first position.

3.d.   *Counter-balance*

From sitting on the knees, rise, lift the arms to third position and shift the weight onto the right buttock. Counter-balance with both arms to the left with the palms turned upwards. Repeat to the left. Take two bars for each 'sit'.

3.e.   *Mazurka*

Introduce mazurka rhythm. There is a strong accent on either the second or the third beat of the bar in this Polish dance.
Tempo 3/4. Mazurka. Clap the rhythm of the step below then execute the step. Prepare the arms to the hips and the right foot to *dégagé devant*.

Bar 1.   &,   Hop on the left leg;
         1,   Step on to the right leg;
         2,   *Plié* on right leg;
         3,   Spring on to two feet in parallel first.

At first, use bar 2 to prepare for the repeat of the step and later repeat the step on the opposite leg in a series.
3.f.   Clap the more developed rhythm.

Bar 1.   &, a,   Two light claps;
         1,   Light clap;
         2,   Strong clap;
         &,   Light clap;
         3,   Slight accent.

Fourth Year

4.a.   *Rocking Boat*

Develop the rocking boat exercise. Sweep the body and arm forward and down then continue the swing round and to the back rising on one knee as the body lifts at the end of the swing. Do one swing in two bars of a waltz and when stability is assured try to complete the swing to both sides in two bars.

4.b. *Figure Eight*

Develop the figure eight exercise using all the zones of movement together with bends of the body. Investigate the widest possible range of movement. Use scarves and feathers to extend the pattern of the arms and body. By now it will be realized that the body must move freely to extend the figure eight and that the impetus comes, in fact, from the body. When using a scarf, the material must float and extend to the end so that the scarf becomes a continuation of the arm.

4.c. *Waltz Rhythm*

Tempo 3/4. Waltz. Prepare by sitting on the knees, hands resting on the knees.
Bar 1. Rise on the knees, lift the arms to parallel first with the palms up;
Bar 2. Keeping the back absolutely straight, hinge back in the knee joints;
Bar 3. Straighten;
Bar 4. Sit back on the knees ready to repeat.

4.d. *Mazurka*

Tempo 3/4. Mazurka. Prepare with *dégagé devant* and the arms in *demi-seconde*.

Bar 1.	&, a,	*Demi-plié*, hop and lift the working leg from *dégagé*;
	1,	Slide, toe first, to fourth *devant*, carry the arms, head inclined over the working foot;
	2,	Transfer the weight into *demi-plié* in *arabesque*;
	&,	Hop;
	3,	Pass the working leg through first position *demi-plié*, head erect;
Bar 2.	&, a,	Hop and extend the working leg;
	1, 2, 3,	Complete the step on the other leg.

Duple Time

There are two crotchets in one bar of the 2/4 time. Use the previous exercises adapted to 2/4 and invent more. Duple time is the tempo of the lively polka which has a very special rhythm of its own.

Second Year

2.a. *Party Polka*

Tempo 2/4. Clap the rhythm of the party polka.

Bar 1.	&,	Clap lightly;
	1,	Accented;
	&,	Lightly;
	2,	Accented.

2.b. Introduce the step. Prepare the hands on the hips or holding the skirt.

Bar 1.	&,	Hop;
	1, &,	Gallop through first position of the feet;
	2,	Step.

This step is done from side to side and later turning, making one complete turn with two party polka steps.

Third Year

3.a. *Classical Polka*
Learn the rhythm of the classical polka.
Bar 1. &, Open the hands in preparation for clapping;
    a, Clap lightly;
    1, Accent lightly;
    &, Lightly;
    2, Accent.

The development of the classical polka is contained in the section on Dance Steps, p. 150.

Compound Duple Time

Six quavers or two dotted crotchets make up six–eight time. In the Second Year count six quavers but in the Third Year introduce the dotted crotchet (and other dotted notes). The dotted note is half the length of the note again and so one dotted crotchet equals three quavers. This means there can be two counts in one bar of 6/8, each of three pulses. It is a very versatile time as it can be slow (*adagio*) or quick (*allégro*). The *gigue* and hornpipe are examples of dances in this rhythm in fast time.

Second Year

2.a. Adapt the exercises for 3/4 to 6/8 by making the movements quicker and counting six quavers with the accents on the first and fourth beats.
2.b. Use word rhythms with or without music, for example:
Tempo 6/8.
Bar 1. 1, *Jump* on two feet in parallel first;
    2, 3, Stretch/stretch;
    4, 5, *Run*/run;
    6, Step;
or *1*, *Step*;
    2, 3, Gallop; (*pas de chat* type).
    4, *Step*;
    5, 6, And skip;
Join the two together.

Third Year

Dotted Notes

3.a. Clap the first and fourth beats of the bar counting the dotted crotchets as three pulses (three quavers).
3.b. *Tempo 6/8*
Bar 1. *1*, *Step*;
    &, Skip;
    a, Step and jump up;

2,	*Land* (on two feet);
&,	Spring up;
a,	Land in *demi-plié*;

or

1,	*Step*;
&, a,	Leap/land;
2,	*Step*;
&, a,	And spin (on one leg).

Join them together.

Fourth Year

4.a. Invent word and step *enchaînements* in 6/8 *tempo* seeing that the impetus is taken from the accents on the first and second dotted crotchet beats so a free flowing on-going feeling is created.

4.b. Do the figure of eight exercises in 6/8 moving more quickly and travelling through general space with, say, triplets.

4.c. *Port de Bras*

Tempo 6/8. Use with *port de bras* to third position.

Bar 1.	1, &, a,	Lift the arms to third position;
	2,	Breathe and open the forearms;
	&, a,	Open to second position;
Bar 2.	1, &, a,	*Allongé* and breathe;
	2, &, a,	Lower to *bras bas*.

4.d. *Swing*

Tempo 6/8.

Bar 1.	1, &, a,	After breathing preparation, make a full *port de bras* through third to *bras bas*;
	2, &, a,	Allow the arms to rise to first position;
Bar 2.	1, &, a,	Reverse the circle to make a swing inwards;
	2, &, a,	Allow the arms to rise to *demi-seconde*.

Take care not to allow the arms to cross over the centre of the body. When mastered in this simple form, add rises on the *demi-pointes* on the counts of 2, &, a,. Later still, add springs instead of rises which will be preceded by a *demi-plié* on 'a' of the first beat.

The swinging movement helps to co-ordinate the arms with the jump and encourages the student to feel the active assistance the arms should give to all springing steps.

4.e. *The Gigue*

Tempo 6/8. Prepare the arms to the hips and the right foot in *dégagé devant*. Hop on the left and pass the right to *cou-de-pied derrière* on the last count of the introduction.

Bar 1.	1,	*Coupé* under;
	&, a,	*Coupé* over and under;
	2,	*Coupé* over;
	&,	*Coupé* under
	a,	Hop and pass the left to *cou-de-pied derrière*.

Zones of Sound and Movement

Zones of movement approximate to the bass, middle and treble sounds and are equated with low, middle and high in space. In the first year it is sufficient to distinguish which zone a sound belongs to and place it in the appropriate physical one. In the later years an understanding of the scale is fostered and melody can be recognized or created.

First Year

1.a.   *Zones*
Clap or walk in the high zone, reaching into the air or walking on tip-toes or both. Use the low zone by walking in a deep *plié* or by crawling.
1.b.   The middle zone is now recognized and included in inventive exercises.

Second Year

2.a.   *Vertical Pattern*
Measure the distance in movement and sound from bass to treble by clapping in the zones as; (1) kneeling, (2) in *demi-plié*, (3) standing, (4) at head height, (5) above the head and on tip-toes. On (6)(7)(8) open the arms and bring them down at the sides in a circular pattern while kneeling or crouching ready to begin the exercise again.

Later, reverse the circle to a descending scale. Relate this exercise to various ideas and things such as blowing up a balloon and letting the air escape again. Low sounds are sad and high ones are happy and so on.

2.b.   *Scale*
Clap the scale in eight counts; (1) low, (2)(3) moving to the middle, (4) in the middle, (5)(6) moving to high, (7) high and (8) on the toes or jumping into the air. Reverse the scale and the movement.

In 3/4 *tempo* use four bars making twelve divisions in space or, if counting only the first beat of the bar, making a broken chord.

2.c.   *Aerial Pattern*
Clap the aerial pattern of a simple melody, say 'Twinkle, twinkle, little star' or 'Pop goes the weasel'. Use one short phrase only then add another until the whole tune becomes a dance in personal then general space.

Third Year

3.a.   *Diagonal Scale*
Clap the scale in a long diagonal line across the body.

3.b.   *Melody*
In the air, draw the melody with the whole body and the arms in both personal and general space. Czerny's Five Finger Exercises make excellent clapping patterns.

3.c.   *Treble and Bass*
Listen to and think about a piece of music, dissect the treble from the bass

before dancing each part. Later, divide into two groups so that A dances the
treble while B dances the bass.
3.d.   Listen to two instruments playing a duet. Dissect the two instrument
parts, dance them then divide into two groups and dance them simultaneously
making the melody pattern in personal then general space.

Fourth Year

4.a.   *Instruments*
Listen to trios and quartets, study the different qualities of the instruments
and dance the various parts so making an orchestration pattern in space. Very
interesting improvisations can be obtained in this manner.

Phrasing

This should be incorporated in *every* exercise but special ones are sometimes
necessary. Decide what the need is and invent an exercise to fulfil that need.

Second Year

2.a.   Sing the melody of 'Twinkle, twinkle, little star' taking a good breath
after 'star' and 'are' and making a longer phrase to 'sky'.
2.b.   Divide into groups for each phrase and see that the exact rhythm is kept
as each group takes up its tune or movement.

Third Year

3.a.   Listen to music and ask the children to distinguish the phrasing.
3.b.   Improvise in conversational form with or without music. Each
'sentence' must be phrased so as to make dance sense.

Fourth Year

4.a.   Work on phrasing in all aspects of the lesson and encourage correct
breathing throughout.

Conducting Dances

Conducting dances are very valuable for musical and special pattern,
phrasing, control of speed and, of course, for observation. The teacher or a
student directs the class with big sweeping movements and gestures which
follow the musical and spacial pattern and the students respond accordingly.
Start simply in the first year with changes of direction and speed in a constant
number of bars. In the second year direct in phrases and in the third and fourth
in various 'voices' as if the conductor is directing an orchestra.

Time Relationships

Many interesting games and exercises can be invented with comparative
speeds and distances of movement. Observation and judgement are
heightened by this means.

Second Year

2.a.   *Tempo 2/4.* Stand the students in straight lines or, later, in a floor pattern. The first line prepares and does four springs in first position while the second line prepares. Then the second line springs while the third prepares and so on. The preparation is most important with the *demi-plié* being on 4, and the spring on &, 1. Later, let each line follow the other after one spring and lastly let each child follow the leader one after the other. This can be done in rhythm patterns as well as in various floor formations such as, V or X, etc. These exercises require real concentration on the part of the students.

Third Year

3.a.   Develop the second year exercises by working in groups and patterns or shapes such as a ship which is divided into four parts; the bow, the middle 1 and middle 2, and the stern which are referred to as A, B, C, D.

This exercise also incorporates the use of zones in space. High is referred to as 1, middle is 3, and low is 5. The intermediate levels are 2 and 4. *Tempo* is 6/8. The ship pitches forward and backward as the dancers move up and down through the levels or zones.

		Bar 1	Bar 2	Bar 3	Bar 4
A.	Zones	3...4...5.../	...4...3.../	...2...1.../	...2...3/
B.	Zones	3...3...4.../	...4...3.../	...3...2.../	...2...3/
C.	Zones	3...3...2.../	...2...3.../	...3...4.../	...4...3/
D.	Zones	3...2...1.../	...2...3.../	...4...5.../	...4...3/

When the mechanics of this game are understood the weather can take an active part so that different qualities are used in both the movement and the music.

3.b.   Work out the same principle for a Chinese Dragon. Practise the undulating movement of the dragon first *sur place* and then move forward with a smooth shuffle.

Fourth Year

Canon
Work out dance games in the form of musical canons, such as 'Three Blind Mice' below.

4.a.   *Tempo 4/4.* Form into four groups; A, B, C, D.

Bar 1.   A.   Hold the hands like mice and do three little runs and a pause; 'Three Blind Mice';

Bar 2.   A.   Step forward, *assemblé* the feet together with a big scratching movement of the arms; 'Three Blind Mice';

       B.   Does as for bar 1;

Bar 3.   A.   Run forward;
         'See how they run';

       B.   As bar 2;

       C.   As bar 1;

Bar 4.   A.   Spin *sur place*;
         'See how they run';

	B.	Bar 3;
	C.	Bar 2;
	D.	Bar 1.
Bar 5.	A.	Four big *jeté* runs; 'They all run after the farmer's wife';
	B, C, D.	Continue one bar behind the other.
Bar 6.	A.	Three springs with the actions of chopping off their tails; 'Who cut off their tails with a carving knife';
	B, C, D.	Follow one bar behind.
Bar 7.	A.	Run in a small circle with one hand in the 'looking' position; 'Did you ever see such a thing in your life?';
	B, C, D.	Continue to follow;
Bar 8.	A.	Step forward into *demi-plié* and cover the eyes with the hands; 'As three blind mice';
	B, C, D.	Finish the dance canon one after the other.

Although games such as this are quite complicated they challenge the children's concentration and make them aware of timing, relationships, mechanical steps and expression. Anything that encourages the child to listen and to react to music is valuable and once an appreciation of music and movement are aroused and educated, interesting and often very beautiful dances emerge in improvisation.

Musical Appreciation

First Year
Play a piece of music and find out what the children think about it. Ask questions such as: Is it fast or slow? Is it happy or sad? Is it high or low? Is it round or spikey? Is it light or dark coloured? And so on.

Second Year
After listening to a piece, discuss it and ask questions. What shape does the tune make, does it bring to mind a colour, an idea, an emotion? What *tempo* is it?

Third and Fourth Years
Continue listening to music of all kinds and discussing its content, quality and style. Start to use simple musical terms such as:

Largo	Slow
Adagio	Slow and peaceful
Andante	Slightly faster
Allégro	Lively, fast
Presto	Fast
Rallentando	Becoming gradually slower
Ritardando	Becoming slower
Accelerando	Becoming faster
Crescendo	Becoming louder

Diminuendo	Becoming softer
Forte	Loud
Piano.......................	Soft
Staccato	Detached and therefore short and sharp
Pizzicato	Plucked, that is, the plucking of a string with a finger
Legato	Smooth

The Awareness of Weight and Quality

The exercises given in this section are only guides for the teacher. In awareness studies, exercises which develop from a need of the moment and are creative, are of more value than set ones repeated over and over again. There are two types of exercises for awareness of weight, one that feels the actual weight of the body or of an object in reality or in imagination, and the other than uses weight related to effort, physical sensitivity and time.

Weight related to Objects and the Body

First Year
1.a.   Pick up and put down various heavy and light objects.
1.b.   Using appropriate music, walk heavily and lightly.

Second Year
2.a.   In imagination, pick up, put down and carry heavy and light objects.
2.b.   Walk or run with the weight of the body affected by emotions such as; sadness, happiness, loneliness, and so on.

Third and Fourth Years
3.a. & 4.a.   Use ideas and situations requiring the feeling of weight in the body and movements, such as: imagine a great bird with large heavy wings and body. Contrast this with a small fluttering one. Improvise a story using various sizes of birds. The possibilities are limitless and both the teacher and the children will enjoy inventing new exercises.

Weight related to Effort and Time

First Year

Firm/sudden and firm/sustained action
1.a.   Using two hands, throw and catch a real ball and later an imaginary one. This involves both firm/sudden and firm/sustained impetus. First, if the ball is heavy, its weight must be felt and the effort gathered for the throw which results in an explosive firm/sudden release as the ball is propelled into the air. Secondly, catching requires a firm/sustained action to accept the weight and absorb it. When the feeling is established, put the exercise to music because rhythm and time will assist the throwing and catching movements.

Tempo 6/8. Prepare on two chords by feeling the weight of the ball and bending the knees in *demi-plié*.

Bar 1. 1, 2, 3, Throw the ball high, stretching the knees;

4, 5, 6, Catch it in two hands, bending the knees.

Bar 2. 1, 2, 3, Stretch the knees;

4, 5, 6, Bend the knees and feel the weight of the ball in preparation to repeat the throw.

1.b. Work in pairs to the same rhythm. One child throws and the other catches. Pause before alternating the roles.

Fine/sudden and fine/sustained action

1.c. *Tempo. 3/4.* Do the same exercise with a real and then an imaginary balloon. The effort actions of the throwing and catching would be fine/sudden and fine/sustained and the movements would be lighter and slower than in the previous exercise. See the children keep their eyes 'on the ball' and feel the rhythm of the throw and the catch. Invent other throwing and catching exercise games.

Second Year

2.a. Continue the same exercises as in First Year but now in groups, say, in a square passing the ball or balloon round and across the square, or in a big circle. Use music and later let the children find the natural rhythm without accompaniment. Concentrate on imaginary objects but revert to real ones if necessary.

Third Year

3.a. Use the same exercises but this time in groups of three or five. Take eight-bar phrases of 3/4 time. Take six bars to throw and two to jump, turn or change places and prepare to repeat the movements.

3.b. *Bouncing Ball*

In 6/8 *tempo* bounce an imaginary ball and catch it in two hands. Make sure to follow the path of the ball with the eyes. Vary the size and weight of the ball.

3.c. *Throw*

In 3/4 *tempo*, throw an imaginary ball from side to side over the head in a semi-circle and catch it in the other hand. This can be done *sur place* or travelling. Alternate the use of firm and light touch according to the weight of the ball.

Fourth Year

4.a. *Simultaneous Action*

Tempo 6/8. Face each other in partners each with a ball.

Bar 1. 1, 2, 3, Both throw their ball simultaneously;

4, 5, 6, Catch simultaneously.

Develop this with three, four or more people. Invent different throws such as under the leg and so on with different weights of balls or balloons.

Fine/Sustained action

4.b.   Blow and catch a feather, imaginary or real.

4.c.   With a light scarf, flick it with a fine/sudden touch and continue to make an aerial pattern with a fine/sustained action. Allow the body to react naturally to the movement as it must be involved in both the effort action and the sustained movement reaction.

Extend this by running forward with the scarf trailing behind. Stop suddenly and, bending forward, let the arm and scarf continue in the line of movement over and down with the body movement. Find out the necessary effort required for the action and the sustained reaction of the scarf.

4.d.   Breathe and rise on the *demi-pointes* lifting the arms over the head. Run backwards with the weight of the body falling forward, make a circular pattern with the arms and body, lift the arms at the sides as the body straightens and rise lightly in the commencing position. This is useful with or without a scarf.

When the use of weight and its relation to effort are understood, apply the same principle to dance steps, for example, a spring is a combination of: A firm/sustained action in the *demi-plié* which is the ACTION resulting in the firm/sudden reaction which propels the body into the air. For a fraction of a second there is a light/sustained feeling as the body is suspended in the air before it changes direction and alights into a soft *demi-plié* which again changes into a firm/sustained action enabling repetition of the spring or the stretching of the knees which completes the movement. The spring is the direct result of the effort put into the *demi-plié*, and that amount of effort is the result of judgement on the part of the dancer using his understanding of weight.

Weight related to Time and Physical Sensitivity

To ensure there is a logical length of time in which to register thought, emotion, action and reaction so as to convince an audience of its intent, work out what kind of action is needed to achieve the required movement and expression, whether it is firm, light, sustained or sudden. The following exercises should be done with music and later, without accompaniment.

First Year

1.a.   *Fright*

Slowly and carefully reach out the hand to touch something hot. Touch it and react suddenly with fright.

1.b.   Creep cautiously and fearfully towards an object, get a sudden fright, freeze, then run away and hide.

Second Year

2.a.   *Reaction*

Tempo 4/4. Work in pairs.

Bar 1.   A slowly approaches the back of B and places a hand on B's shoulder;

Bar 2. 1,   B abruptly brushes the hand away and turns towards A;

      2, 3, 4, The arms of both float down in a light sustained manner as the eyes hold each others. Various emotional reactions can be expressed such as hostility, pleasant surprise, recognition or laughter.

2.b.   *Tempo 3/4*. Work with partners.

Bars 1–2.   A affectionately strokes B's arm;

Bar 3.   B offers both hands to A;

Bar 4.   A gently takes the offered hands.

Third Year

3.a.   *Fear and Surprise*

Tempo 4/4. To express fear and surprise.

Bar 1.   With the eyes leading, slowly turn the head over one shoulder;

Bar 2. 1,   Quickly turn the body in the same direction;

      2, 3, 4, Sustain the pose and the feeling of fear or surprise.

3.b.   *Touch*

Stroke an imaginary cat following the line of the body with a gentle light/sustained action. Contrast this with stroking the neck of a horse which will require a more firm/sustained action.

Fourth Year

4.a.   *Fear and Escape*

Tempo 4/4.

Bar 1.   Slowly turn the body from *en face* to profile leaving the head and eyes concentrated on an object *en face*.

Bar 2. 1,   Suddenly turn the eyes and head to profile;

      2, 3, 4, Run away.

4.b.   *Greeting*

Develop 3.a. into a mime sequence say, 'I hear my friend coming' which uses the slow turn of the head. Quickly turn the body and run to meet the friend.

4.c.   *With Partners*

A turns the head quickly and calls a friend's name then slowly turns the body in the friend's direction;

    With a slow turn of the head, B looks to A then quickly turns the body to recognize and greet A.

    Greetings of various kinds can be expressed in this way.

The Awareness of Space

To assist in understanding stage directions and general orientation in space it is helpful to teach the points of the stage or studio early in the training (see p. 26).

Exercises in General Space: Floor Patterns

First Year

Circle

Place the children in a circle holding hands with the arms stretched. The teacher stands in the centre of the circle which must also be in the centre of the studio. It is helpful to do exercises for Body Awareness in this pattern as the children do not feel isolated and can all see the teacher equally well. Working in a circle establishes the feeling for this shape which is essential when the students begin to travel in it.

A difficulty that can arise from the use of the circle is that some children become confused between, say, pointing the right foot and copying the opposite child, as a mirror image, and pointing the left. To overcome this, give an exercise in pairs making first a mirror image, then a 'different person' image.

1.a.   *Tempo 2/4.* Stand in a circle and note carefully the exact position of the individual in relation to the points of the room. Also, be aware of who is on either side.

Bars 1–4.   Run anywhere in general space to find 'a place of one's own';

Bars 5–8.   Turn to look at the place in the circle from which each started;

Bars 9–12.   Run back to that place;

Bars 13–16.   Correct the circle then stand still.

Should a child find it difficult to look directly at a certain place, give eye exercises first.

1.b.   Hold hands facing the centre of the circle. Turn and walk in an anti-clockwise direction for, say, eight bars. Take eight bars to turn and prepare then another eight to walk in a clockwise direction.

This should also face the outside of the circle.

1.c.   Walk, run, skip, etc., in a circle without holding hands.

Second Year

2.a.   From a circle, alternate children move in to make a smaller circle while the others move out to make a bigger one. Return to the original circle and then reverse the circles. Make sure the original pattern is established before reversing the movement. This can be done in small groups of eight or more. Use various *tempi* and different steps and arm movements.

2.b.   *Semi-circle*

Learn to make a semi-circle. This can be done by closing up the gaps in a circle or by placing children in the spaces. The semi-circle can be *en face*, in profile or across the diagonal which gives an interesting pattern.

Third Year

3.a.   *Figure Eight*

Make a figure eight by walking, running, skipping, galloping, etc. Make sure the figure crosses in the centre of the room. Use the arms in interesting ways.

Fourth Year

4.a. *A Chain*
Make a chain. At first, hold hands on passing by the right. Later pass without taking hands. Walk, run, skip, gallop, etc., and use the arms and head in an appropriate manner.

4.b. Walk backwards in a circle, a square or *en diagonale*.

4.c. Make a spiral pattern and unwind it.

4.d. Walk, run, etc., in a small individual circle making sure to return to the original position. Use steps that move forward, sideways and backwards.

Exercises for the eyes in general space
It is most important to look in the direction of movement and travel, but the child cannot be relied upon to do this naturally.

First Year
1.a. Look to the points of the room with the eyes only then turn the head and body.

1.b. Before setting out, give the child time to focus on the spot to which he will travel then walk, run, skip or gallop to that spot.

Second Year
2.a. Look to a spot in space then dance to it and hold a pose. Make sure that the exact spot is decided upon before setting out and that it is reached.

Third Year
3.a. *Tempo 4/4.*

Bars 1–2.	A and B walk in individual paths;
Bars 3–4.	They meet and really make contact by looking at each other;
Bar 5.	A indicates a chosen direction with a turn of the eyes and head;
Bar 6.	Both face the indicated direction;
Bars 7–8.	They walk towards that direction.

Fourth Year
4.a. The teacher or student gives directions with eye and head movements only for groups to move in various pathways and patterns.

Straight Lines

First Year

1.a. *Lines*
Place the children in lines of five with one child in the centre and two on either side, equally spaced. See that the lines form a correct grid pattern. This requires the children to orient themselves in two directions, in line forward and sideways.

1.b.   *Grid*

Place four children in a line from point 8 to point 6 on the Prompt side of the stage. They then walk the required number of steps to reach the position of the first grid line on the O.P. side. Follow this with each successive line walking fewer steps to reach their place in the pattern. Later this can be done to music, each line starting at the appropriate bar to match the number of steps needed. To vary this, make a train travelling through three stations to its terminus. One passenger drops off at each station

1.c.   *A Square*

Walk, run, skip or gallop in a square round the room starting from either point 4 or 6. Make a pause at the corners to give time to make an exact ninety degrees turn.

1.d.   *Cross*

Stand in the pattern of a cross, either straight or diagonal, disperse then return to the original place in the pattern.

Second Year

2.a.   *Grid*

Make a grid pattern with an even number in each line and a space in the centre.

2.b.   Form the grid by walking in from both sides. Later pass to the opposite sides.

2.c.   Form lines across the back and walk forward line by line into the grid pattern.

2.d.   *Cross*

Walk the cross patterns in pairs and then use steps to dance in the pattern. Use greetings of various kinds in different *tempi*.

Third Year

3.a.   *Grid*

Run quickly into the grid pattern either in even or staggered lines with five in the first and uneven lines and four in the even ones.

3.b.   *Grand March*

Follow the leader in two groups from points 4 and 6 to meet in the centre at point 5. Turn and move in pairs downstage to point 1 then out to the points 2 and 8. Exit or return to the original points

3.c.   *Diagonale*

In two groups follow the leader *en diagonale*. Cross with the opposite number in the exact centre of the stage; the right side passing in front of the left.

3.d.   *Butterfly*

Make a butterfly pattern from points 4 and 6 to meet centre stage then move to points 2 and 8 then up the sides of the stage to the starting point.

Fourth Year

4.a. *Formation*
In pairs, threes, fours and fives dance along pathways previously studied. The formation of each group must be maintained during the making of the floor pattern.

4.b. *The Wheel*
Form a cross and, with the arms on each others waist or shoulders, make the spokes of a wheel. Each line should look to the centre of the cross and later to the outside so as to keep the pattern as the wheel turns in a full circle.

Body Levels

First Year
1.a. *Tempo* 2/4. Prepare in the middle level with the arms and feet in parallel first positions.

Bar 1.	Crouch down in low level;
Bar 2.	Stay low;
Bar 3.	Stand in middle level;
Bar 4.	Stay;
Bar 5.	Stretch up to high level;
Bar 6.	Stay;
Bar 7–8.	Return to middle level

Second Year
2.a. *Tempo* 4/4. Prepare in a *demi-plié* in a slightly turned out first position. Hold the arms in *bras bas*.

Bar 1.	1,	Jump into high level lifting the arms to high parallel;
	2,	Land in a crouching position in low level;
	3, 4,	Hold the position.

Third Year
3.a. Travel in various levels.
Tempo 4/4. Prepare in a set level.

Bar 1.	Travel, with various steps, in that level;
Bar 2.	Change the level;
Bar 3.	Move in the new level;
Bar 4.	Change the level.

Continue in this manner. Use the imagination in this exercise and most interesting things will develop.

Fourth Year
4.a. Use a lunge and a rise to change the level with each step taken while moving forward, sideways or backwards.

Levels with the Arms
Arms which are held at the same level throughout a dance become very

monotonous. These exercises make the young dancer aware that there is great variation in the height of arm movements and positions. A simple rule for the aesthetic use of the arms is that low positions are used with small steps, middle level is suitable for grander steps and *adage* and high positions are harmonious with big jumps and *adage*.

First Year

1.a.   Using shoulder level as middle, below that as low and above as high levels, move the arms from one level to another, pausing in each for the position to be registered and remembered. Make the movements to the front and to the sides of the body. Different speeds and qualities can also be used. Later travel using the arms in different levels.

Second Year

2.a.   Develop the previous exercises with curved arm positions and with more complex travelling steps.
2.b.   Combine arm and body levels.
2.c.   Develop diagonal positions with one arm in low and the other in high.

Third Year

Bends, Rises and Springs
3.a.   Add bends of the body in various levels.
3.b.   Develop with rises and springs.

Fourth Year

4.a.   *Travelling*
Develop with travelling steps moving in directions and patterns.
All these basic exercises can be made more interesting by using various themes such as:

1.   Enact the exploding of a star from a group in the centre dispersing to the various points of the room. Use levels and quality.
2.   Work with partners doing the same or the opposite movements.
3.   Use different shapes in each level.
4.   Use different time signatures and instrument accompaniments.
5.   Call on the children's imagination for ideas and representations.

In fact, explore space and be aware of it in all dancing movements.

Using both Personal and General Space

Of course dancing or any movement must use both general and personal space but it is the awareness of this which makes it part of the creative experience. The teacher and the student should always be conscious of space and these exercises are suggestions for special exercises to heighten this awareness.

First Year

1.a.   Start in a group huddled up in low level in the centre of the studio. Spread out in all directions to a high level and spin in an individual space with the arms extended to the sides. This could represent an exploding star, a water fountain, a fire cracker or sparkler. Use touch qualities, shapes, time and speed, levels, effort and energy and so on to understand the different expressive qualities which can be put into the same movements when they are governed by different ideas and attitudes.

Second Year
2.a. Progress to the relation of each student's personal space to that of the others thus creating patterns in general space.
2.b. Starting from a set spot in the studio, move, on the direction of the teacher, to specified places or points of the room. Use speeds, qualities and levels. This will encourage judgement of the effort required to reach a certain spot in a given time as well as the ability to arrest movement when required. Both these attributes are essential to the dancer.

Third Year
3.a. Work in partners or groups to make symmetrical patterns, meeting, passing and crossing.

Fourth Year
4.a. Work in groups in asymmetrical patterns developing the understanding and use of space, time, weight and flow.

Space Relationships
It is necessary for the dancer to understand being part of a static pattern but being aware of his part in the general movement pattern is even more important. The good dancer, sportsman and car driver, is always aware of all that is happening around him and of his relationship to the general spacial movement pattern.

First Year
1.a. Place the children in a circle round the centre of the room. Move in a circle:
  (a) as trains by holding the waist of the child in front;
  (b) as a caterpillar by placing the hands on the shoulders of the child in front;
  (c) as children in a folk dance holding hands;
  (d) following freely as in, 'follow my leader'.
These suggestions will help the individual to feel his place in the general space pattern.

Second Year
2.a. Follow movement patterns and poses set by a leader.

Third Year
3.a. In a circle, the leader initiates a movement which can be passed on to the next person who copies it and, in turn, passes it on right round the circle.

3.b.   Pass on the original movement to the next person. She develops it before passing it on to the next person and so on right round the circle by which time all concerned should be able to dance the compound movement.

It is wise to start with a small number in the circle!

Fourth Year

4.a.   In various patterns, pass on movements from different touch qualities and emotions.

4.b.   React in contrast to the movement being passed on.

4.c.   Improvise in pairs working on continuous flow of movement.

Conducting Dances

On p. 128 conducting dances have been described as applied to time. General space, as well as the use of levels in personal space, must play a great part in this exercise. Eventually these dances should combine pathways and directions, levels, aerial pattern, rhythm and phrasing, and shapes, in fact, all the elements of the dance. It must be remembered that all the principles of dance should be applied in all sections even though each section concentrates on one special aspect.

Dance steps

Part IV

Flow of Movement

Dance Steps

This group of exercises has an entirely different purpose from that of purely academic ones. The steps studied allow the student to dance with a reasonably sized repertoire which does not require adherence to the strict demands of academic steps. However, they do prepare the student for the time when these must be executed in the strict academic matter. The quality and style, as well as the correct rhythm, of the finished form should be used in the dance step. As the arms gain freedom, fluidity and rhythm from the use of *allongé* and the breathing movement in the preparation, so steps are moved into by simple and easy preparations. The general picture of the step is understood and experienced before perfection in every detail is demanded and studied.

The use of dance steps in a freely moving, flowing, co-ordinated and musical style will ensure that, when the strict demands of technique have to be met, the dance quality and musicality of the step will not be lost. This does not mean that it can be done in a careless manner. The legs must work correctly with soft *demi-plié* then fully stretched legs and feet. Springs must be strong, high and light and return to the floor softly through the feet. The body must be carried correctly and the arms and head must be co-ordinated, flowing, expressive and beautiful. In fact, the whole body must perform well both functionally and aesthetically.

Walking Steps

These are to co-ordinate walks with arm movements, to use floor patterns and changes of directional *épaulement*.

First Year

1.a.   *Tempo* 4/4. Face point 2. Prepare with the right leg in *dégagé devant* and the arms in low position.

Bar 1.	1, 2,	Take two steps *en diagonale* to point 2, lift the arms to *demi-seconde*, look in the direction of travel;
	3, 4,	Take two steps in the same direction, lower the arms to low;
Bar 2.	1, 2,	Two steps, lift the arms to *demi-first*;
	3, 4,	Two steps and lower the arms to low position.

Continue across the room *en diagonale* and finish in a pose of the child's own choice. Of course, a simple walk *en diagonale* should be taught before introducing the use of arms.

Note: Remember to work on the opposite pattern so the student can learn to work with either leg equally well and be able to reverse steps and patterns.

143

Second Year

With changes of *épaulement* directions.

2.a.　*Tempo* 4/4. Stand in corner 6 facing point 2 and prepare the left foot in *dégagé devant croisé*. Lift the arms to *demi-first* then open the left to *demi-seconde*, turn both palms to the floor with *allongé* into *demi-arabesque* position.

Bar 1.	&,	Lift the working foot a little, breathe, look to point 1;
	1, 2, 3,	Three walking steps, change the arms through *bras bas*;
	4,	*Dégagé* the right foot *devant*, look to point 1;
Bar 2.		Hold the pose *effacé*;
Bars 3–4		Repeat bars 1 and 2 holding the pose *croisé*;
Bars 5–6		Repeat bars 1 and 2 holding the pose *effacé*;
Bar 7.	1, 2,	Close the right foot into first position, close the arms to *bras bas* and look into the palm of the right hand;
	3, 4,	Change the direction of the body to face front, look to point 1;
Bar 8.	1, 2,	Turn to face point 8;
	3, 4,	Prepare the right foot in *dégagé devant croisé* and the arms to *demi-arabesque*.

Repeat the whole on the diagonal from point 4 to point 8. This exercise can also be done moving backwards with the *dégagé* still *devant*.

Third Year

3.a.　*Tempo* 4/4. Prepare facing point 2 with *dégagé devant croisé* and the arms in *demi-seconde*.

Bar 1.	&,	Lift the well-pointed working foot a little, *allongé* the arms and breathe in;
	1, 2, 3, 4,	Three walking steps and *dégagé*, carry the arms through *bras bas* and *demi-first* to pose *effacé*, look into the palm of the left hand;
Bar 2.		Hold the *dégagé effacé* and open the left arm to *demi-seconde* following it with the head and eyes;
Bar 3.	&,	Lift the working foot and *allongé* the arms with a deep breath;
	1, 2, 3, 4,	Repeat bar 1 with the *dégagé croisé*;
Bar 4.		Repeat bar 2 *en croisé*;
Bars 5–6		Repeat bars 1 and 2;
Bar 7.	1,	Close in first position of the feet, lower the arms to *bras bas* as the body turns *en face*;
	2, 3,	Rise on *demi-pointes*;
	4,	Lower the heels maintaining rotation;
Bar 8.	1, 2,	Turn to face point 8;
	3, 4,	Repeat the preparation for *diagonale* from point 4 to point 8.

This exercise can also be done walking backwards with the *dégagé* still *devant*.

For Pas Marché

3.b.　*Tempo* 4/4. Prepare *en face* with the right foot in *dégagé devant*. Open the arms to *demi-seconde*, look to the left hand.

Bar 1. &, Lift the foot, *allongé* the arms and breathe deeply looking to the left hand;

1, Place the right foot in fourth position *devant*, lower the arms to *bras bas*;

2, *Demi-plié*, hold the arms in *bras bas*, look to the left hand;

3, Transfer the weight on to the right foot and draw the left to it in *demi-plié* in first position, lift the arms to *demi-first* and look to the right hand;

4, *Dégagé* the left foot *devant* as the right knee straightens, open the arms to *demi-seconde* following the right hand;

Bar 2. Repeat with the left foot.

3.c. *Tempo* 4/4. Prepare with the right leg in *dégagé derrière*. Open the arms to *demi-seconde*.

Bar 1. 1, *Battement passé* through first position, both arms begin a small downward circle, head inclines to the right looking to the left palm;

2, *Dégagé devant* with the right leg, complete the circle of the arms to *demi-first* position, look to the left palm;

3, *Demi-plié* in fourth position, hold the arms;

4, Transfer to the right leg and *dégagé* the left *derrière*, open the arms to *demi-seconde* and follow the left arm;

Bars 2–4. Repeat with alternate legs.

Fourth Year

4.a. *Tempo* 4/4. Prepare facing point 2 with the left foot in *dégagé devant croisé*, open the arms to *demi-seconde*.

Bar 1. &, Lift the foot with a *piqué* movement, *allongé* the arms breathing in;

1, 2, 3, 4, Three walking steps and *dégagé effacé*, carry the arms through *bras bas* to *demi-first* looking into the palm of the right hand;

Bar 2. Repeat bar 1 with the *piqué* lift of the foot and the *dégagé croisé*, open the arms to *demi-seconde* following the right hand with the head and eyes;

Bar 3. 1, 2, Close into first position turning to face point 4 lower the arms to *bras bas* following the right hand;

3, 4, Turn to face point 6 hold the *bras bas* and look to point 6;

Bar 4. 1, 2, Turn to face point 8.

3, 4, Prepare to repeat on the opposite *diagonale*. Reverse this exercise but with the *dégagé* still *devant*.

Notes: The arms in all these exercises should move slowly and continuously during the walking steps and should not move in jerks. Make sure the turns of the body are made as one unit holding the feet in first position and turning on the ball of one foot. A turn to the right on the right foot is *en dedans* and on the left, it is *en dehors* and, of course, the reverse to the left.

These basic exercises can be varied in many ways: in the degree and direction of the turn, with different use of head and arms, with running steps, skips, gallops, etc.

For Pas Marché
4.b.   Do the exercise 3.b. in the same manner and timing with the exception that on the count of 3, the working foot passes into the *cou-de-pied* position on the *demi-pointe* in first and, from there, extends to the *pointe dégagé* on 4.
4.c.   In the same manner and timing as for 3.c., *développé* the working foot through the *cou-de-pied* position *en l'air* on the count of 1. Use only the arm opposite the working leg to make the movement to first position and open it to *demi-seconde* on 4. The other arm remains in *demi-seconde*.

For Triplets
These rhythmic running steps encourage a smooth, thrusting, free movement through space. The head and arms are carried with the movement of the body so they also feel that they are travelling through space.

First Year
1.a.   *Tempo* 3/4. Polonaise. Prepare for this step by learning the rhythm. Clap each beat of the bar then the first beat only. See Time/Music p. 121.

Second Year
2.a.   *Tempo* 3/4. On each beat of the music, take even steps, the first in *demi-plié* and the second and third on *demi-pointes*. Hold the arms in a given position such as parallel first or second. Look in the direction of the movement which can be *en diagonale* or in a circle. Introduce the step *sur place* until the rhythm is understood.

Third Year
3.a.   *Tempo* 3/4. In this year, encourage stepping out with even paces to develop later into triplets proper. Move the arms to the required position on the count of 1, and hold it for the following two counts. Change the position of the arms or return to *bras bas* on the second triplet. Follow the arms with the head and eyes.

Fourth Year
4.a.   *Tempo* 3/4. *En diagonale*, one triplet travels facing forward and the second moves backward on the same diagonal facing the back corner. Use arms in a simple *port de bras*.
4.b.   Develop the step into running triplets in a faster *tempo*. Be sure to hold the body and arms without reflected movement.
Note: Try to reverse all the exercises and patterns.

Waltz
The waltz is a very beautiful step of many aspects and is akin to the classical *balancé*. It can be elegant or boisterous, fast or slow, with or without turning and can be done *sur place* or travelling forward or backward in any *épaulement* direction. It consists of three steps, the first stepping out into *demi-plié à la seconde*. Whereas the second step of *balancé* is on the *demi-pointe* and the third

again on a melting *demi-plié*, in the stage waltz both these steps may be on the *demi-pointe*.

In contrast to the triplet, the legs are rotated instead of parallel and the second and third steps are in fifth position instead of passing through first. Because the first step of the waltz is to the side it moves forward and backward along two parallel lines whereas triplets travel along one line.

The use of the head, arms and body is an integral part of the waltz step. The bend of the body and the incline of the head, may be over the *tombé* of the first step or away from it. The arms vary from a simple opening of both to their alternate use through the same movement pattern. The opening can be through *demi-first*, first or third positions.

First Year
1.a.   Introduce the understanding of 3/4 time through clapping exercises as shown in the Time music section, p. 121.

Second Year
Introduce the waltz step in a simple form *sur place* with the arms held in *demi-seconde*. Allow the head to incline a little over the first step.
2.a.   *Tempo 3/4.* Slowly. Stand in a slightly rotated first position and on the introductory chords *dégagé* the right leg to the second and open the arms to *demi-seconde*.

Bar 1	1,	Step into *demi-plié* on the right leg to the side, incline the head over the right leg;
	2,	Bring the left foot to the *cou-de-pied* position *par terre* in first position and step on to the *demi-pointe*, lift the right fully pointed to the *cou-de-pied* position *en l'air* in first, hold the position of the head and arms;
	3,	*Coupé* onto the *demi-pointe* on the right in first, hold the arms and head;
Bar 2.	&,	Extend the left leg to the side in preparation for the step *tombé* to the left.

Third Year
3.a.   *Tempo 3/4.* Slowly. Stand in rotated third position, with the left foot in front and prepare with *dégagé* to the second and the arms in *demi-seconde*.

Bar 1.	1,	Step into *demi-plié* on the right leg, place the left on *demi-pointe* in the *cou-de-pied* position in third *derrière*, close the arms to *bras bas* and incline the head to the right;
	2,	*Coupé* onto the *demi-pointe* on the left leg lifting the right fully pointed to *cou-de-pied* position *devant*, lift the arms to *demi-first* looking into the palm of the left hand;
	3,	*Coupé* on to the *demi-pointe* on the right and lift the left to *cou-de-pied derrière*, hold the arms and head;
Bar 2.	&,	Extend the left leg fully pointed to the second, lift the head upright;

1,	*Tombé* on to the left leg and repeat the leg movements to the left, open the arms to *demi-seconde* and incline the head to the left;
2, 3,	Repeat as bar 1 but *allongé* the arms on the count of three.

Bars 3–4.   Repeat bars 1 and 2.

On three finishing chords, step to second and close in third with the right in front.

Repeat the exercise starting to the left so that the use of the arms is reversed. When mastered with the working foot *derrière*, place it *devant*.

3.b.   *Tempo 3/4.* Slightly faster. Prepare *effacé* with the right foot front in third position. *Dégagé* to point 2 and open the arms with the breathing preparation, pass through *bras bas* to *demi-first*.

Bar 1.   1,   *Tombé* forward to point 2 on the right leg, place the left in *cou-de-pied derrière* on the *demi-pointe*, open the arms to *demi-seconde*, look slightly above eye level to point 2.

2,   *Coupé* onto the *demi-pointe* on the left and lift the right, hold the arms in *demi-seconde*;

3,   *Coupé* on to the *demi-pointe* on the right, hold the arms in *demi-seconde*;

Bar 2.   &,   Extend the left leg *derrière* to point 6. *Allongé* the arms;

1,   *Tombé* back to point 6 on the left leg placing the right *sur le cou-de-pied devant*, close the arms to *bras bas* and look down inclining over the left leg;

2, 3,   Repeat the *coupés* on *demi-pointe*, lift the arms to *demi-first* on the count of 3.

Repeat the step to points 8 and 4 with the left foot in front.

3.c.   *Tempo 3/4.* Prepare with *dégagé à la seconde* and the arms in *demi-first*.

Bar 1.   1,   *Tombé* on to the right leg, open the right arm to *demi-seconde*, incline the head to the right;

2,   *Coupé* as before and hold the arms and head;

3,   *Coupé* and close the right arm to *demi-first* and look upright;

Bar 2   Repeat to the left opening the left arm.

Later, this may be done opening the arms to second position from third. A simple combination is to execute two waltz steps then change feet by a step to second, *dégagé* and close on bars 3 and 4.

Fourth Year

4.a.   *Tempo 3/4.* Slightly faster. Prepare with the right leg in *dégagé à la seconde*, the right arm in *demi-first* and the left in *demi-seconde*.

Bar 1.   &,   Lift the right leg slightly, open the right arm to *demi-seconde*;

1,   *Tombé*, close the left arm to *demi-first* and look into its palm;

2,3,   *Coupé* under and over, hold the position of the arms and head;

Bar 2.   &,   Extend the left leg, open the left arm and look forward;

1, 2, 3, Repeat the step to the left.

4.b.   The waltz step now travels forward and backward by stepping in to the *tombé* slightly forward or behind the second position and placing the working foot *devant* when travelling forward and *derrière* when travelling backward. Use the arms in a simple *port de bras*.

4.c.   Waltz turning can be done with four waltz steps making a quarter turn on each step or half turns with two waltz steps. In this course it is sufficient to achieve the waltz turning by quarter turns.

Tempo. 3/4. Slowly. Introduce *en face* and when understood do the step *en diagonale.*

Bar 1.	&,	Turn on the ball of the left foot to face point 3;
	1, 2, 3,	Waltz step;
Bar 2.	&,	Turn on the right foot to face point 5;
	1, 2, 3,	Waltz step;
Bar 3.	&,	Turn on the left to face point 7;
	1, 2, 3,	Waltz step;
Bar 4.	&,	Turn on the right to face point 1;
	1, 2, 3,	Waltz step.

The step must also turn to the left.

Polka

This is a very charming step with a very special rhythm of its own in 2/4 time. It has many aspects from light, delicate and elegant to comic. There are the classical and the party polkas to be studied in this course.

First Year

1.a.   For this introduction to the classical polka, use four slow counts. Prepare the arms to *demi-seconde*, hold the skirt or place the hands on the waist. *Dégagé* the right foot *devant.*

Bar 1.	&,	Lift the right foot a little from the floor, hop on the left;
	1, 2, 3,	Take three steps forward, hold the arm position;
	4,	Lift the left knee to parallel *retiré*;
Bar 2.	1, 2,	Close in parallel first;
	3, 4,	*Dégagé* the right foot *devant.*

Repeat the step three times on the right then four times on the left.

The step looks pleasing in a circle or *en diagonale*. Be sure to reverse the direction. Later alternate the feet. When mastered moving forward, try moving backward.

Second Year

2.a.   Clap the rhythm as described in the section on Music and the Awareness of Time.

2.b.   Do the party polka as in the music section.

2.c.   For the classical polka.

Tempo 2/4. Prepare the right leg to *dégagé devant* and the arms to *demi-seconde*, *demi-plié* on the left leg.

Bar 1.	&,	Lift the right foot a little and hop on the left;
	1, &,	Take two steps forward on the *demi-pointes*, hold the arms, look *en face*;
	2,	Step in to *demi-plié* on the right leg, pass the left through parallel *retiré* and extend *devant.*

2.d.   In the same manner and timing, do the step from side to side the steps being to second, first and second.

Third Year

3.a.   Now do the party polka turning with a gallop in fifth, two polka steps to one full turn. Hold the skirts or place the hands at the waist.

3.b.   Learn the steps of the classical polka in conjunction wth the rhythm (see p. 125).

Tempo 2/4. Now working in rotated positions, prepare with *dégagé devant* and the arms as desired.

Bar 1.   &,   Lift the working foot, incline the head over the lifted foot;
        a,   Hop, hold the head position;
        1,   Step on to *demi-pointe*, head inclined;
        &,   Close in fifth on *demi-pointes*, head held;
        2,   Step in to *demi-plié*, head erect;

3.c.   Classical polka with arms.

Prepare with *dégagé devant* and the arms in *demi-first*.

Open the right arm to *demi-seconde* with the step on the right leg.

Join them in *demi-first* on the hop in the second bar, then repeat on the left.

3.d.   Side polka.

The side polka is now done stepping into fifth position. The arms may be used in various ways, for example, as in 3.b. or hold the arms in *demi-seconde* on the step in to fifth and close one either into *demi-first* on the hop or use the arms high.

Fourth Year

4.a.   Do the party polka turning, in all directions, with partners and in *enchaînements*.

4.b.   A variation on the classical polka.

Tempo 2/4. Prepare as before.

Bar 1.   a, 1, &,   Hop step, close in fifth as before;
        2,   *Jeté devant* from *demi-pointe* to *demi-plié*;

4.c.   Speed up the *tempo* and work to improve neatness and quality. Vary the use of the arms. Make combinations with other steps and movements. Do not neglect to move in all directions and many patterns, with partners or in groups.

Bar 1.   &,   Hop with the head erect, arms in third;
        1,   Step, open the right arm to *seconde*, incline the head to the right;
        &,   Step in to fifth, hold the head and arm positions;
        2,   Step in to *demi-plié*, join the arms in third and bring the head erect.

Sways

Swaying is a natural dancing movement. It is aesthetically pleasing to watch and to execute. It is excellent training in rhythm and freedom of movement. One part of the body can make the movement independently or the whole body can take part. The expression and dynamics can be varied and the potential artistry of the student can be brought into play in this action.

First Year

1.a. *Tempo* 6/8. Stand *en face* in parallel first position of the feet. Prepare the arms with the right in parallel first and the left in second.

Bar 1. 1, 2, 3, Close the arms to *bras bas*, look to the front arm with the head and eyes;

      4, 5, 6, Swing the arms to the opposite positions with the left in first and the right in second, look to the left hand with the head and eyes.

The exercise can be done from four to eight times.

Second Year

2.a. *Tempo* 6/8. Prepare in second position of the feet and the arms as for 1.a.

Bar 1. 1, 2, 3, *Demi-plié* in the second position, lower the arms to *bras bas*, look to the movement of the front hand;

      4, 5, 6, Transfer the weight on to the left leg and stretch the knee, *dégagé* the right in parallel *seconde*, swing the right arm to first position parallel and the left to second, look to the right arm with the head and eyes;

Bar 2. 1, 2, 3, *Demi-plié* in second and lower the arms to *bras bas*;

      4, 5, 6, Transfer the weight to the right leg and change the arms and head;

From four to eight times gives time to enjoy this movement.

Third Year

3.a. *Tempo* 6/8. Prepare in *dégagé* to the second in a slightly rotated position with the weight directly over the left leg and the right fully pointed. Prepare the right arm to parallel first and the left to the second.

Bar 1. 1, 2, Step in to *demi-plié* in second position, lower the arms to *bras bas*;

      3, Draw the left leg to the right on *demi-pointes* in first position the arms are in *bras bas*, look in to the left palm;

      4, Step in to *demi-plié* in second with the right leg, begin to lift the arms to the *arabesque* position as previously and look to the left hand;

      5, 6, Transfer the weight directly on to the right leg and stretch the knee, *dégagé* the left in second position, complete the arm swing so that the left is in first and the right in second;

Bar 2. Hold the pose.

Later continue immediately to the left.

3.b. Now the step is done with a spring instead of a rise. See that the feet are fully stretched in the spring in first position, later in a well-crossed fifth with the front foot masking the back one. The body must show no reflection of the activity of the feet and should make one smooth flowing movement throughout the whole step.

Fourth Year

4.a. *Tempo* 6/8. To 3.a. add a gentle rise on the count of 5 and a soft *demi-plié* on 6. To 3.b. add a spring on 5 and a soft *demi-plié* on 6.

4.b *Tempo* 6/8. Add a turn on the *demi-pointes* or on the spring on the count of 2 landing in a soft *demi-plié* on 3, when travelling to the right on the left leg and when travelling to the left landing on the right.

Note: The arms must be taken through the first or third position during the turn and then make a slight swing down and up to the final arm position.

Sways Changing Direction

Second Year

2.a. *Tempo* 6/8. Stand in second position *en face*. Make the breathing preparation on four chords introduction.

Bar 1. 1, 2, 3, Transfer the weight to the ball of the right foot and turn to face point 3, stretch the left leg in *dégagé derrière*, lift the arms to first position and look into the left palm;

4, 5, 6, With the weight directly over the right leg, *allongé* the arms to *arabesque a deux bras*, that is, the right arm is extended in front of the right shoulder with the hand at head height while the left is in front of its shoulder at shoulder height, the eyes look along the right arm and beyond it;

Bar 2. 1, 2, 3, Lower the arms to first position;

4, 5, 6, Turn on the ball of the right foot to face front and transfer the weight in to second position, lower the arms to *bras bas*, look to the hands;

Bars 3–4 Repeat to the left.

When mastered do the whole step in two instead of four bars of music.

Third Year

3.a. *Tempo* 6/8. Prepare in *arabesque a deux bras* facing point 3.

Bar 1. 1, Step on to the left foot to face front, lower the arms to *bras bas*, look to the left palm;

2, Rise on the *demi-pointe* on the left and join the right to it in first position, *bras bas*;

3, Lower the heel of the right foot as the body is turned to face point 7 extend the left foot *devant*, lift the arms to first position, look to the right hand;

4, Step on to the left foot and *dégagé* the right *derrière*, begin the *allongé* movement of the arms;

5, 6, Complete the arm movement to *arabesque a deux bras*;

Bar 2. Repeat to the right to point 3.

Note: Make sure the weight is correctly placed and that the movement is free, flowing and continuous. The speed can be regulated with the accomplishment of the class. Later add a spring in first position on the count of 2.

Fourth Year

4.a. Add a spring in the *arabesque* position.

4.b. Spring with the feet in fifth on the count of 2 and join the arms in first and later in third on the spring.

4.c. Turn in the spring in fifth on 2 with the arms in first position.

4.d. Take the arms to third during the turn.

For Pas de Bourrée

A *pas de bourrée* is a quick, lively joining movement made up of three small running steps. It requires very exact movements of the legs and feet and rapid transference of weight from one foot to the other, as the weight is never on two feet at one time during this step. The variation in the placing of the steps in *pas de bourrées* is vast and the brain must work quickly to direct the feet into the correct position and direction. However, in this introduction, the stage *pas de bourrée* merely gives the understanding of the weaving movements of the feet and the quality and rhythm of the step in a general, not in an academic sense. Introduce this step in the third year when the student has become familiar with quick changes of weight. The *pas de bourrées* included in this course also help in the understanding of *dessous* or under and *dessus* or over which descriptions apply to many steps. The steps of *pas de bourrée dessous* are behind, side, front, while those of *dessus* are front, side, behind.

Third Year

Introduction to *pas de bourrée dessous*.

3.a. *Tempo 4/4.* Stand in a rotated third position of the feet facing point 8 with the right foot in front. Prepare the arms to *demi-seconde*.

Bar 1. &, Extend the left foot to point 4 of the individual square;

1, Step back on the left leg, *allongé* the arms and look to point 8;

2. Step to the side *en face* on the right leg, close the arms to *bras bas*, look to the front;

3, Step forward to point 2 on the left leg, lift the arms to first position, look to the palm of the left hand;

4, Close in third position *derrière*, open the arms to *demi-seconde*, look to the left hand;

Bar 2. Hold the position;

Bars 3–4 Repeat to the other side.

When mastered, delete the bar holding the position or substitute a pose.

Introduction to *pas de bourrée dessus*.

Teach *pas de bourrée dessus* stepping forward to point 8 with the right foot, to second with the left then back on the right facing point 2.

3.b. *Dessous*

Tempo 4/4. Prepare facing point 2 with the right foot *sur le cou-de-pied par terre derrière*, *demi-plié* on the left, open the arms to *demi-seconde*.

Bar 1. 1, Step on to the *demi-pointe* of the right foot, lift the left to *cou-de-pied devant*, close the arms to *bras bas*;

2, Step to the second on the *demi-pointe* of the left and place the

153

right on the *cou-de-pied devant*, lift the arms to *demi-first*, follow the right hand with the head and eyes;

3,   *Coupé* over onto the right leg in *demi-plié*, open the arms to *demi-seconde*, follow the right hand with the head and eyes;

4,   Hold the position with the left foot in *cou-de-pied derrière* ready to repeat to the other side or to take a pose.

When understood do the step *dessus*.

Fourth Year

4.a.   *Tempo 4/4*. Develop 3.b. by making the first step exactly into fifth position and the *coupé* exactly over the fifth. Speed the step up and encourage the light running character of a *pas de bourrée* proper.

4.b.   *Tempo 4/4*. Complete the *pas de bourrée* on the count of 1. Prepare on four chords. Chord 1 and 2 breathing preparation; chord 3, *demi-plié* on the supporting leg; chord 4, take the first step into fifth;

Bar 1. &,   Step to second;

1,   *Coupé* over;

2,   Stretch the supporting knee;

3,   *Demi-plié*;

4,   Commence the *pas de bourrée* to the other side.

Use the arms as before once the step is mastered at this speed. Until that time hold them in *demi-seconde* and use the head only. Also execute the *pas de bourrée dessus*.

4.c.   This *pas de bourrée* is based on a character dance step and should have a light and happy quality.

Tempo 4/4. Prepare on four introductory chords from parallel first position of the feet.

Intro. 1,2,   *Dégagé* the right leg to parallel second, open the arms to *demi-seconde*;

3,   *Demi-plié* and lift the right leg slightly, hold the arms;

4,   Step into parallel first on the *demi-pointe*, on the right;

Bar 1. &,   Step into second on the left *demi-pointe*, hold the arms;

1,   *Coupé* into *demi-plié* in first on the right and extend the left leg to the side, hold the arms in *demi-seconde*;

2, &, 3,   Repeat to the right, hold the arms throughout;

4,   Commence the next step to the left.

This is done in a continuous series. The body and head are allowed to lean slightly away from the extended foot and is then held upright on the little running steps. The face and eyes are to the audience.

Note: The steps of all *pas de bourrées* are up/up/down and should have a light skimming-across-the-floor quality.

For Glissades

A *glissade* is a gliding movement with a light, quick and small gliding spring over the floor which prepares the body and legs for a bigger step to follow. These exercises are designed to establish the helping role and the correct quality of the future classical *glissade*.

First Year

1.a. *Tempo* 2/4. Prepare in parallel first position of the feet with the arms in *demi-seconde*.

Bar 1. &, Step forward, sideways or backwards, hold the arm position;

1, Join the other foot in parallel first;

2, Pause;

Bar 2. Prepare to repeat the step on bar 3, etc.

Second Year

2.a. *Tempo* 4/4. Prepare in parallel first with the arms in *demi-seconde*.

Bar 1. 1, *Demi-plié*, hold the arm position;

2, Extend the right foot in the required direction, hold the arms;

&, 3, Step with a lift of the body and stretching the knees, forward, sideways or backwards and close in *demi-plié*. Close the arms to *bras bas*;

4, Stretch the knees, hold the *bras bas*;

Bar 2. Prepare to repeat the step on the same leg.

After practising four times with each leg, alternate them.

Third Year

3.a. *Tempo* 4/4. Prepare in a rotated first position of the legs. The feet work as in 2.a. but add arm movements.

Bar 1. 1, *Demi-plié*, close to *bras bas*;

2, Extend, lift the arms to *demi-first*;

&, 3, Step and close, open to *demi-seconde*;

4, Stretch, *allongé*.

Fourth Year

4.a. *Tempo* 4/4. Prepare in a rotated third position of the feet with the arms in *demi-seconde*.

Bar 1. 1, *Demi-plié* and extend, *bras bas*;

&, 2, With a small spring, step and join the feet in *demi-plié* in third position, carry the arms through *demi-first* to *demi-seconde*;

3, Stretch the knees;

4, *Allongé*.

4.b. *Tempo* 4/4. Prepare as for 4.a. but *demi-plié* on the last chord holding the arms in *demi-seconde allongé*.

Bar 1. &, 1, Spring, close into third and lower the arms to *bras bas*;

2, 3, Stretch the knees, open the arms to *demi-seconde*;

4, *Demi-plié*, *allongé*;

Bar 2. Repeat.

This is the correct timing for the finished form of a *glissade*.

Russian Coupé Step

This step should be very light in character and the arms and head used with charm. The back is held easily erect with no strain and with a dignified bearing. The arm movements are usually in *demi-* positions and are not exaggerated in any fashion. The head inclines over the foot executing the *coupé* into *demi-plié* or follows one arm as it opens or lifts. Introduce the step in the second year.

Second Year
2.a.   *Tempo* 4/4. On four chords, place the hands on the hips and lift the right foot to *cou-de-pied* in parallel first *par terre*.

Bar 1.	1,	Step into *demi-plié* on the right leg without travelling and lift the left to the *cou-de-pied* position;
	2,	Step on to the low *demi-pointe* on the left and release the right slightly from the floor;
	3,	Step in to *demi-plié* on the right;
	4,	Step on to the *demi-pointe* on the left;
Bars 2–3.		Repeat bar 1 twice;
Bar 4.	1,	*Demi-plié*;
	2,	Close the working foot in *demi-plié* in first;
	3, 4,	Stretch both knees.

Repeat starting on the left leg.

Third Year
3.a.   Repeat 2.a. slightly faster and in a rotated third position of the feet. Travel a little on the *coupé* into *demi-plié* in all directions *en croix* and in *épaulement*. Use the arms opening to *demi-seconde* on the first bar of music and hold until the closing of the feet when the arms also close to *bras bas*.

Fourth Year
4.a.   Add various uses of the arms, for example, lift the arms to third position and open them slowly to second; lift them to third *arabesque* position; use a reverse *port de bras* to third position or any arm movement thought suitable by the teacher.

4.b.   The step can now turn. First take one step in each of the eight directions to make one turn. Then do two steps in quarters to make one turn. Later take one step to each of the quarter marks *en croix* or *en diagonale*. Turn first to the right then to the left. Use the arms as desired by the teacher.

There are two ways of using the head in this step; either turn the head with the body in the same direction as the turn; or, turn the head over the leading shoulder and lead with the crown of the head.

Stage Pas de Basque
This is based on a traditional step used in the national dances of the Basque country where it is done either *par terre* or *sauté*. In the classical dance it has many aspects but in this course we concentrate on the preparation for only one of them, *pas de basque par terre*. This is a light, gliding step with a soft and elastic quality in which the head and arms must move in the same style as, and in harmony with, the leg movements.

Although the finished form consists of three steps and is done in 3/4 *tempo*, in order to give time for thinking in this course, it is prepared in 4/4 *tempo*.

Begin to teach *pas de basque* in the Second Year.

Second Year

2.a.   *Tempo* 4/4. Stand in a slightly rotated first position of the feet. Open the arms to *demi-seconde*.

Bar 1.   1,   Step to the side with the right foot, *allongé*;

2,   Close the left into first position, lower the arms to *bras bas*;

3,   Step forward on the left leg, lift the arms to *demi-first*;

4,   Close the right leg into first position, open the arms to *demi-seconde*;

Bars 2–4.   Repeat to the right.

Note: When introducing *pas de basque* give a bars rest between each step to allow time for thinking of repeating the movements. When mastered, the step should also move backward.

Third Year

3.a.   *Tempo* 4/4. Stand in a rotated third position of the feet. Prepare by opening the arms to *demi-seconde* and then *dégagé* the right leg *à la seconde*.

Bar 1.   &,   Lift the right leg slightly from the floor, *allongé*;

1,   *Tombé* on to the right leg in *demi-plié*;

2,   Place the left foot on the *cou-de-pied* position *devant*, close the arms to *bras bas* and look in to the palm of the left hand;

3,   Step forward on to the left leg, lift the arms to *demi-first*, look in to the left palm;

4,   Close the right leg behind in third position, open the arms to *demi-seconde* following the left hand with the head and eyes;

Bar 2,   1, 2, 3,   Pause;

4,   *Dégagé* the left leg to the second, hold the arms and head;

Bars 3–4   Repeat to the left.

When mastered, do the step moving backwards.

Fourth Year

4.a.   *Tempo* 3/4. Prepare as for exercise 3.a.

Bar 1.   &,   Lift the foot and *allongé*;

1,   *Tombé* and place the left foot in the *cou-de-pied* position, close the arms;

2,   Step forward, lift the arms to *demi-first*;

3,   Close in third, open the arms to *demi-seconde*.

Also do the step moving backwards.

4.b.   *Tempo* 3/4. Prepare as before.

Bar 1.   &,   *Dégagé*, lift and *allongé*;

1,   *Tombé* as in 4.a.;

2,   Step forward on to the *demi-pointe*, use the arms as before;

3,   Close the leg in to third position on the *demi-pointes*, open the arms to *demi-seconde*;

Bar 2.   1,   Hold the pose;

2,   Lower the heels;

3,   *Dégagé*.

When understood vary the arm movements. Also do the step moving backwards.

Country Pas de Basque

This step is similar to the waltz but is done with a slight spring and bounce. Its quality is more lively and robust.

Second Year

2.a.   *Tempo* 3/4. Use two bars preparation.

Bar 1.	Prepare in parallel first position of the feet and place the hands on the hips;
Bar 2.	Lift the right leg to parallel *retiré, demi-plié* on the left;
Bar 1. &, 1,	Spring on to the right leg in *demi-plié* lift the left to parallel *retiré*, hold the arm position and incline the head over the right shoulder;
2,	Step on to the *demi-pointe* on the left and lift the right a little, hold the head position;
3,	Step into *demi-plié* on the right and lift the left to parallel *retiré*;
Bar 2.	Repeat on to the left leg with the head inclined to the left.

2.b.   *Tempo* 3/4. To 2.a., add a turn of the eyes and head to point 2 when springing on to the right leg and to point 8 when springing on to the left.

Third Year

3.a.   *Tempo* 3/4. Prepare as for Second Year.

Bar 1. 1,	Turn the body on the spring to face point 2 leave the head looking to point 1;
2, 3,	Complete the step with the body facing point 2;
Bar 2. 1,	Spring, turning the body to face point 8 leave the head to point 1;
2, 3,	Complete the step.

Use the arms as required, on the hips, holding the skirt or behind the backs.

3.b.   *Tempo* 3/4. With quarter turns, prepare as before.

Bar 1.	Turn on the spring to face point 3;
Bar 2.	Face point 5;
Bar 3.	Face point 7;
Bar 4.	Face point 1.

Also turn to the left. The turn can be done to points 2, 4, 6, 8 if desired.

Fourth Year

4.a.   *Tempo* 3/4. From a rotated third position, *dégagé devant* and prepare the arms to first position.

Bar 1. &,	Lift the right leg to a small *attitude devant*, *demi-plié* on the left;
1,	Spring on to the right leg and lift the left to a small *attitude devant*, hold the arms in first; incline the head to the right;
2,	*Coupé* over on to the *demi-pointe* on the left foot, open the right arm to *demi-seconde*;
3,	*Coupé* under in to *demi-plié* on the right lifting the left to small *attitude devant*;

Bar 2. &,   Join the arms in *demi-first* position;
        1, 2, 3,   Repeat the step to the left.

The arms may be varied by opening through third position.

4.b. *Tempo 3/4.* Do the step with straight legs in the air, passing directly in front of the body.

Spring Points

These difficult steps are frequently given to very young children who find them almost impossible to execute correctly as so many elements are combined in them. The demands on the brain are as complicated as those on the body, so a very detailed set of progressions has been developed to help the child understand and execute each piece of the puzzle as they are gradually put together. Spring points should be very light and buoyant. There should be no reflected movement in the body or arms during the spring and the body must always be correctly aligned. Introduce the step in the Second Year after brushes have been studied.

Second Year

2.a. *Tempo 4/4.* Stand in first position, slightly rotated. Prepare the arms to *demi-seconde.*

Bar 1. &,   Transfer the weight on to the left leg, hold the arms and incline the head over the left shoulder;
       1, 2, 3, 4, Extend the right leg to fourth *devant* with fully stretched ankles, insteps and toes;
Bar 2. 1, 2, 3, 4, Four taps in fourth with the fully pointed right foot;
Bar 3. 1, 2, 3, 4, Close in first position, lift the head upright;
Bar 4. 1, 2, 3, 4, Centre the weight on both legs, hold the arms and the head.

Repeat with the right leg three times then do four times with the left.

Note: The hands could be on the hips or hold the skirts.

2.b. *Tempo 4/4.* Prepare as before.

Bar 1. &,   Transfer the weight;
       1, 2,   Extend the *dégagé*;
       3, 4,   *Plié* on the supporting leg;
Bar 2. 1, 2, 3, 4, Do four taps in fourth *devant* holding the *demi-plié* on the supporting leg;
Bar 3. 1, 2,   Stretch the supporting knee;
       3, 4,   Close to first position;
Bar 4. 1, 2, 3, 4, Centre the weight.

Practise four times on each leg then alternate the sides.

2.c. *Tempo 4/4.* Prepare as before.

Bar 1. &,   Transfer the weight to the left leg;
       1, 2,   *Dégagé* the right leg to the fourth *devant*, hold the arms in *demi-seconde*, incline the head over the left shoulder;
       3, 4,   Join the feet in first position on the *demi-pointes*, lift the head upright;
Bar 2. 1, 2,   Lower the heels slowly and lightly, hold the position of the arms and head;

3, 4,   Pause.

Repeat three times on the right then four times on the left.

Third Year

3.a.   *Tempo* 4/4. Prepare in rotated first position, open the arms to *demi-seconde*.

Bar 1. 1, 2,   *Dégagé* to fourth *devant*;

        3, 4,   *Demi-plié* on the supporting leg allowing the working toe to slide further out along the floor;

Bar 2. 1, 2,   Draw the feet together in first position on the *demi-pointes*;

        3, 4,   Lower the heels gently.

Use alternate legs and do the step from four to eight times.

3.b.   *Tempo* 4/4. Prepare with *dégagé devant* and the arms in *demi-seconde*.

Bar 1. 1, 2,   Rise on the *demi-pointes* in first position, close the arms to *bras bas* and look forward;

        3, 4,   Lower the right heel and *dégagé* the left leg *devant*, open the arms through *demi-first* to *demi-seconde*, look to the right palm;

Bar 2.   Pause.

Repeat three times, rest and repeat.

3.c.   *Tempo* 4/4. Prepare with *dégagé devant* in *demi-plié* and the arms to *demi-seconde*.

Bar 1. 1, 2,   Rise as in 3.b.;

        3, 4,   *Demi-plié* on the supporting leg after the heel has been lowered;

Bar 2.   Pause until balance is sure then continue without the pause.

At first hold the arm position after the first opening and close after the end of the series of steps. Later open the arms on every alternate step.

3.d.   *Tempo* 4/4. Prepare with the right foot in *dégagé devant* and *demi-plié* on the left. The arms open to *demi-seconde* looking to the palm of the right hand.

Bar 1. 1, 2,   Rise on the *demi-pointes* in first position, close the arms to *bras bas* and look ahead;

        3, 4,   *Dégagé* the left leg and *demi-plié* on the right, open the arms through *demi-first* to *demi-seconde*, look to the left palm;

Bar 2. 1, 2,   Stretch the right knee and lift the left foot slightly from the floor maintaining a fully pointed foot, hold the head and arm positions;

        3, 4,   *Demi-plié* and place the working toe again on the same spot on the floor, hold the arm and head positions;

Bar 3.   Repeat bar 2.

Bar 4. 1, 2,   Rise on both feet in first position, lower the arms to *bras bas* and look forward;

        3, 4,   Lower the right heel and *dégagé* the left leg *devant*, open the arms to *demi-seconde*, look to the left palm and so prepare to repeat the step commencing with the left leg.

From two to four times is sufficient for this exercise.

Note: It is useful to introduce these exercises at the *barre* to help the student gain the feeling of equilibrium during the change of weight from one leg to the other. Remember the body must remain upright and well-lifted throughout and should show no strain or reflected movement.

Fourth Year

4.a.   *Tempo* 4/4. Prepare in rotated first position of the feet and the arms with the breathing movement.

Bar 1. 1,   *Demi-plié* in first position, close to *bras bas*, look erect;

        &,   Spring in first position, lift the arms to *demi-first*, keep the head erect;

        2,   Land in a soft *demi-plié* on the right leg and *dégagé* the left *devant*, open the arms to *demi-seconde*, look to the left palm;

        3, 4,   Hold the position;

Bar 2. 1, 2,   Stretch the supporting knee and draw the working toe in a little, hold the head and arm positions;

        3, 4,   Close in first position, *allongé* and close to *bras bas*.

Repeat three times then do the exercise four times commencing with the left leg. Later eliminate the pause and complete the step in one bar of music.

4.b.   *Tempo* 4/4. Commence as for 4.a.

Bar 1. 1, &, 2, *Plié* and spring as before;

        3,   Stretch the supporting knee;

        4,   Hold the *dégagé*;

Bar 2. 1,   *Demi-plié* on the supporting leg and lift the working one from the floor a little, hold the arms in *demi-seconde*, look to the palm on the side of the *dégagé*;

        &,   Spring, bringing the feet together in first position in the air, *allongé* the arms and look erect;

        2,   Land lightly in *demi-plié* in first position, close to *bras bas*;

        3, 4,   Slowly stretch the knees.

Alternate the legs when ready.

Later the exercise should be completed in one bar without pauses using the fourth count to finish with both knees straightening in first position. Later, add a small tap of the pointed toe with a *sauté* on the supporting leg before closing. Gradually increase the number of taps to three.

4.c.   Final Form of Spring *Pointes*

Tempo 2/4. Stand in first position and prepare the arms with the breathing movement.

Bar 1. 1,   *Demi-plié* in first, arms in *bras bas*;

        &,   Spring in first in the air, lift the arms to *demi-first*;

        2,   Land in a soft *demi-plié* on one leg while the other extends to *dégagé devant*, open the arms to *demi-seconde* and look into the palm of the hand on the side of the *dégagé*;

Bar 2.   Repeat with the other leg.

Continue, changing the feet five times and finish with a *sauté* into first, then slowly stretch the knees on the fourth bar. The arms may be held during the step or moved in a simple *port de bras* making sure they co-ordinate with the leg movements and are of active assistance to the step. Later, the step can be done with quarter turns and may be combined with other steps.

Pas de Chat
Fourth Year
4.a.　*Tempo 4/4.* This is like a rotated *pas de chat* gallop. Prepare in third position with the right leg behind. Make the breathing movement and take the right arm through *bras bas* to *demi-first* look over the right elbow.

Bar 1.　1, 2,　　*Demi-plié*, hold the head and arm positions;

　　　　&, 3,　　Do a rotated gallop lifting the back leg and land without changing feet in a soft *demi-plié* in third, the front foot very slightly later than the back one. Hold the positions of the head and arms;

　　　　4,　　　Stretch the knees.

Bars 2–4.　　Repeat three times.

Repeat four times with the left leg at the back and the left arm in *demi-first*

Stage Sissonne
Stage *sissonne* is a free *relevé* or *sauté* into first *arabesque* and allows the young student to copy a pose frequently seen in a favourite photograph. The step should be done, initially, from the child's own observation and ability to copy accurately, and it is from this point of view that corrections should be made. The line differs from that of a normal first *arabesque* in that the body is lifted more upright, the front arm is higher and the leg lower. It should have a light, lively dance quality.

　　Introduce stage *sissonne* toward the end of the Fourth Year if and when the student has developed sufficient strength of posture and has a good sense of line in the arms, head, body and legs.

4.a.　*Tempo 6/8.* Prepare facing the *barre*, six small paces from it. *Dégagé* the right foot *devant* and open the arms to *demi-seconde*.

Bar 1.　1, 2, 3, 4, 5, 6,　　Six small runs on *demi-pointes*, lift the arms to *demi-first*, look to the left palm;

Bar 2.　1, 2,　　*Demi-plié* in third position with the right leg behind, place the hands on the *barre* looking to the left hand;

　　　　3,　　Spring in *arabesque*, keep the hands on the *barre*, lift the head and eyes slightly above head height;

　　　　4,　　Land in a soft *demi-plié* in *arabesque* on the left leg, hold the *barre*;

　　　　5,　　Hold the position;

　　　　6,　　Close in third and stretch the knees;

Bar 3.　　Six small runs on *demi-pointes* backwards, reverse arm movement from first to *demi-seconde*, *allongé*, follow the right hand;

Bar 4.　　Prepare with *dégagé devant* with the left leg ready to repeat the spring on the right leg.

Teach the step according to the general rule of repeating it on the same leg before alternating the legs.

4.b.　*Tempo 6/8.* Prepare in corner 6 facing point 2. *Dégagé* the right foot *devant* and open the arms to *demi-seconde*.

Bar 1. 1,   Step into a *demi-plié* in a small fourth, lift the arms through *bras bas* to first, look into the left palm;

        2,   Spring into first *arabesque*, look along the right arm;

        3,   Land softly in *demi-plié* in *arabesque*, hold the arms;

        4, 5, 6,   Three small runs on *demi-pointes*, gather the arms to first and look into the left palm;

Bar 2.   Repeat the preparation;

Bar 3.   Repeat bar 1;

Bar 4.   Finish in a pose.

Later, do the step without the second preparation and run off the stage.

4.c.   *Stage Sissonne Relevé*

In the exercises 4.a. and b. substitute a *relevé* on *demi-pointe* for the spring.

4.d.   *Tempo* 3/4. Slowly. Prepare in third position with the right foot in front facing point 2. Open the arms with the breathing movement.

Bar 1.   Waltz on the left leg; use the arms simply;

Bar 2.   Waltz on the right leg;

Bar 3.   Step to point 2 on the left leg in *demi-plié* stage *assemblé* landing in third with the right leg in front, arms through *bras bas* to *demi-first*, look to the right palm;

Bar 4.   Stage *sissonne relevé* and hold the pose as long as possible before running off the stage.

Note: This is just an example of an *enchaînement* using three of the dance steps from the Fourth Year repertoire. The teacher should compose many *enchaînements* so the student learns to pick up and memorize quickly.

Sauté in Arabesque

This step differs from the stage *sissonne* in that *sissonnes* spring from two feet whereas this *sauté* springs from one.

4.a.   *Tempo* 6/8. Prepare facing point 3. *Dégagé* the right leg *devant*, open the arms with the breathing movement.

Bar 1. 1,   *Tombé* into *demi-plié* in fourth position on the right leg, lift the left to *arabesque* and the arms to first position, look to the right palm;

        2,   Spring into *arabesque*, extend the arms to first *arabesque* and look along the right arm;

        3,   Land in a soft *demi-plié* on the right holding the *arabesque* pose with a feeling of still lifting in the arms and leg;

        4,   *Chassé* with the left leg to second *en face*, close the arms to *bras bas* and look *en face*;

        5,   Spring *coupé* bringing the right leg into first or fifth in the air, lower the arms to *bras bas*;

        6,   Facing point 7 land softly in *demi-plié* on the right leg, lift the arms to first position.

Bar 2.   *Tombé* on the left leg to repeat the step to the left;

Bars 3–4.   Repeat to the right and left finishing by closing the right leg in front in third position facing point 7.

Note: This step can also be done with a *relevé* in the *arabesque*.

Grand Jeté en Avant

This is also to allow the young student to do a step which is often seen in illustrations of dance books and encourages reproduction from observation. It gives a free, flying, thrusting feeling of movement covering space. Introduce in the Fourth Year.

4.a.   *Tempo 6/8*. Face point 2 standing in corner 6. *Dégagé* the left leg *devant*, open the arms to *demi-seconde* and look to point 2.

Bar 1.   Six small runs on the *demi-pointes*, take the arms through *bras bas* to first position, follow the left hand with the head and eyes;

Bar 2.   1, 2,   Two more small runs, slowly open the arms to second *arabesque*, look along the left arm to point 2;

3,   Step into *demi-plié* on the left leg and spring as for a high-flying skip, then extend the working leg to the front in the air, hold the arm position;

4,   Land in a soft *demi-plié* on the right leg in the *arabesque* pose;

5, 6,   Take two steps, bring the arms to first position and look into the left palm;

Bar 3.   Take a pose and hold it;

Bar 4.   Walk making an exit from the stage.

Repeat on the diagonal from point 4 to point 8 commencing with the right leg in *dégagé croisé*.

4.b.   In the same timing do the *jeté* with a *grand battement* instead of a high skip so that the working leg is straight during the spring from the floor.

Interpretation

The amount of individual interpretation expected of or allowed to a dancer greatly depends on the choreographer or producer and can lead to a wonderful rapport or be a constant cause of discord between them.

Some choreographers depend on their dancers for inspiration. The manner in which the dancer uses his body, that is, his body language, and his approach to the character of the movements being created, contribute to the variety of materials available to the choreographer. He does not have merely a physical instrument with which to draw the outline of his movements but has a live, emotional and intelligent human being to add colours to his creation. It depends on the character and artistic development of the dancer how vivid those colours can be. Other choreographers seem to expect their dancers to act as pawns to be moved about the stage without any life of their own.

Some producers of the great classical ballets look for interesting and creative individuals to cast in important leading roles. With the co-operation of the dancers they develop a personal approach to the production which is new and stimulating and which is therefore a 'production' and not another 'reproduction'.

Other producers look for dancers who fit their idea of the roles and will either guide and coach the dancers until they feel at home, or will impose their will so rigidly that the creative individuality of the artist is stifled.

Most dancers want to dance because they have something to express and should be able to contribute part of their inner selves as well as their physical bodies, to their chosen art and, in so doing, give inspiration to the choreographer or producer. It is unrewarding for all concerned to treat dancers as unthinking instruments and yet, at the same time, expect them to be sensitive artists.

Therefore, I believe that individual interpretation, within the framework of the dance in question, should be encouraged from the beginning of training. This helps the mind of the student to mature, to discriminate and to understand the bounds and discipline of the art as it is dictated by taste. It also gives creative satisfaction.

Solo Work

A solo dance in pure movement can show the performer's personal interpretation of the music in the way her body reacts to the content, accents, phrases and climaxes of the work. However, the producer must actually 'produce' the dancer, that is, he must develop the dancer's talents and show how to hear the music and how to express it from within.

Compositions with characters and stories should not dictate when the dancer must, say, smile or be sad, because the music and the composition itself should provide the vehicle for the dancer's emotional reactions and the foundation on which to create a character. Here again, the producer draws out what is within the dancer to give life to his creation.

Group Work

As no two people are totally alike so no two dancers should dance so alike that they become replicas of one another. To see individuals dancing together with the same style and musical understanding is more satisfying than watching a well-drilled corps of automatons. The interpretation of pure movement by a group must be a team effort and the individuality must be disciplined to conform to the group.

If the dance composition is portraying live beings, a certain amount of personal interpretation can be permitted to each member of the corps as long as this adds to the quality of the whole and is not a disruptive element. Therefore, I believe, the ability to subdue, but not necessarily annihilate, individuality should also be developed in early training.

Body Language

Animals use body language more naturally than humans and much can be learnt from watching them. People who live closely with their pets have no difficulty in understanding what they want. It is easy to distinguish between the desire of a dog to play and to attack. Curiosity, fear, uncertainty, disappointment and joy are beautifully expressed by body attitudes and movements. So, too, do humans react to their emotions and the influences around them. Observation of animals and people, the way they move and the attitudes they adopt in different situations greatly enlarges the vocabulary of body language. In this course, improvisation provides the opportunity to explore this side of dancing.

165

Mime

Mime is acting without words and is an extension of body language. Naturalistic mime takes everyday movements and reactions then refines and enlarges them to become significant enough to carry in the theatre. When the movements become stylized gestures they become an art form in themselves, the most important example being the Commedia dell'Arte with its delightful characters of Harlequin, Columbine and Pantalon. These gestures were adopted by the classical ballet but are seldom used today, being replaced by more naturalistic gestures. However, elementary gestures from classical ballet as described in this section, are still the basis of good natural looking dance mime.

These gestures are based on the classical *port de bras en dehors* or *en dedans* commencing through *bras bas* and first or through second positions. The head and eyes always reflect the movement of the arms. The finish of the gesture is held for a moment after which the arm is allowed to fall unhurriedly to the rest position. There should be no bending forward from the waist. Should a forward movement be required, it should be an inclination of the whole weight of the body in the desired direction. The artificial simpering, bending, bobbing and pointing which often passes for mime should not be encouraged as it is completely unconvincing and is inclined to give the child a precocious air.

It is useful to speak the meaning of mime gestures so that timing and phrasing convey its full meaning. Once the feeling for timing has been established it is no longer necessary to speak aloud. However, dancers should always speak the words to themselves. When teaching mime gestures introduce them with music so the movements are controlled and not hurriedly glossed over with consequent loss of meaning. There must be time for thought to take place before the gesture is made and, in conversation, time for the reaction before the reply. The tone of voice used should also be reflected in gesture.

Some Mime Gestures

I or Me. With a reverse *port de bras*, bring one hand from *bras bas* through second to nearly touch the centre of the chest. Follow the arm with the head and eyes then look at the person being addressed. The gesture can also be done with two arms together.

You. Lift one arm to *demi-first* position and open it out to *demi-seconde*, palm up, in the direction of the person being spoken to. Follow the movement with the head and eyes. If speaking to many people, the gesture can be made with both arms simultaneously or one after the other.

Him, Her, It. Make the same circular movement with the palm turned down and the fingers pointed either softly or strongly according to the tone of voice being used.

Come.	Lift the arm into *arabesque* position at head height. Make a circular movement inwards (like a reverse *allongé* movement) and finish with the arm in an open third position. Follow the movement with the head and eyes making sure to look directly at the person being addressed.
Go or There.	Look to the person being addressed, place the hand on the opposite shoulder from the direction required by the command, 'Go'. The fingers are pointing and the palm turned down. Then, keeping the hand in the same position, draw a circular movement to finish pointing in the required direction. Look to that direction and, while holding the pose, turn once more to the person being given the command. Again, this gesture can be made in various tones of voice according to the situation in the mime scene.
Here.	Lift the arm to a high *arabesque* position, Look to the person receiving the command, then down to one's own feet. Release the elbow and draw the hand down in the same line to point in front of the feet. As the arm is being lowered, look up again to the other person.
Look.	Make a reverse *port de bras* to third position, bend the forearm so the palm of the hand shades the eyes but be careful not to cover them as the whole head must be visible under the arm. Place the weight well forward on the supporting leg so the whole body inclines forward.
Please.	Lift both arms to first position with the palms facing each other. Bend the elbows and place the palms together. With a small circular movement downward return to a more extended position. Follow the gesture with the head and eyes.
To Plead.	Make the same gesture as for *please* but with the hands clasped and use a stronger movement and a feeling of urgency.
Yes.	Make one slow nod of the head or two sharp ones for urgency, the first being emphatic and the second small to reinforce the meaning.
No.	Slowly turn the head from one side to the other and return to centre. For more emphasis turn the head strongly once then a second time more softly.
Yes.	Lift the arm to first position with the palm turned down, look down. Turn the palm up and lower the arm slowly while the head and eyes lift to look at the person being answered.
No.	Lift one arm to first position with the palm turned down, look down. Look up as the palm is turned

	outwards. Hold the upper arm in place and move the hand from one side to the other. The head turns in the direction in which the hand moves. If this gesture is made with both hands simultaneously, they cross once only with the accent on the opening of the last movement.
Why? Who? What?	Make a small *port de bras* with both arms through *demi-first* to *demi-seconde* and finish with the palms turned up. Follow the movement of one hand with the eyes and head then look *en face*.
Goodbye.	Look to the person being bid farewell. Lift the arm to *arabesque* position at head height following the movement with the head and eyes. Then gently wave the slightly upturned hand from side to side once or twice. Hold for a fraction of a second then allow the arm to float down to the rest position.

When a question is asked, the gesture should finish on an uplift and be sustained to give the same feeling as the raised tone of voice at the end of a question. To give credibility to mime, the placement of weight should be correct so as to give freedom of movement as the body turns to face or away from the person being addressed. Usually the weight is placed on one leg with the other slightly relaxed and ready to take the weight when required. Do not be afraid to turn the body and change the weight as long as there is not so much movement that it creates restlessness. Do not allow the student to stand in a rigid pose while trying to give meaning to a gesture, as this results in a stilted, unrealistic scene with no meaning for the audience. Remember: THINK, ACT, REACT.

As a feeling for mime develops, the reliance on music should become less dominant. Mime should never appear to be done 'on the beat' but should be contained within the musical phrases while flowing freely with its own rhythm.

Greetings, with various kinds of emotions or a story line, make most interesting exercises. These can be improvised or set by the teacher or students. Both ways have great merit. Short conversations should follow which can be extended as the story unfolds. If two or more students can perform a mime scene and the rest of the class understand what is being said then an appreciation of credible and expressive gesture is being nurtured. The following mime scene between two people can be gradually built up and performed with or without music.

Example of a Mime Scene

Tempo 6/8.	B is sitting centre stage playing.
Bars 1–4.	A walks from point 2 past B towards point 6. She stops suddenly with the weight on the left leg;
Bar 5. 1,	A turns the head to the right to look at B with the firm/sudden action of decision;
2, 3, 4, 5, 6,	A turns the body to face B;

Bars 6–7.		A walks towards B who, with a slow turn and lift of the head and eyes, looks to A and with a light/sudden uplift of recognition, smiles at A;
Bar 8.	1, 2, 3,	A offers a hand to B;
	4, 5, 6,	B takes the offered hand and is helped up;
Bar 9.	1, 2, 3,	A looks at B;
	4, 5, 6,	A places the right hand on B's left shoulder;
Bar 10.	1, 2, 3,	A turns her head and eyes to look to point 2;
	4, 5, 6,	A lifts her left arm to indicate point 2;
Bar 11.	1, 2, 3,	B turns her head and eyes quickly to look in the direction of point 2;
	4, 5, 6,	A lowers her arm but still looks to point 2 while B points in that direction;
Bar 12.	1, 2, 3,	B still indicating point 2, turns her head to question A who looks at B;
	4, 5, 6,	A nods once for YES and B lowers her arm;
Bar 13.	1, 2, 3,	Both A and B turn to look to point 2;
	4, 5, 6,	Both turn their bodies to 2;
Bar 14.		B walks to point 2; A watches her;
Bar 15.	1, 2, 3,	B turns the head slowly to look at A;
	4, 5, 6,	B turns her body to face A and they both wave GOODBYE;
Bar 16.	1, 2, 3,	B turns her body to 2 and A hers to 6;
	4, 5, 6,	Both turn their heads to the direction of travel and exit to opposite corners.

When time for thinking has become habitual, the exercise can be done in a more flowing manner. Incorporate various stories and characters, for example; a mother finds her child and sends her home for tea or two friends meet and one gives a message to the other and so on. The gestures can be done in a happy, friendly manner or in an angry, commanding one. It will be realized that the exercises suggested have developed the free and independent movement of the head from the body. Work out other exercises for the transference of weight. There is plenty of opportunity for creative mime built on the foundation of basic gestures as described in this section.

Folk Dance

I recommend that a thorough study of folk dance be undertaken by the teacher as it is from folk dance, with its ritual and work dances, that inspiration for all kinds of dance originates. There are many good books on folk and character dance.

All aspects of dance previously studied are contained in folk dance, and as these dances should be well controlled, rhythmic and stylish and never rough and untidy, they show the end result of this preparatory training. They also provide a valuable contrast to improvisation as they require the child to learn set work and show the necessary discipline to be able to work with others. Of course, self discipline is also essential to make an art form of group improvisation but working with others in folk dance adds another dimension to team work.

I have not presented any authentic dances in the following exercises. They use the type of steps and patterns found in many folk dances and, while providing a set of dances to perform, should be a preparation for more serious study.

Care should be taken to prepare the arms and feet correctly and to see that the head and eyes look in the direction of the movement.

First Year

1.a.   *Walking Dances*
Tempo 4/4. This can be done in a circle holding hands or separately or in couples. Prepare facing round the circle in an anti-clockwise direction. Point the right foot and place the arms as required.

Bars 1–2. Eight walking steps;
Bar 3. 1, 2, Step on the right and close the left to it;
  3, 4, Turn to face the centre of the circle with the feet in parallel first;
Bar 4. 1, 2, Turn to face clockwise;
  3, 4, Prepare to repeat in the opposite direction.

1.b.   *Tempo* 4/4. Holding hands, prepare in a circle facing the centre. *Dégagé* the right foot *devant*.

Bar 1 Four walks towards the centre of the circle;
Bar 2. Feet together and swing the arms up to parallel third;
Bar 3. Four walks backwards;
Bar 4. Feet together and swing the arms down and prepare to repeat.

1.c.   *Gallops with Rises*
Tempo 4/4. Prepare in a circle holding hands and with the feet in parallel first.

Bar 1. 1, Step to the side with the right leg;
  2, Join the left to it;
  3, Rise on *demi-pointes*;
  4, Lower the heels;
Bar 2. Repeat to the left;
Bar 3. Four side gallops;
Bar 4. Step, together, rise, lower.

1.d.   *Running Dance*
Tempo 4/4. Prepare in a circle, holding hands and facing anti-clockwise. *Dégagé* the right foot *devant*.

Bars 1–2 Eight running steps;
Bar 3. 1, 2, Jump bringing the feet together;
  3, 4, Jump in parallel first, to face the centre;
Bar 4. 1, 2, Jump to face clockwise;
  3, 4, Prepare the left foot to repeat in the opposite direction.

This can also be done with two small springs on the turn, one to each beat.

These four exercises can be put together, as they are learnt, to make a small dance.

Second Year

2.a. *Stamping*

Tempo 4/4. Prepare in a circle, holding hands and with the right feet in *dégagé devant*.

Bars 1–2.   Eight walks in an anti-clockwise direction;
Bar 3.   1,   Step on the right foot facing the centre;
         2,   Join the left in parallel first;
         3, 4,   Stamp right, left;
Bar 4.   1,   Step to the side on the right;
         2,3,4,   Turn to face clockwise and *dégagé* the left in preparation to repeat.

When teaching the stamp, stand in parallel first and slightly bend the knees. Lift one foot off the floor, flexed and keeping the lower leg perpendicular, then place it down firmly in first while lifting the other. Maintain the *demi-plié* so as not to jar the body on the stamp. Practise different weights in the stamp from very light to sharp and loud but never HEAVY!

2.b. *Gallop*

Tempo 2/4. In a circle or in lines, prepare the right foot to the side.

Bar 1.   Two side gallops;
Bar 2.   Step right then stamp left;
Bar 3.   Step left, stamp right;
Bar 4.   Step right and *dégagé* the left in preparation to repeat to the left.

2.c. *Chassés*

Tempo 2/4. Prepare in a circle or in a line. Hold hands and *dégagé* the right foot *devant*.

Bar 1.   Two *chassés* forward;
Bar 2.   Step forward on the right and stamp the left in third *derrière*, lift the arms;
Bars 3–4.   Reverse, moving out of the circle or backwards in the line. Lower the arms.

2.d. *Running Dance*

Tempo 2/4. This can be done *sur place* or travelling in a circle or in a line.

Bar 1.   Three little running steps and a pause;
Bars 2–3   Repeat twice;
Bar 4.   Two small springs in parallel first changing direction with a quarter turn on each spring.

Third Year

3.a. *Gallops and Stamps*

Tempo 4/4. Prepare in a circle facing in. Hold hands or place them on the hips. *Dégagé* the right foot to the side.

Bar 1.   Four side gallops;
Bar 2.   Two side gallops and three stamps, right, left, right;
Bars 3–4.   Repeat bars 1 and 2 to the left;

Bar 5. 1, 2, *Sur place*, with hands on the hips, two skips turning to the right to face anti-clockwise;

        3, 4, Two skips to face outside the circle;

Bar 6. 1, 2, Two skips to face clockwise;

        3, 4, Three stamps facing the centre;

Bars 7–8. Repeat bars 5 and 6 taking the hands again before repeating the whole.

3.b. *Heel–Toe Steps*

Tempo 4/4. Hold hands with partners facing front. *Dégagé* the right foot to the side.

Bar 1. 1, Bend the left knee and place the heel of the right foot, with the toe flexed, in second position;

        2, Maintain the *demi-plié* and place the toe of the right foot across the left foot;

        3, 4, Three *petit jetés*, right, left, right;

Bar 2. Repeat with the left leg;

Bar 3. 1, 2, &, Holding hands or linking arms, face clockwise and do four little running steps round each other starting with the right foot;

        3, 4, Step and jump with the feet in first; changing direction.

Bar 4. Repeat bar 3, anti-clockwise.

3.c. *Slow Dance*

Tempo 2/4. In lines facing *en diagonale*. *Dégagé* the right foot *effacé devant*. Hands on hips or arms folded.

Bar 1. Three walking steps and swish the left through first on *demi-pliè*;

Bars 2–3. Repeat twice;

Bar 4. Lightly stamp the left foot in first and, changing direction, prepare to repeat to the left;

Bars 5–8. Repeat to the left;

Bars 9–12. Turn to the right with six Russian *coupé* steps and two stamps facing front;

Bars 13–16. Six snatch skips back and two light stamps.

3.d. *Pas de Basque*

Tempo 3/4. Do this step *sur place* or travelling forward. Prepare in lines. *Dégagé* the right foot *devant* and place the hands on the hips.

Bars 1–4. Two country *pas de basques*; step *sauté* in *attitude devant*, twice;

Bars 5–8. Three *pas de basques* making a complete turn and a light stamp.

Fourth Year

4.a. *Changing Directions*

Tempo 3/4. Prepare, holding hands, in a circle or in lines. *Dégagé* the right foot *devant*.

Bar 1. Step and *sauté* in *attitude devant* facing the line of travel;

Bar 2.	One country *pas de basque* turning to face the opposite direction and travelling backwards;
Bars 3–6.	Repeat twice;
Bars 7–8.	*Chassé* back on the right and prepare to the left to repeat clockwise.

4.b.   *Heel–Toe Dances*

Tempo 2/4. Prepare with the hands on the hips or folded. Stand in third position.

Bar 1.	1,	Spring, landing in *demi-plié* on the left foot with the toe of the right turned in, in second position;
	2,	With a small spring place the heel of the flexed right foot in second;
Bar 2.	1, &, 2,	Three stamps;
Bars 3–4.		Repeat on the left;
Bars 5–6		Four snatch skips with a quarter turn on each;
Bars 7–8.		Small runs backwards on the heels and a stamp.

4.c.   *Tempo 2/4.* Prepare in third position of the feet, hands on the hips or holding the skirt.

Bar 1.	1, &, 2,	With a small spring on each movement, place the toe then the heel of the right foot in second position then across the left toe;
Bar 2.	&,	One snatch skip back;
	1, 2, 3,	Three stamps with alternate feet in third position;
	&,	Spring in preparation to repeat to the left;
Bars 3–6.		Repeat twice;
Bar 7.		Step forward into second position on the left heel then the right;
Bar 8.	1, &, 2,	Step back on the left and do two stamps. Prepare to repeat.

4.d.   *Fast Dance*

Tempo 2/4. Stand in a circle holding hands and facing anti-clockwise. *Dégagé* the right foot *devant*.

Bar 1.		Two skips leaning well forward with the body and with the head looking to the centre;
Bar 2.		Four fast running steps, body and head held in the same position;
Bars 3–6.		Repeat twice;
Bar 7.	1,	Jump into full *plié* in parallel first facing anti-clockwise;
	2,	Staying in the *plié* make a small jump to face the centre;
Bar 8.	1,	Small jump in *plié* to face clockwise;
	2,	Spring up and *dégagé* the left foot ready to repeat clockwise.

As this is a fast moving step, it requires good discipline and control to make it look spectacular.

Improvisation

Subjects for improvisation are so numerous and varied that they should not be difficult for teachers and students to devise. It is important that some knowledge and experience be gained from every improvisation as well as it being a pleasant release for personal feelings and ideas. The examples given show how the simplest idea can be developed so as to introduce and explore many aspects of dance.

Nature

First Year

1.a.   A Garden. A flower grows, opens and blooms then dies. This involves simple form with a beginning, a middle and an end.

    (a)   Introduce this without accompaniment so the children think about the speed of growth and control their movements to represent this. Think of the shape of the flower and show this in the body and arms.

    (b)   Listen to suitable music, practise movements to fit the time and quality.

1.b.   The Wind. A soft gentle breeze develops into a strong wind and dies down. Again do this without, then with, accompaniment of music, voice sounds or instruments.

1.c.   Bees look for honey, find the flower, gather honey and fly away. Use voice sounds then musical accompaniment.

1.d.   Divide the class into groups of flowers, wind and bees, and combine them. The flower grows, the wind blows, the bees take honey and the flower dies.

Second Year

The Air. Practice these exercises with and without accompaniment. Find words to illustrate the qualities needed.

2.a.   Perhaps use light scarves to portray clouds, big fluffy ones, thin streaky ones or storm clouds.

2.b.   Be small birds on a calm day then on a windy one.

2.c.   Be large birds and feel the contrast of their big heavy wing movements as against the light fluttering ones of the small birds.

2.d.   Invent movements to show the sharp darting flight of insects.

2.e.   Make a composite scene from all the previously studied subjects.

Third Year

The Sea. Find words to illustrate the type of movement required. Work with breath rhythm and then with music.

3.a.   Dance waves in a calm sea and in a storm.

3.b.   Be seaweed waving gently in the swell then being torn up by the roots in a storm and floating away.

3.c.   Be small fish. Work in pairs swimming, turning, twisting, darting and resting together.

3.d.   Be a sting ray lying still then swimming away with a sudden dash and undulation of the wings.

3.e.   Make a composite picture with a story line.

Fourth Year
The Seasons. Continue working with and without music. Find words, sounds, shapes, qualities and patterns to express the idea to be danced.

4.a.   Spring. Show the feelings and emotions associated with spring, pleasant warmth, a fresh cool breeze, a spring shower, energy, vitality, life.

4.b.   Summer, with long sunny days, the lassitude of heat, summer rain and humidity, hot, dry winds.

4.c.   Autumn. Winds and the beginning of chill in the air, calm with the presentiment of approaching fate.

4.d.   Winter. Cold, ice and snow, frost and stillness.

4.e.   Introduce people, animals and birds and show their reactions to the various seasons.

People

First Year
1.a.   Happy girls and boys at the beach in summer, and in the snow in winter.

1.b.   Sad, cold and hungry people.

Second Year
2.a.   People frightened of someone or something. Lost and lonely children.

2.b.   In pairs be friends, then enemies.

Dance from Natural Movements

Third Year
Discover how to make natural movements into dance.

3.a.   Play tennis and make serving, returning and falling, using rolling, jumping up sideways, forwards and backwards, turning and twisting, into a dance for four.

3.b.   A picnic. Mother, father, uncles, aunts, big sisters and brothers and younger children eat and drink, play chasing, have races, ride ponies and play hide and seek. This makes a big group improvisation.

A Story Line

Fourth Year
Work in groups of three portraying Cinderella, her Stepmother and the Fairy Godmother.

4.a.   Study the characters of all three and find movements to suit them. Work out a simple conversation between them such as; Cinderella asks her stepmother if she can go to the ball, the stepmother refuses her. Cinderella appeals to the Fairy Godmother who agrees to help her. Set a rhythm, without music, for the conversation say; six beats for Cinderella, three for the stepmother, six for Cinderella and six for the Fairy Godmother. Make the statements short and concise. Several groups can do this following on one after the other with no pause so the rhythm becomes continuous and flowing.

4.b.   Extend the time duration of each statement and elaborate on the characters and their movements.

4.c.   Find suitable music and further develop the characters and movements into a reasonably lengthy dance for three people.

Dance Composition and Choreography

No doubt the teacher will be required to arrange dances or compose ballets for students. I refrain from using the word 'choreograph' as this ability springs from natural talent whereas the skill of arranging dances can be taught. The choreographer should also study these skills but the inspiration which makes a choreographer is inherent in that person. Artists must study their craft, but it is the way in which they use that craft that makes them mere practitioners or real artists.

A competent piece of work is better than a bad one. A well-constructed dance can be very pleasing to an audience and is nothing to be ashamed of. So the teacher also should study the craft of composition, put it into practice and see if inspiration reveals a choreographer.

Study of dance as explained in this book, will provide a basis for dance composition. The experience gained in improvisation and from folk dance together with the use of imagination, lead directly to composition.

Performances

Performances are good for students as, in them, they can participate in the end product of their study. Confidence is gained in conducting themselves with assurance, in public. Encouragement is given to express themselves freely in front of others.

Performances develop team spirit because the success of the whole depends on each individual dancer. Great self-control is required to concentrate fully on technique while performing in front of an audience and at the same time giving expression to the dance. The nervous child will learn to master his nerves and the carefree one will learn that thought and control are necessary if anything is to be successfully achieved.

Work Suitability

The skilful producer sees that the work presented is within the capabilities of the dancers. He should choose a theme or story suitable for each age-group. Nothing is more distateful than seeing children perform unsuitable dance subjects looking precocious and unchildlike.

Choice of Music

The choice of music for the production must also reflect the qualities of the specific age-group and be easily understood by the children.

In composition, unlike in exercises, where the music reflects the movement, the music dictates the type of movement to be used.

Costumes

Do not overload small children with elaborate costumes. Allow them to experience various shapes and cut of costumes making sure the choice of fabric is suitable to the design.

Neatness and immaculate grooming should always be insisted upon. Shoes must be clean and tidy and tied properly. Hair must be neat and dressed close to the head so that the proportions of the body are not disturbed. Over-large and heavy head-dresses should be avoided, rather use a small light one firmly secured so as not to slip or fall off.

Settings

As most school performances are, of necessity, run by friends of the school, and as expense should be considered, a more professional appearance is achieved if scenery is kept to a minimum. If necessary, use self-standing props which can be quickly put in place and as quickly removed thus avoiding long delays between items. Of course, make quite certain that the pieces are firmly braced. Also see that the dancers have time to become completely familiar with them.

Lighting

Over-ambitious lighting is costly and time-consuming in rehearsal often to the disadvantage of the dancers who need as much rehearsal on stage as possible. Use a simple lighting plot with changes of general colour for different moods but keep changes during the dance to a minimum as the stage manager or lighting technician must have time to learn what is happening on stage and this again costs time and money.

Rehearsal

When rehearsing a dance for performance give time to think and prepare movements. Rehearse thoroughly so every nuance is known and practised until the performers have completely mastered all aspects of the dance. The dancers will not become bored with repeated rehearsals if they know what they are trying to achieve and are challenged to get everything involved, both technically and aesthetically, correct every time the dance is repeated and experienced. Experiencing movement and quality is pleasurable and so repetition also can be pleasurable.

Remember that dancing is a joyous thing for the performer and audience alike and should give fulfilment to the teacher and producer.

First Year Study Programme

First Year Progressions
First
Basics

Develop all aspects learnt of time/music, weight/quality, space, folk dance and improvisation.

Second Year Study Programme

Second Year Progressions
First

Basics

Isolation

Control

Transference

Elevation

Time/Music

Weight/Quality

Space

Fourth

Fifth

Seventh

Third Year Study Programme

	Progression	**Page**
Isolation		
1. Feet, ankles, toes	3.a. Astride sitting. Flex and stretch 1	51
	3.b. Sit or lie. Lift, flex, stretch 2	51
	3.c. Lift, stretch, flex 4	51
	3.d., 3.c. rotated. Also on back to	
	side 6	51
	3.e., 3.d. on stomach to the back 7	51
2. *Demi-pointes*	3.a. *Demi-plié*, rise. With arms 1	53
3. Knees and hips	3.a. Sitting. *Retiré*, pointed foot. 4/4 1	54
	3.b., 3.a. lying on back 4	54
	3.c. *Retiré*. Standing 7	54
4. *Pliés*	3.a. At *barre*. Add third, rotated 5	57
	3.b. With arm swings in centre 2	57
5. Back, stomach, waist		
Resiliences	3.a. In all positions. Chords to	
	change 2	60
Cat stretch	3.a. Divided 1	61
Sphinx	3.a. Turning head 5	61
6. Head and eyes	3.a. Look up and down forty-five	
	degrees 1	63
Turning	3.b. Turn 180 degrees without	
	pauses 6	63
Inclined	3.a. With and without arms 2	64
Eyes	3.a. Diagonal cross 5	65
7. Waist and shoulders		
Shoulders	3.a. Forward 1	65
Waist turns	3.a. Add arms to 2.a. Increase turn 6	66
Side bends	3.a. Arms by sides 7	67
8. Hands and fingers	3.a. Alternate and opposite	
	movements 1	68
Fingers	3.a. Roll into fist and unroll 2	69
	3.b. Repeat plus rotation of wrists 5	69
Wrists	3.a. Figure eights on floor and in air 6	70
Arm waves	3.a. Flower shape, not touching 7	70
Control		
1. Brushes	3.a. Off the floor, without pauses 1	72
	3.b. Toe held on floor 5	72
	3.c. Rotated. To front and side 7	72
2. *Cou-de-pied*	3.a. Lifted, ankle height 6	75
3. For *pas de cheval*	3.a. Parallel, *en l' air* 8	76
4. For *relevé lent* and *développé*		
Relevé lent	3.a. Lying. 2/4 *tempo* with pauses. 1	77
Développé	3.b. Lying. In parallel 5	78

Third Year Progressions
First

Fourth Year Study Progressions
First

Basics

Third

Bibliography

Allcock, Rita *and* Bland, Wendy, *Dance in education*. London: Dance Books, 1981.

Adshead, Janet, *The study of dance*. London: Dance Books, 1981.

Boorman, J., *Dance and language experiences with children*. Ontario: Longman.

Bruce, Violet, *Movement in silence and sound*. London: Bell, 1970.

Barlow, Wilfred, *The Alexander principle*. London: Arrow, 1975.

Cornazano, Antonio, *The book on the art of dancing*. London: Dance Books, 1981.

Cohen, Selma Jeanne, *Dance as a theatre art*. London: Dance Books, 1977.

Canner, Norma, *And a time to dance*. Boston: Beacon Press, 1968.

Carrol, Jean *and* Lofthouse, Peter, *Creative dance for boys*. London: Macdonald & Evans, 1969.

Ellfeldt, Lois, *A primer for choreographers*. London: Dance Books, 1974.

Exiner, Johanna *and* Lloyd, Phyllis, *Teaching creative movement*. Sydney: Angus & Robertson, 1973.

Featherstone, Donald, *Dancing without danger*. London: Kaye & Ward, 1969.

Farley, M. *A teacher's guide to creative movement*. Melbourne: Reed.

Gelb, Michael, *Body learning, an introduction to the Alexander technique*. London: Aurum Press, 1981.

Grant, Gail, *Technical manual and dictionary of classical ballet*. New York: Dover, 1967.

Humphrey, Doris, *The art of making dances*. London: Dance Books, 1978.

Hughes, L., *The first book of rhythms*. London: E. Ward.

King, Bruce, *Creative movement*. New York: Bruce King Studios, 1968.

Kersley, Leo, *and* Sinclair, Janet, *A dictionary of ballet terms*. London: A. & C. Black, 1977.

Laban, Rudolf, *Modern educational dance*. London: Macdonald & Evans, 1975.

Lawson, Joan, *Mime*. Brooklyn: Dance Horizons.

Lawson, Joan, *A history of ballet and its makers*. London: Dance Books, 1973.

Manthorp, Beryl, *Towards ballet*. London: Dance Books, 1980.

Preston-Dunlop, Valerie, *A handbook of modern educational dance*. London: Macdonald & Evans, 1980.

Rowen, Betty, *Learning through movement*. New York: Teachers College Press, 1963.

Shawn, Ted, *Every little movement*. Brooklyn: Dance Horizons, 1974.

Stebbins, Genevieve, *Delsarte system of expression*. Brooklyn: Dance Horizons, 1977.

van Praagh, Peggy, *and* Brinson, Peter, *The choreographic art*. London: A. & C. Black, 1963.

Wood, Melusine, *Historical dances*. London: Dance Books, 1982.

Wiener, Jack, *and* Lidstone, John, *Creative movement for children*. New York: Van Nostrand Reinhold, 1969.

Woodland, E. J. M., *Poems for Movement*. London: Bell & Hyman, 1984.

Glossary

À deux bras	With two arms.
À la seconde	To the side
Allégro	Bright lively steps of elevation.
Allongé	Extended. Extending the arms from a curved to a straight line.
Arabesque	A basic pose in classical dance. A flowing line through the body from the fingers to the toes of the working leg *par terre* or *en l'air*.
Assemblé	Gathered together.
Battement	Beating action away from and to the supporting leg.
Battement tendu	*Battement* stretched.
Bras bas	Arms low.
Changé	Changed.
Cou-de-pied	The neck of the foot. The ankle.
Coupé	Cutting the weight from one foot to the other *sur place*.
Croisé	Crossed. The body faces diagonally across the stage with the legs crossed to the audience.
Dégagé	Disengaging the leg to an open position with a stretched leg and pointed toe.
Derrière	At the back. With no change of feet.
Dessous	Under. The front foot changes to the back.
Dessus	Over. The back foot changes to the front.
Devant	In front. With no change of foot.
Développé	Unfolding. A gradual unfolding of the leg to an open position after being drawn up to *retiré*.
Écarté	Separated. Thrown open. The body faces diagonally on stage with the working leg in second.
Échappé	Escaped. Opening the legs from a closed to an open position and returning, *relevé* or *sauté*.
Éffacé	Shaded. The body faces diagonally on stage with the legs open to the audience.
En arrière	Travelling backwards.
En avant	Travelling forwards.
En croix	In the shape of a cross. Front, side, back, side.
En dedans	Inwards or towards the supporting leg.
En dehors	Outwards. Away from the supporting leg.
En l'air	In the air.
Épaulement	The use of the shoulders.
Épaulement direction	Facing *croisé*, *effacé* or *écarté*.
Glissade	A gliding step preparatory to another.

Grand battement	Big beating. A throw of the leg from a closed to an open position *en l'air*.
Jeté	Thrown. A spring from one leg to the other.
Par terre	On the floor.
Pas	A step.
Pas de chat	Step of the cat.
Pas de cheval	Step of the horse.
Pas de basque	Step from basque dancing.
Pas de bourrée	A small running step.
Pas marché	Marching step in classical style.
Passé	Passed. The leg passes through first, *cou-de-pied* or *retiré*.
Piqué	Pricked.
Plié	A bending of the knees.
Relevé	Raised.
Relevé lent	A slow raising of the leg to an open position.
Retiré	Drawn up. The toe of the working leg is drawn up the supporting leg to the height of the knee.
Rond de jambe	A circular movement of the leg.
Sans changé	Without changing.
Sauté	Jumped.
Souténus	Sustained.
Sur place	In place.
Temps levé	Time raised. A spring.
Temps lié	Connected movement.
Tombé	Fallen.